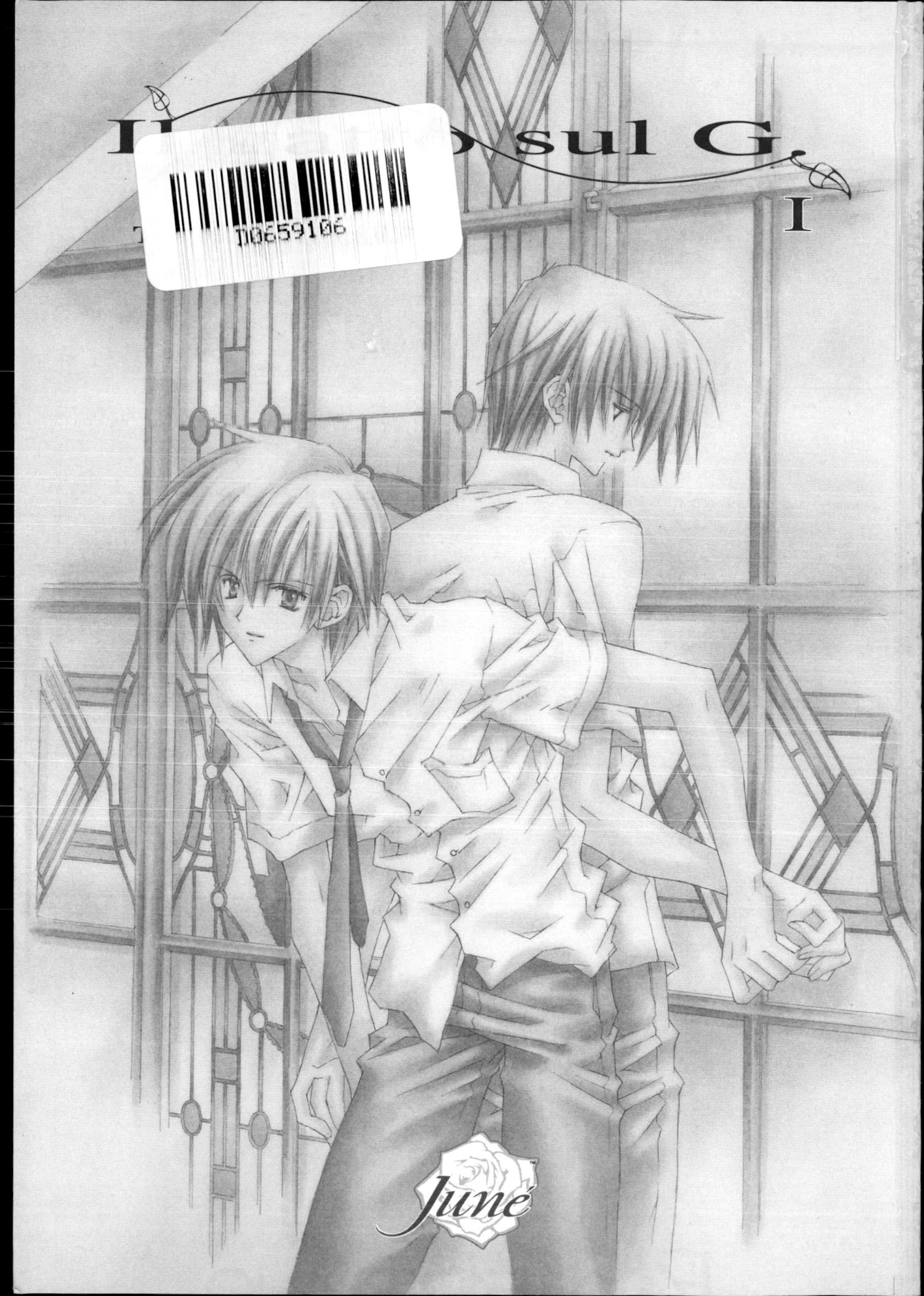

I
Juné

Il gatto sul G

I

❧ INDICE

IL GATTO SUL G. (NERO)......005

THE PRACTICE ROOM......083

IL GATTO SUL G. (BIANCO)......091

Translation	**Duane Johnson**
Lettering	**Replibooks**
Editing	**Bambi Eloriaga**
Editor in Chief	**Fred Lui**
Publisher	**Hikaru Sasahara**

English Edition Published by
DIGITAL MANGA PUBLISHING
A division of DIGITAL MANGA, Inc.
1487 W 178th Street, Suite 300
Gardena, CA 90248

www.dmpbooks.com

First Edition: March 2006
ISBN: 1-56970-923-8

1 3 5 7 9 10 8 6 4 2

Printed in China

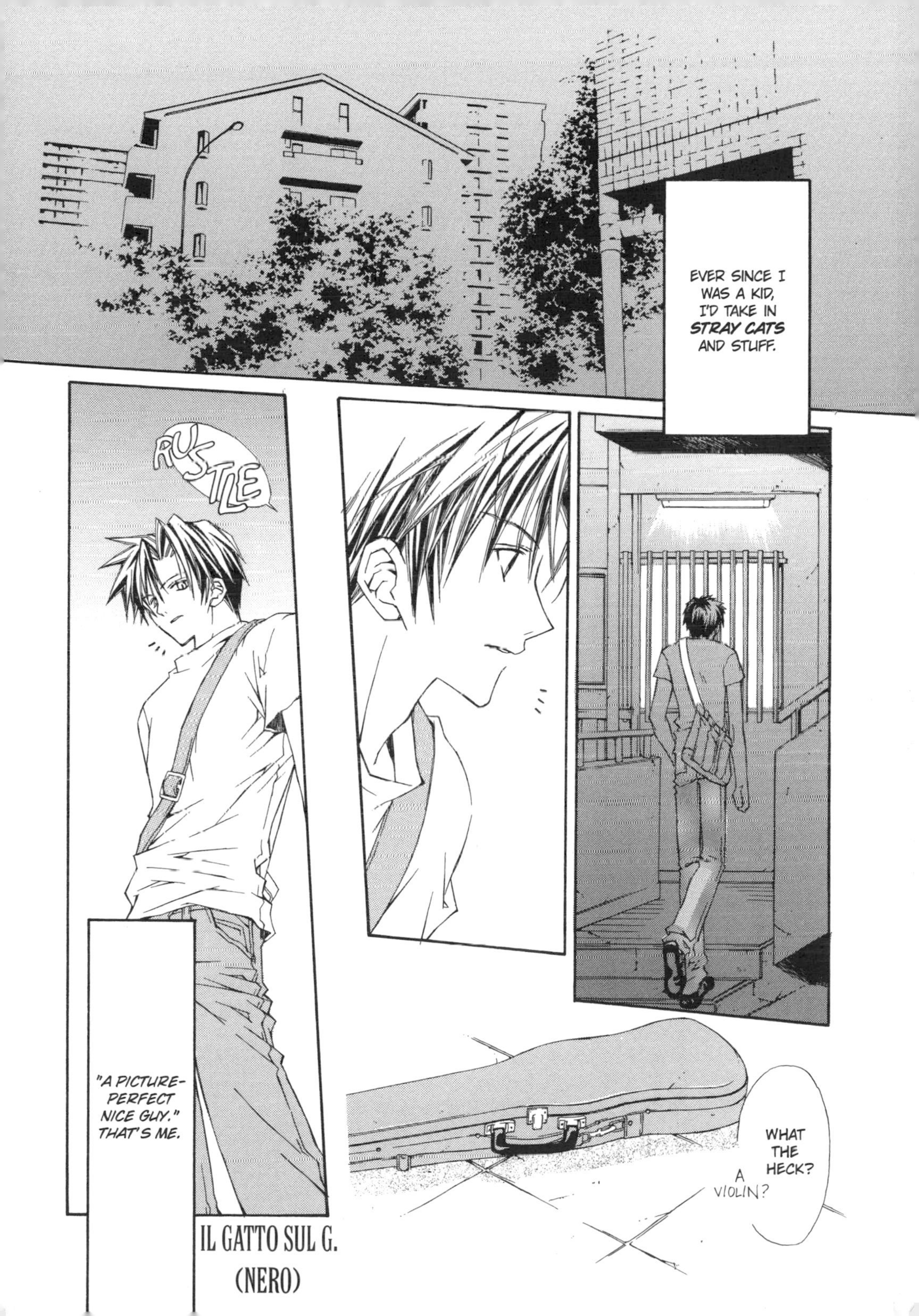
EVER SINCE I WAS A KID, I'D TAKE IN **STRAY CATS** AND STUFF.
RUSTLE
WHAT THE HECK?
A VIOLIN?
"A PICTURE-PERFECT NICE GUY." THAT'S ME.
IL GATTO SUL G.
(NERO)

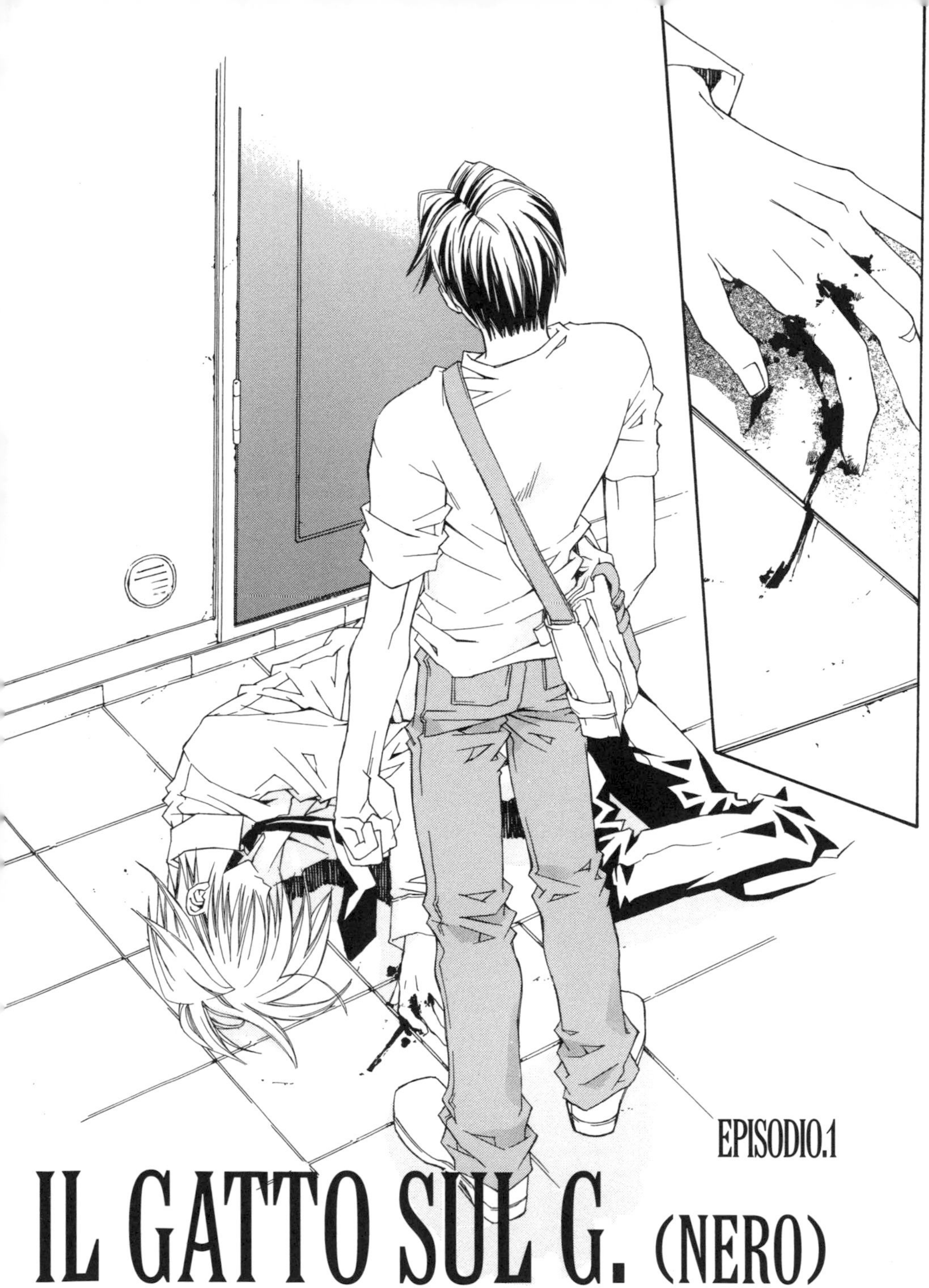

EPISODIO.1

IL GATTO SUL G. (NERO)

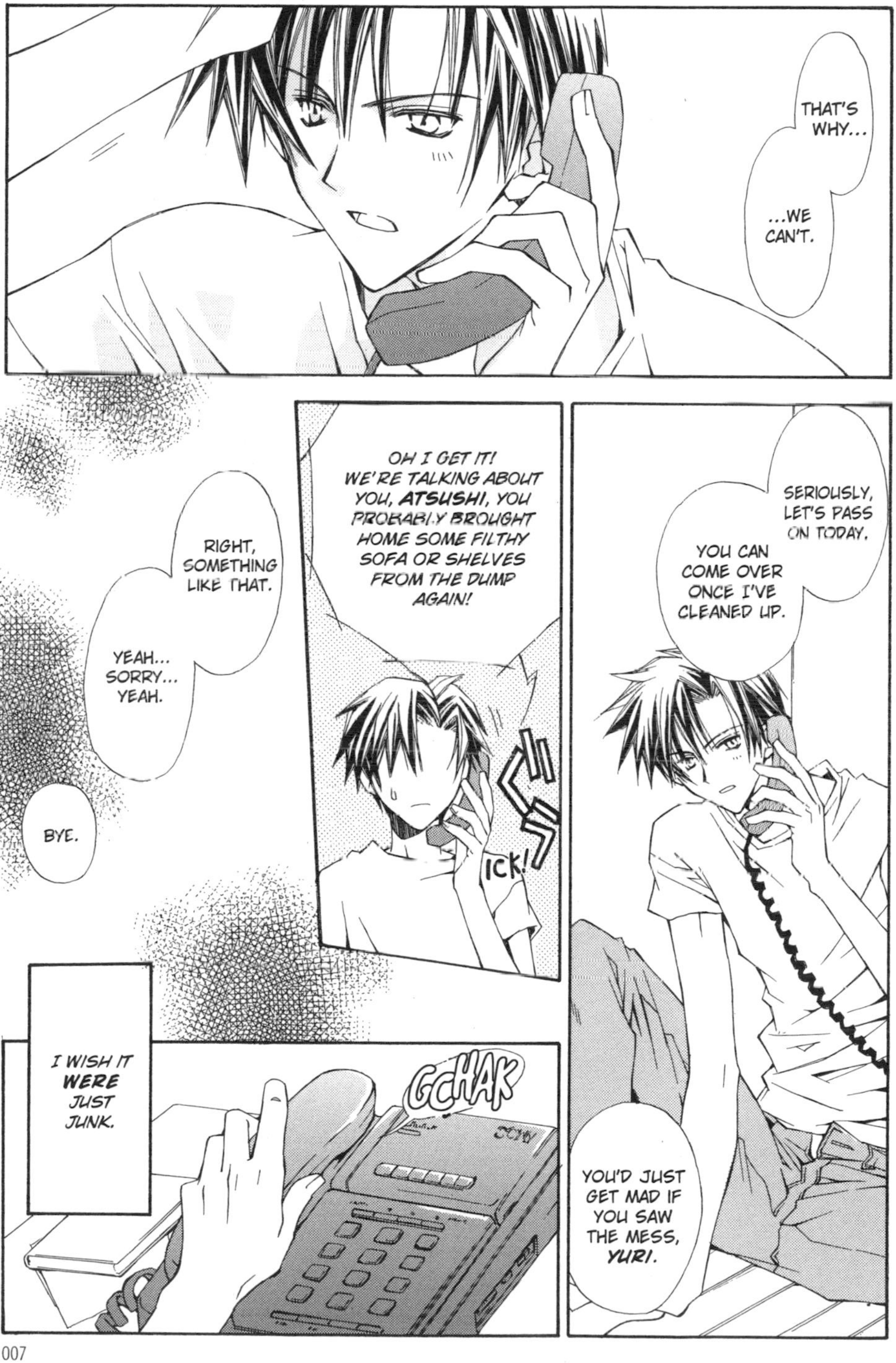
THAT'S WHY...
...WE CAN'T.
SERIOUSLY, LET'S PASS ON TODAY.
YOU CAN COME OVER ONCE I'VE CLEANED UP.
YOU'D JUST GET MAD IF YOU SAW THE MESS, YURI.
OH I GET IT! WE'RE TALKING ABOUT YOU, ATSUSHI, YOU PROBABLY BROUGHT HOME SOME FILTHY SOFA OR SHELVES FROM THE DUMP AGAIN!
ICK!
RIGHT, SOMETHING LIKE THAT.
YEAH... SORRY... YEAH.
BYE.
GCHAK
I WISH IT WERE JUST JUNK.

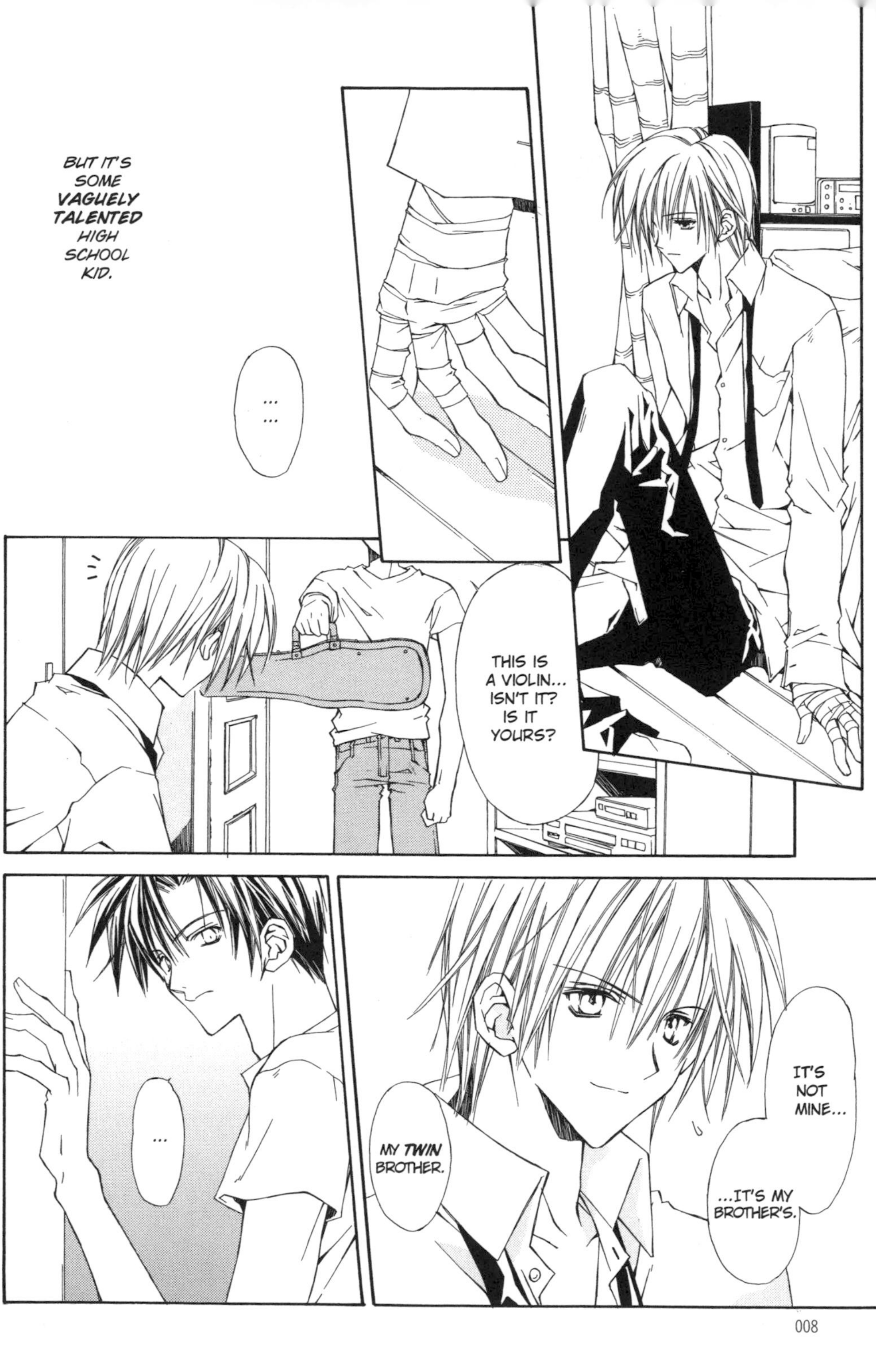

BUT IT'S SOME VAGUELY TALENTED HIGH SCHOOL KID.
... ...
THIS IS A VIOLIN... ISN'T IT? IS IT YOURS?
IT'S NOT MINE...
...IT'S MY BROTHER'S.
MY TWIN BROTHER.
...

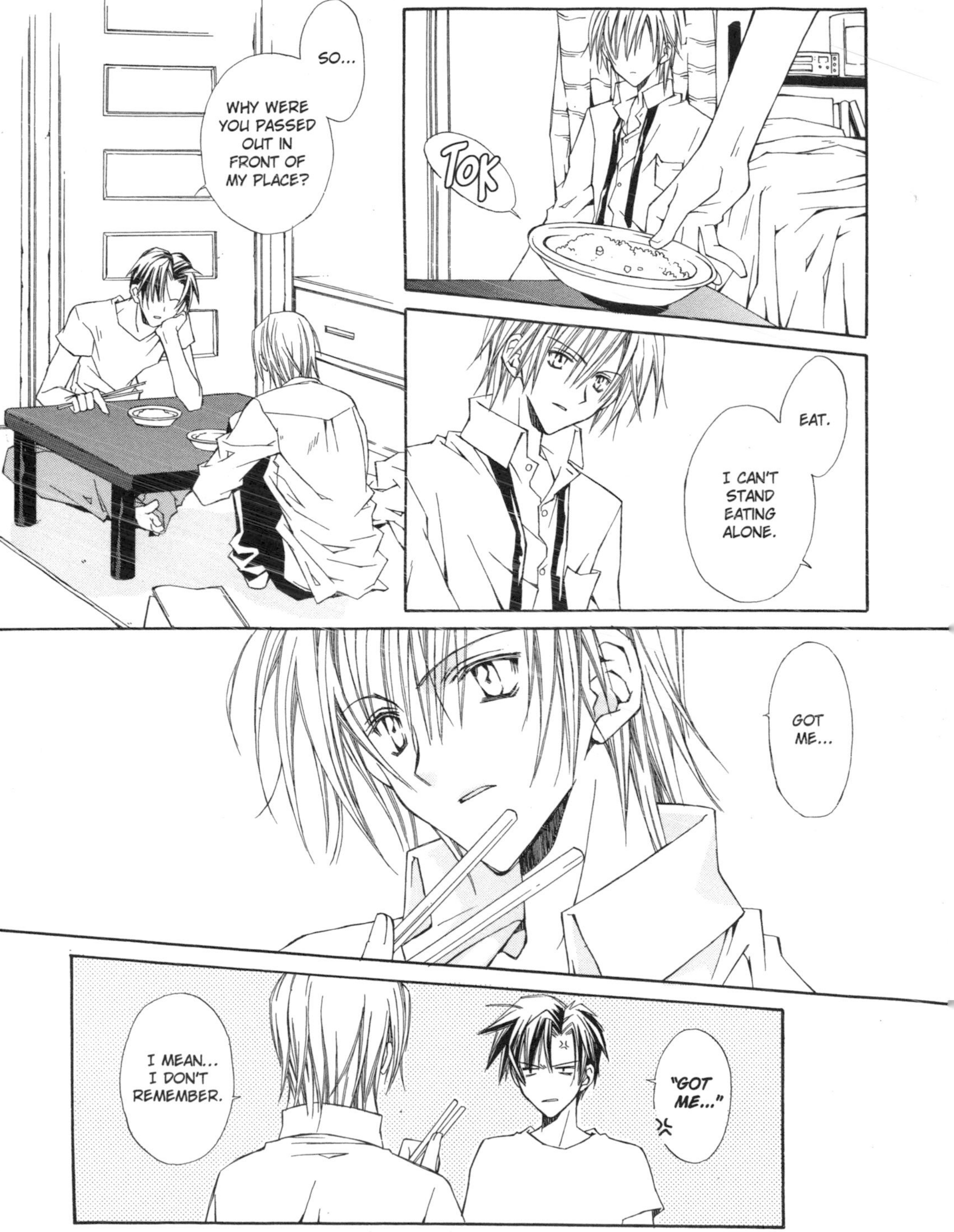
TOK
EAT.
I CAN'T STAND EATING ALONE.
SO...
WHY WERE YOU PASSED OUT IN FRONT OF MY PLACE?
GOT ME...
"GOT ME..."
I MEAN... I DON'T REMEMBER.

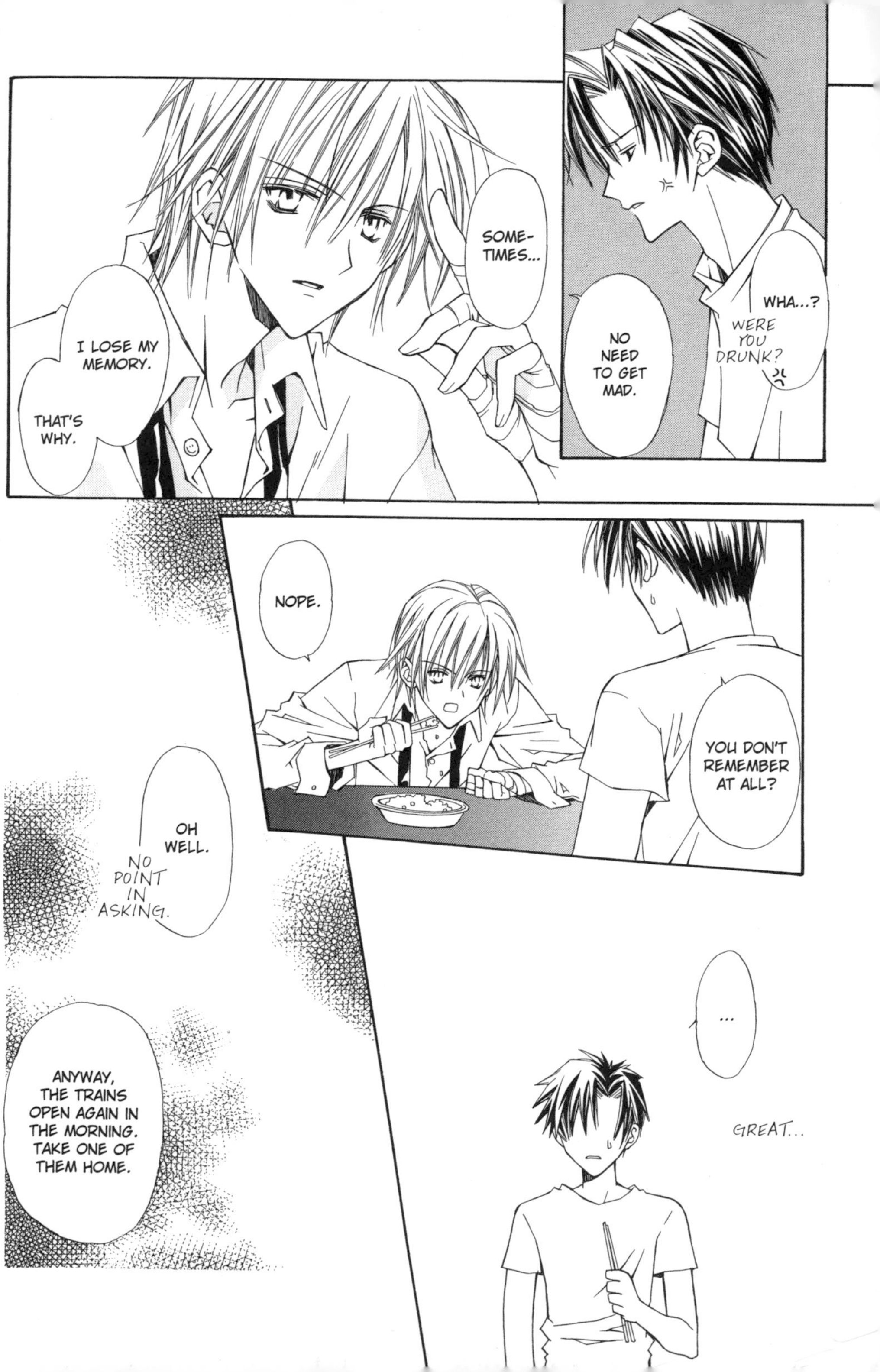
WHA...?
WERE YOU DRUNK?
NO NEED TO GET MAD.
SOME-TIMES...
I LOSE MY MEMORY.
THAT'S WHY.
YOU DON'T REMEMBER AT ALL?
NOPE.
OH WELL.
NO POINT IN ASKING.
...
GREAT...
ANYWAY, THE TRAINS OPEN AGAIN IN THE MORNING. TAKE ONE OF THEM HOME.

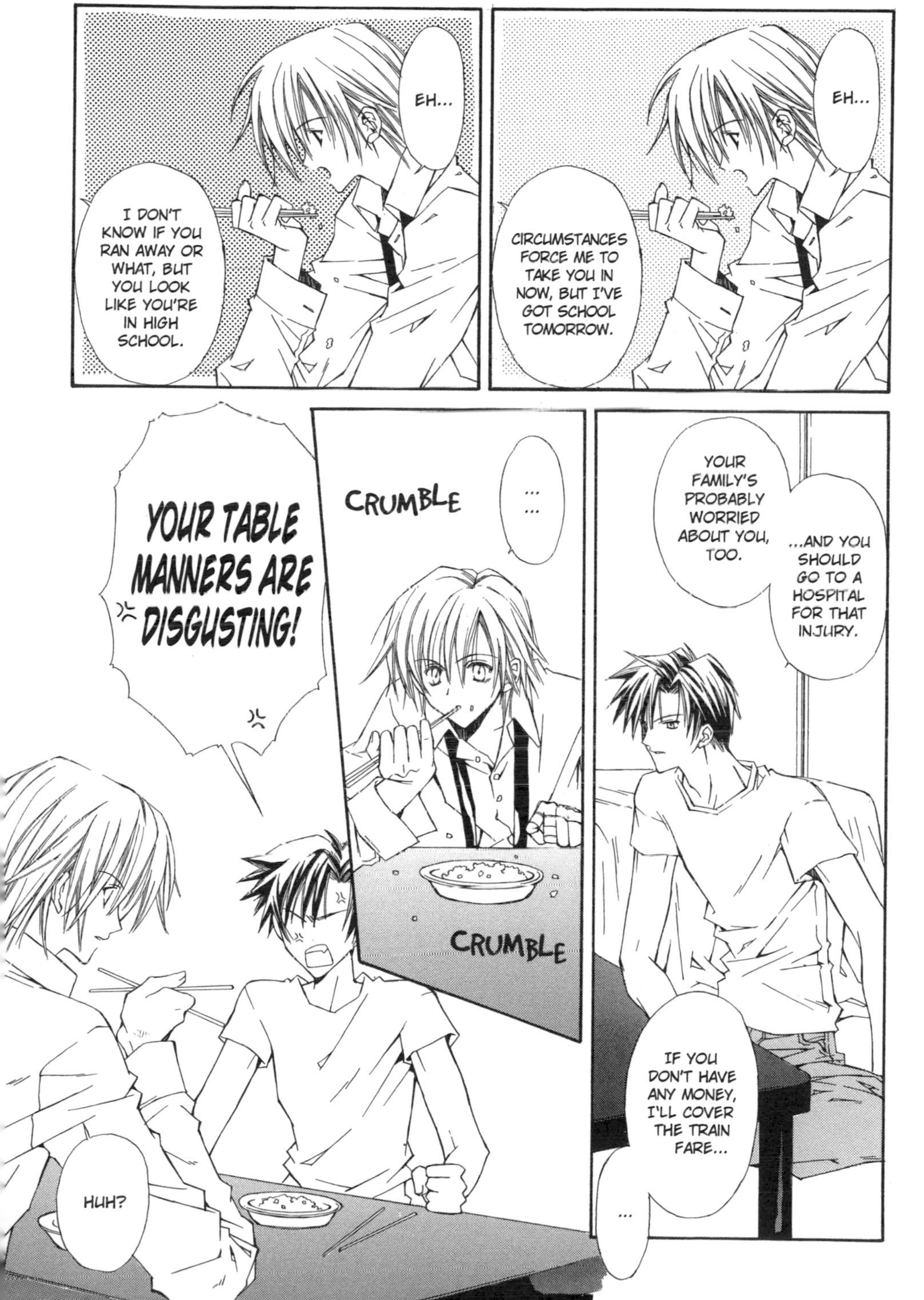
EH...
CIRCUMSTANCES FORCE ME TO TAKE YOU IN NOW, BUT I'VE GOT SCHOOL TOMORROW.
EH...
I DON'T KNOW IF YOU RAN AWAY OR WHAT, BUT YOU LOOK LIKE YOU'RE IN HIGH SCHOOL.
YOUR FAMILY'S PROBABLY WORRIED ABOUT YOU, TOO.
...AND YOU SHOULD GO TO A HOSPITAL FOR THAT INJURY.
IF YOU DON'T HAVE ANY MONEY, I'LL COVER THE TRAIN FARE...
...
CRUMBLE
... ...
CRUMBLE
YOUR TABLE MANNERS ARE DISGUSTING!
HUH?

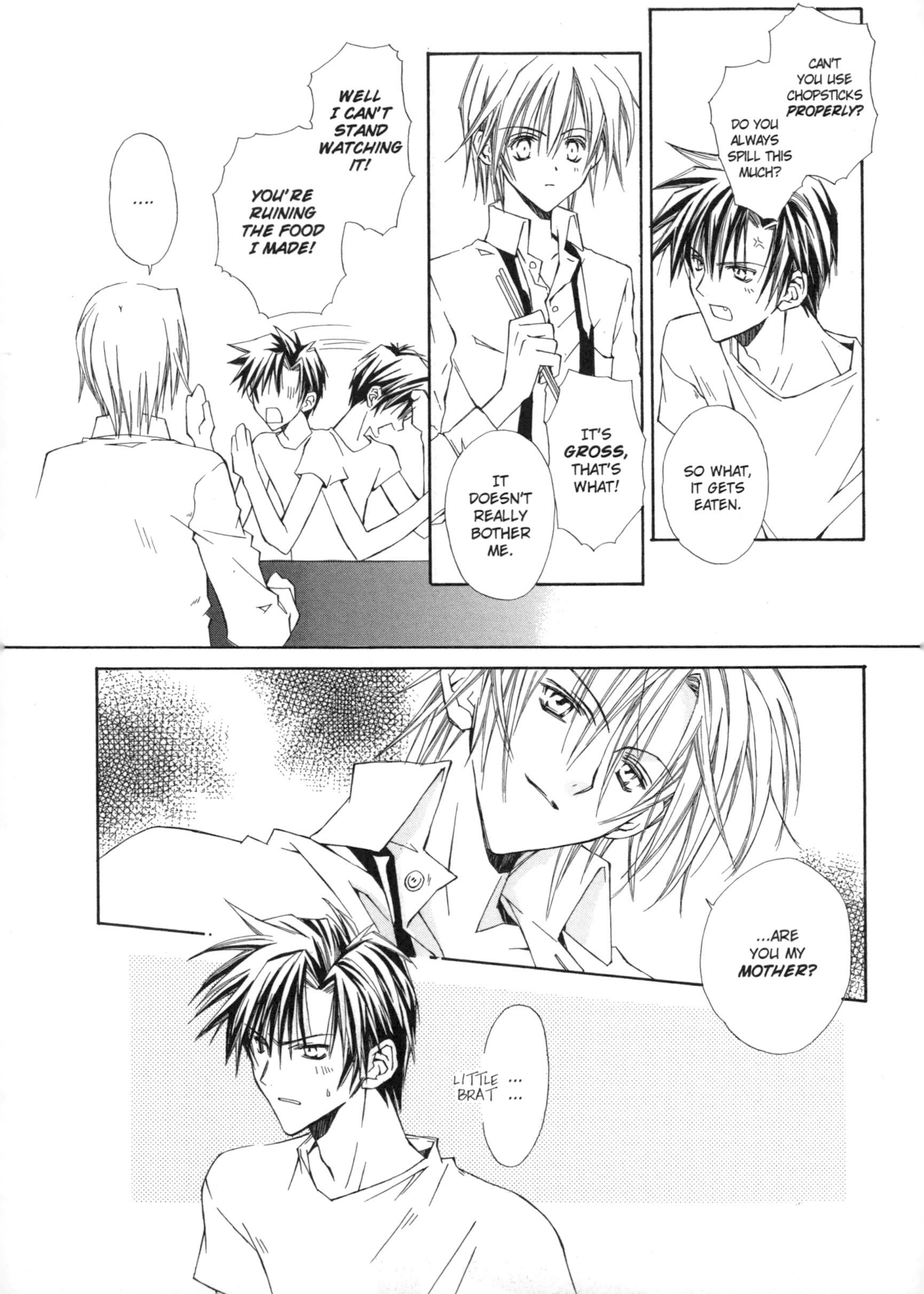
CAN'T YOU USE CHOPSTICKS PROPERLY?
DO YOU ALWAYS SPILL THIS MUCH?
SO WHAT, IT GETS EATEN.
IT'S GROSS, THAT'S WHAT!
IT DOESN'T REALLY BOTHER ME.
WELL I CAN'T STAND WATCHING IT!
YOU'RE RUINING THE FOOD I MADE!
....
...ARE YOU MY MOTHER?
LITTLE ... BRAT ...

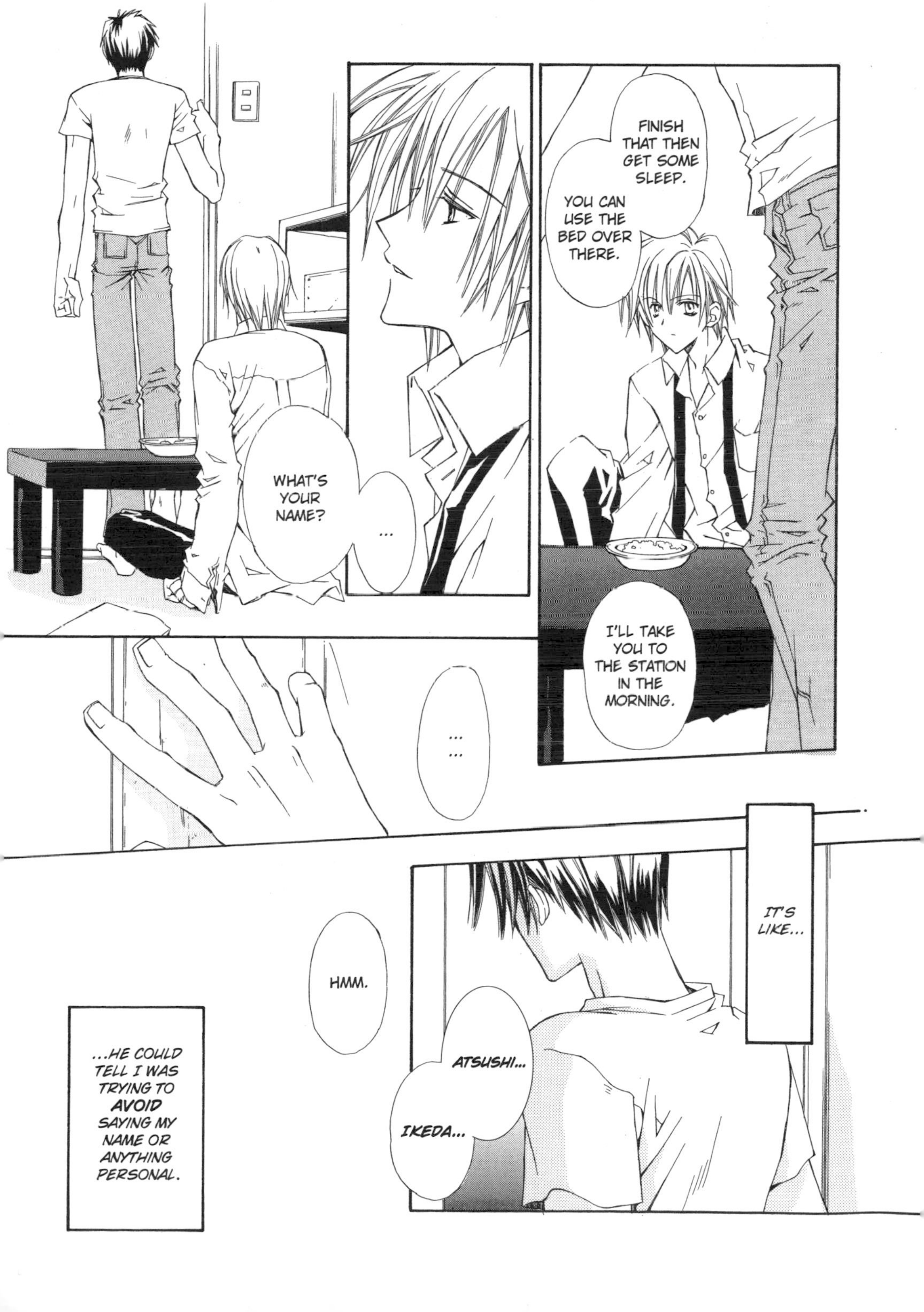
FINISH THAT THEN GET SOME SLEEP.
YOU CAN USE THE BED OVER THERE.
I'LL TAKE YOU TO THE STATION IN THE MORNING.
WHAT'S YOUR NAME?
...
...
...
ATSUSHI...
IKEDA...
HMM.
IT'S LIKE...
...HE COULD TELL I WAS TRYING TO **AVOID** SAYING MY NAME OR ANYTHING PERSONAL.

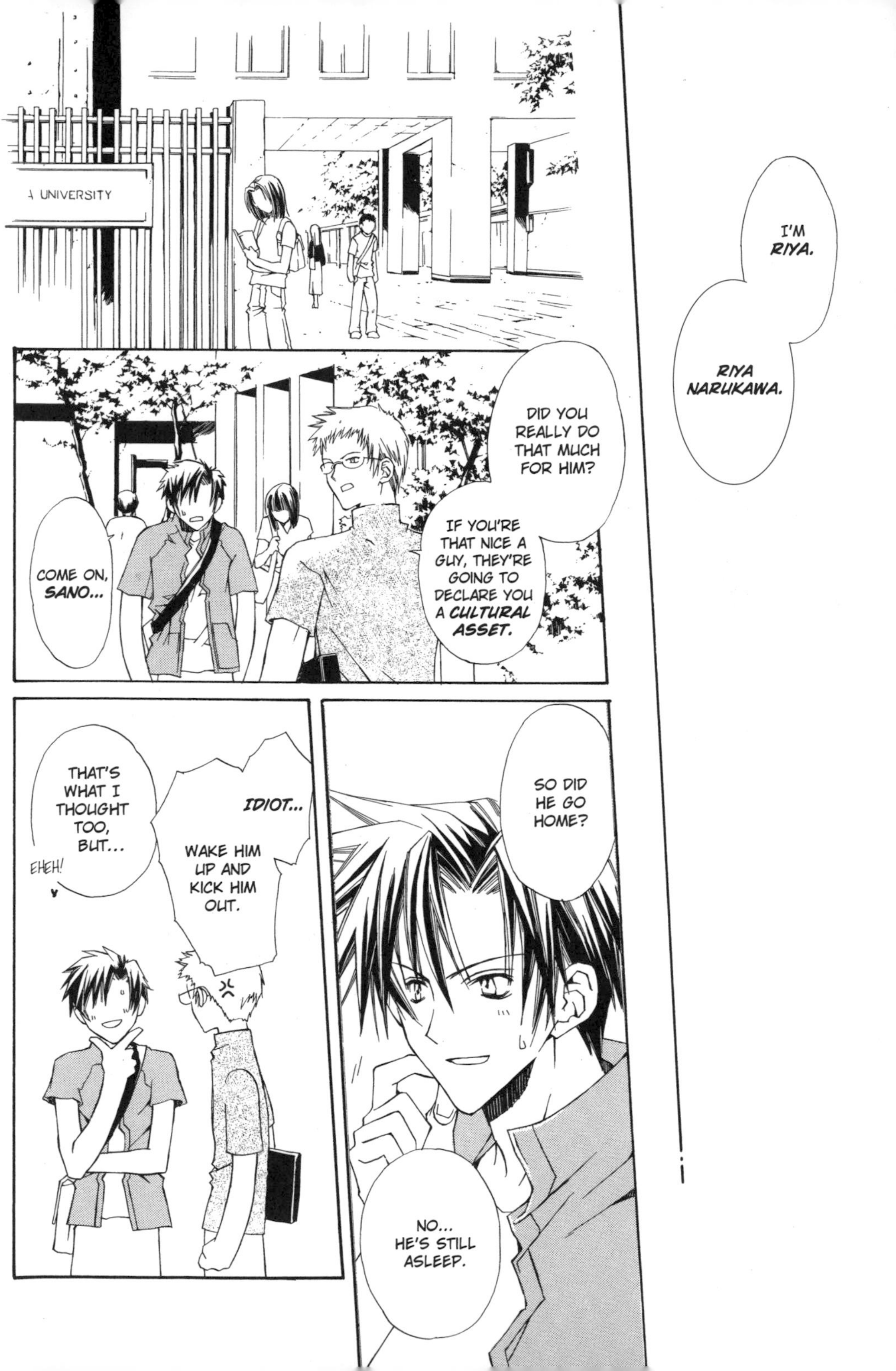
I'M RIYA.
RIYA NARUKAWA.
A UNIVERSITY
DID YOU REALLY DO THAT MUCH FOR HIM?
IF YOU'RE THAT NICE A GUY, THEY'RE GOING TO DECLARE YOU A CULTURAL ASSET.
COME ON, SANO...
SO DID HE GO HOME?
NO... HE'S STILL ASLEEP.
IDIOT...
WAKE HIM UP AND KICK HIM OUT.
THAT'S WHAT I THOUGHT TOO, BUT...
EHEH!

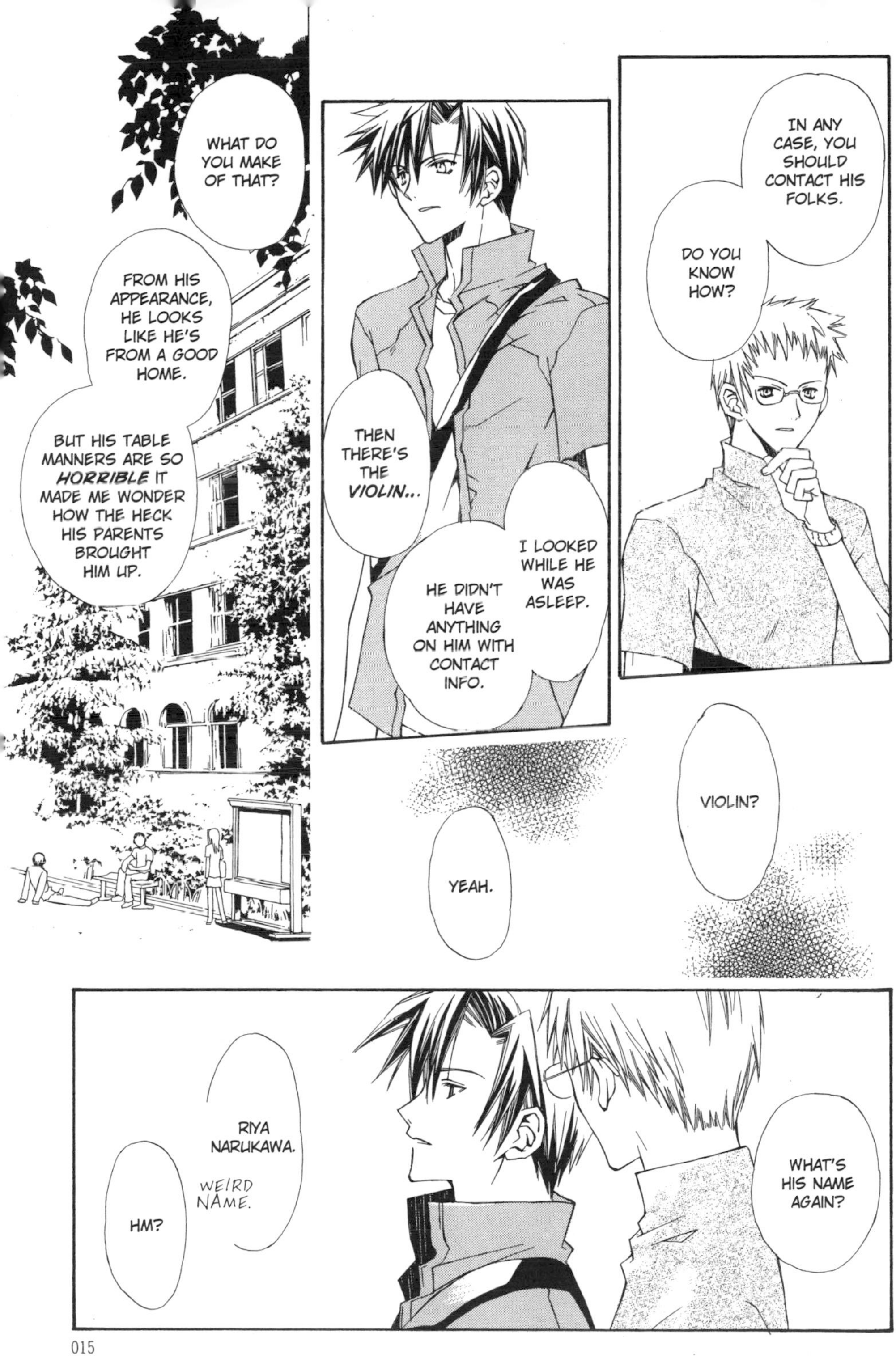
IN ANY CASE, YOU SHOULD CONTACT HIS FOLKS.
DO YOU KNOW HOW?
I LOOKED WHILE HE WAS ASLEEP.
HE DIDN'T HAVE ANYTHING ON HIM WITH CONTACT INFO.
THEN THERE'S THE *VIOLIN*...
VIOLIN?
YEAH.
WHAT DO YOU MAKE OF THAT?
FROM HIS APPEARANCE, HE LOOKS LIKE HE'S FROM A GOOD HOME.
BUT HIS TABLE MANNERS ARE SO *HORRIBLE* IT MADE ME WONDER HOW THE HECK HIS PARENTS BROUGHT HIM UP.
WHAT'S HIS NAME AGAIN?
RIYA NARUKAWA.
WEIRD NAME.
HM?

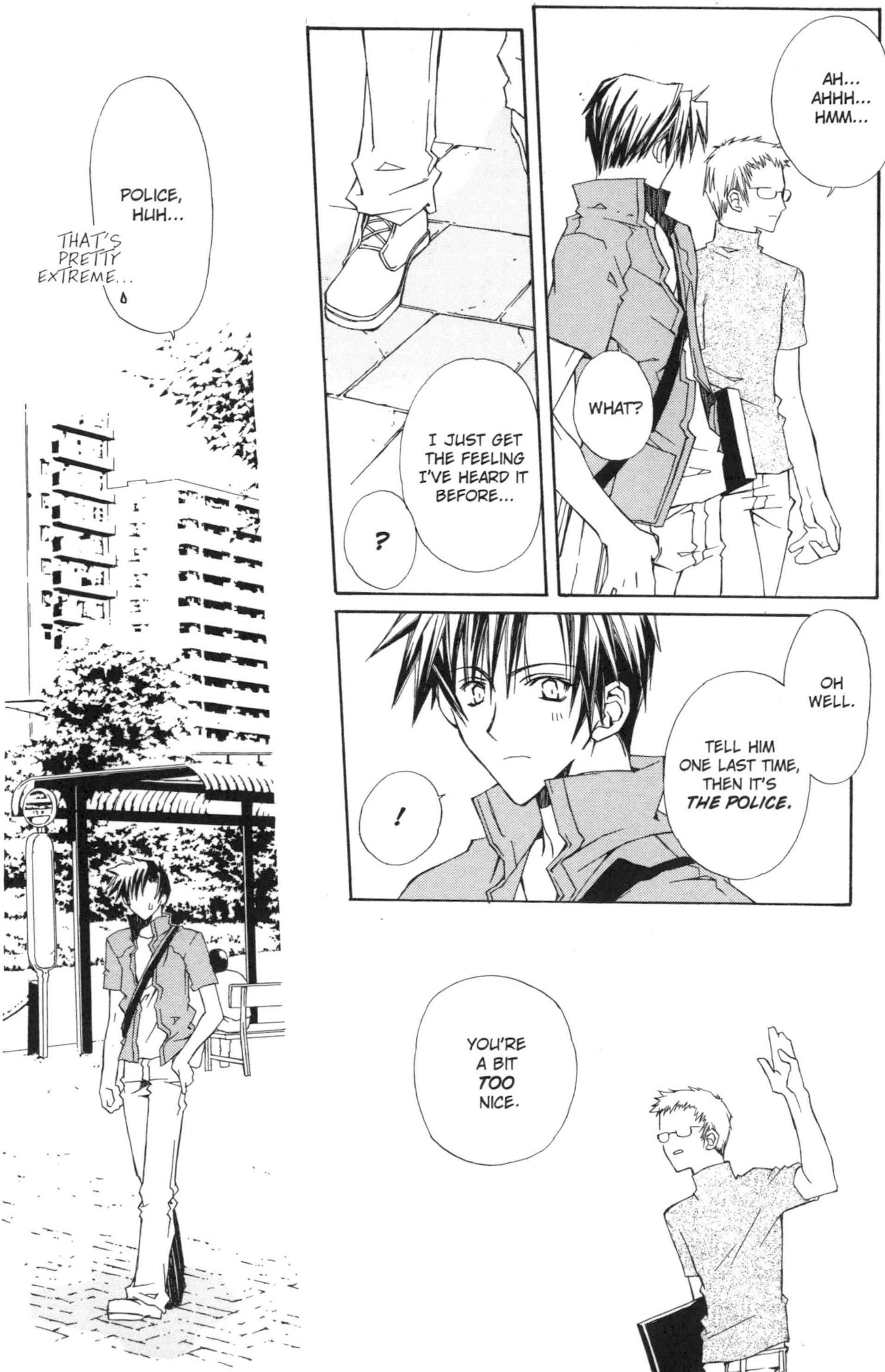
AH... AHHH... HMM...
WHAT?
I JUST GET THE FEELING I'VE HEARD IT BEFORE...
?
OH WELL.
TELL HIM ONE LAST TIME, THEN IT'S ***THE POLICE.***
!
YOU'RE A BIT ***TOO*** NICE.
POLICE, HUH...
THAT'S PRETTY EXTREME...

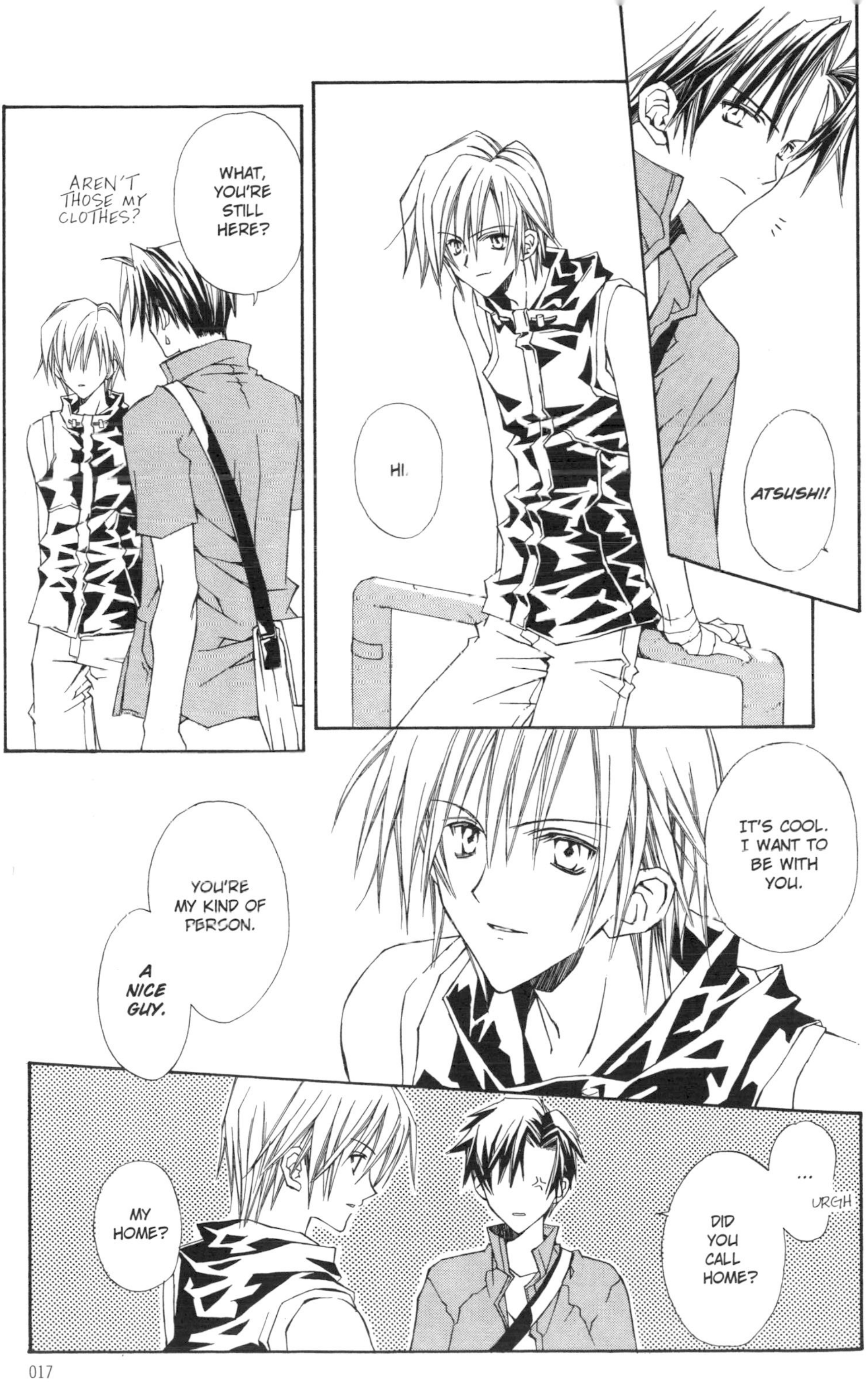
ATSUSHI!
HI.
WHAT, YOU'RE STILL HERE?
AREN'T THOSE MY CLOTHES?
IT'S COOL. I WANT TO BE WITH YOU.
YOU'RE MY KIND OF PERSON.
A NICE GUY.
...
URGH
DID YOU CALL HOME?
MY HOME?

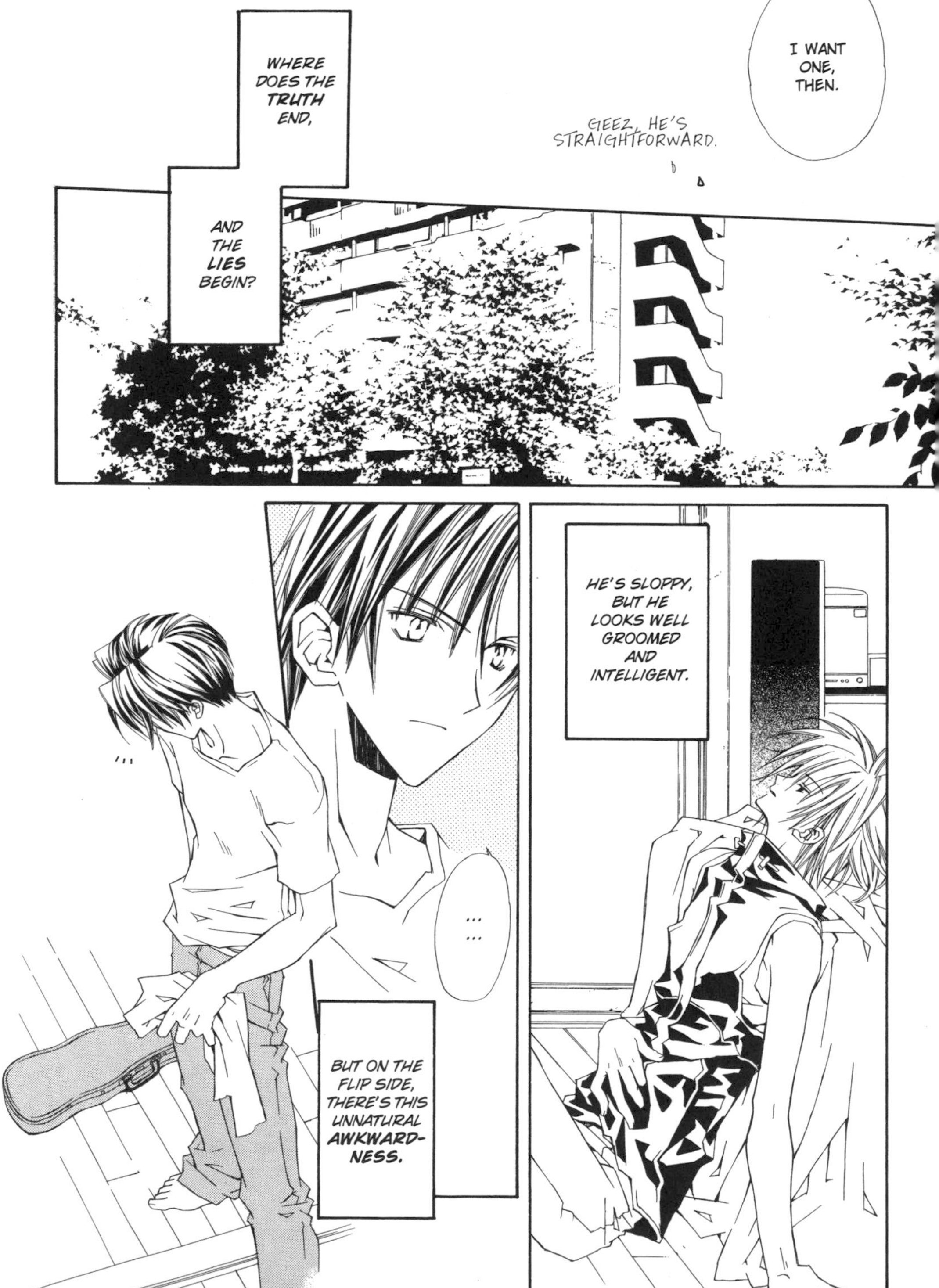
I WANT ONE, THEN.
GEEZ, HE'S STRAIGHTFORWARD.
WHERE DOES THE TRUTH END,
AND THE LIES BEGIN?
HE'S SLOPPY, BUT HE LOOKS WELL GROOMED AND INTELLIGENT.
......
BUT ON THE FLIP SIDE, THERE'S THIS UNNATURAL AWKWARDNESS.

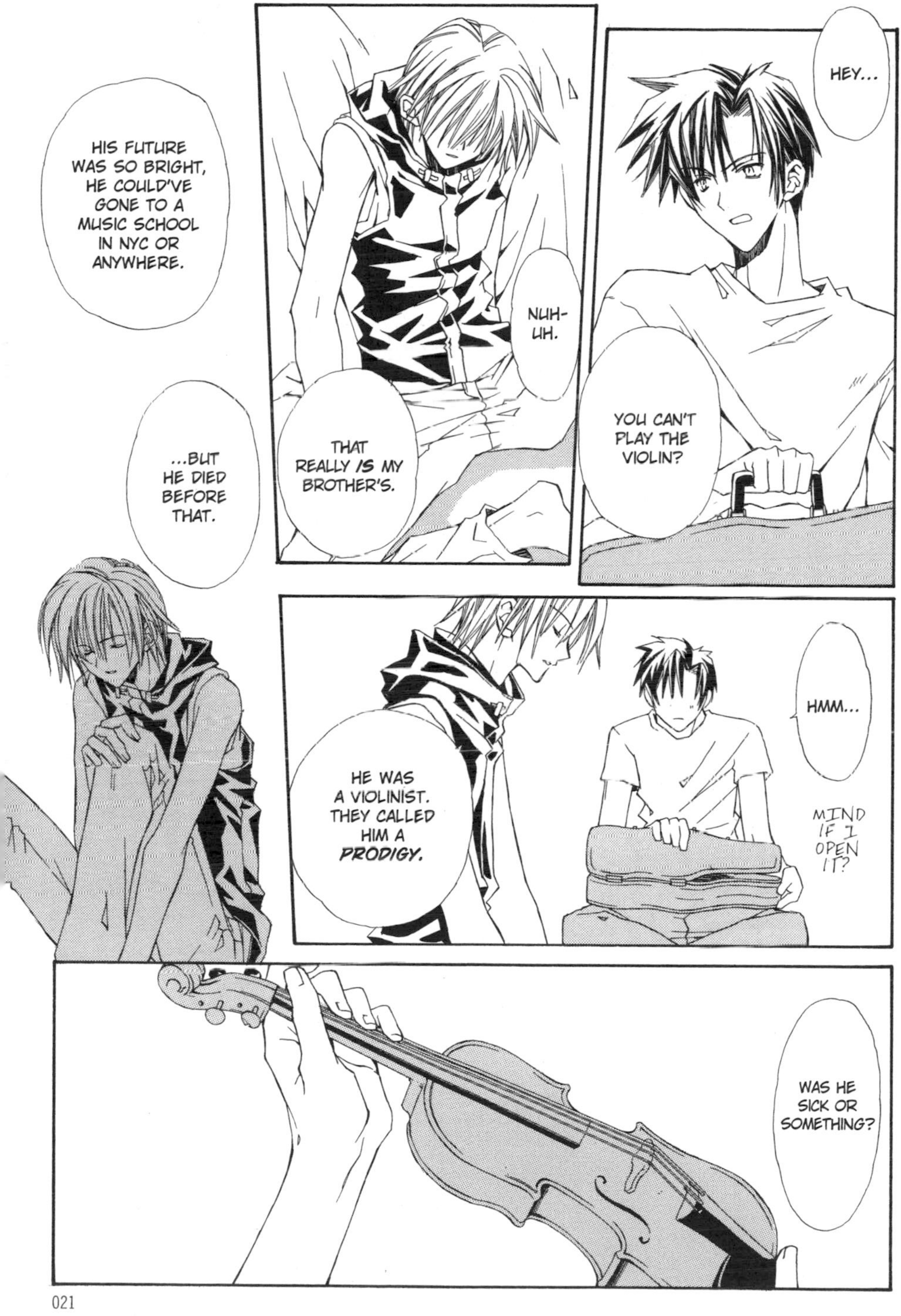
HEY...
YOU CAN'T PLAY THE VIOLIN?
NUH-UH.
THAT REALLY *IS* MY BROTHER'S.
HMM...
MIND IF I OPEN IT?
HE WAS A VIOLINIST. THEY CALLED HIM A *PRODIGY.*
HIS FUTURE WAS SO BRIGHT, HE COULD'VE GONE TO A MUSIC SCHOOL IN NYC OR ANYWHERE.
...BUT HE DIED BEFORE THAT.
WAS HE SICK OR SOMETHING?

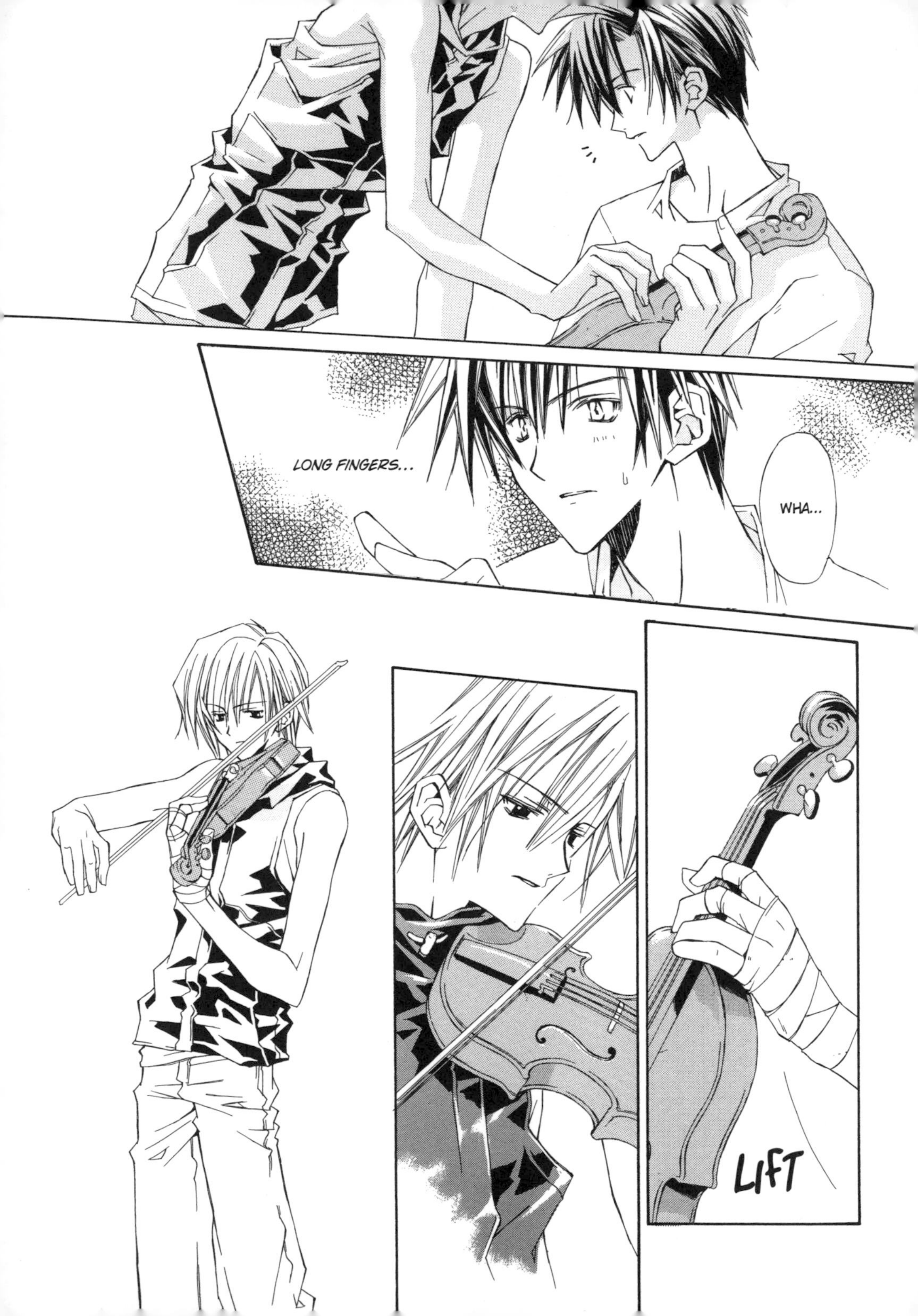
WHA...
LONG FINGERS...
LIFT

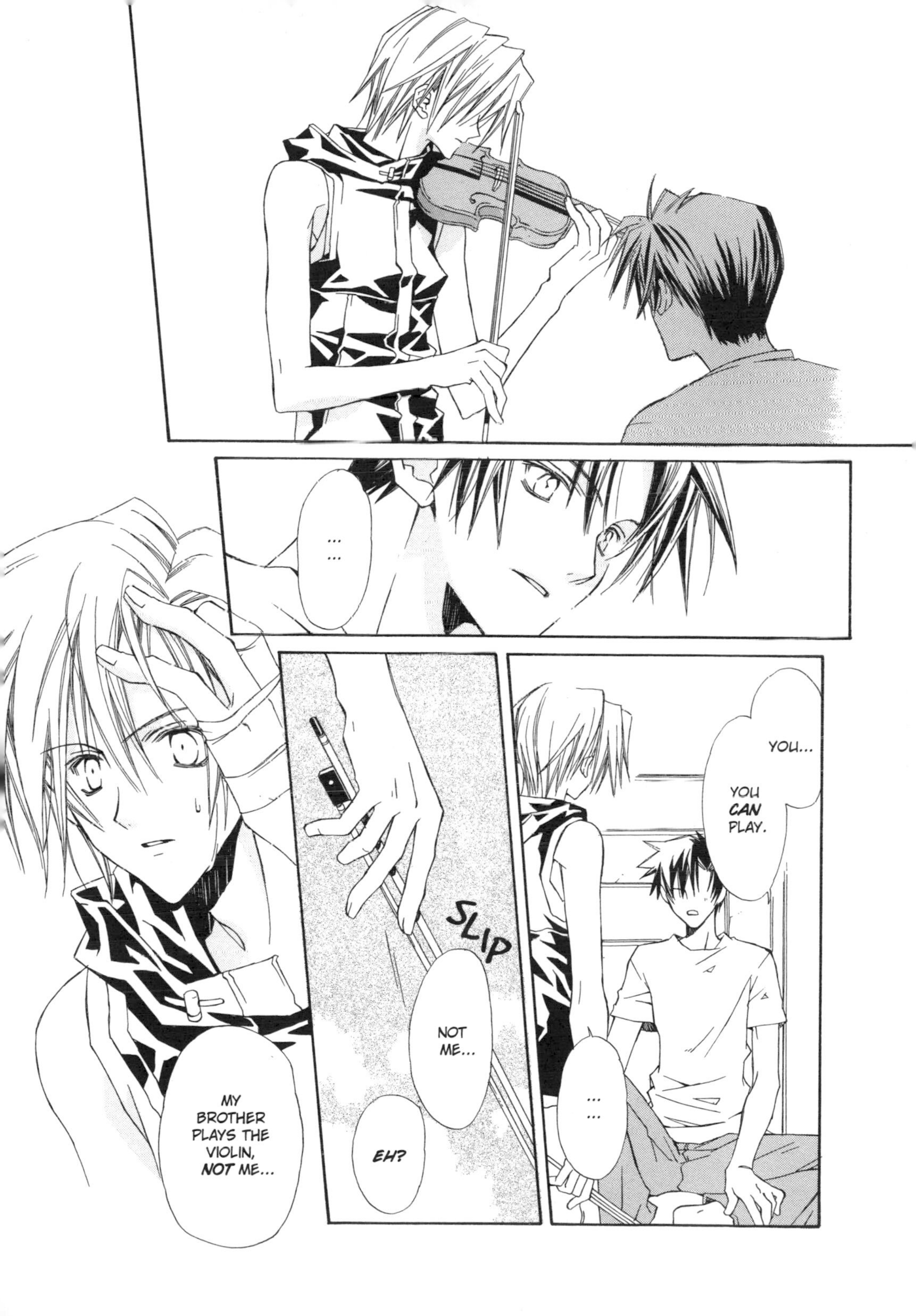
... ...
YOU...
YOU CAN PLAY.
... ...
SLIP
NOT ME...
EH?
MY BROTHER PLAYS THE VIOLIN, NOT ME...

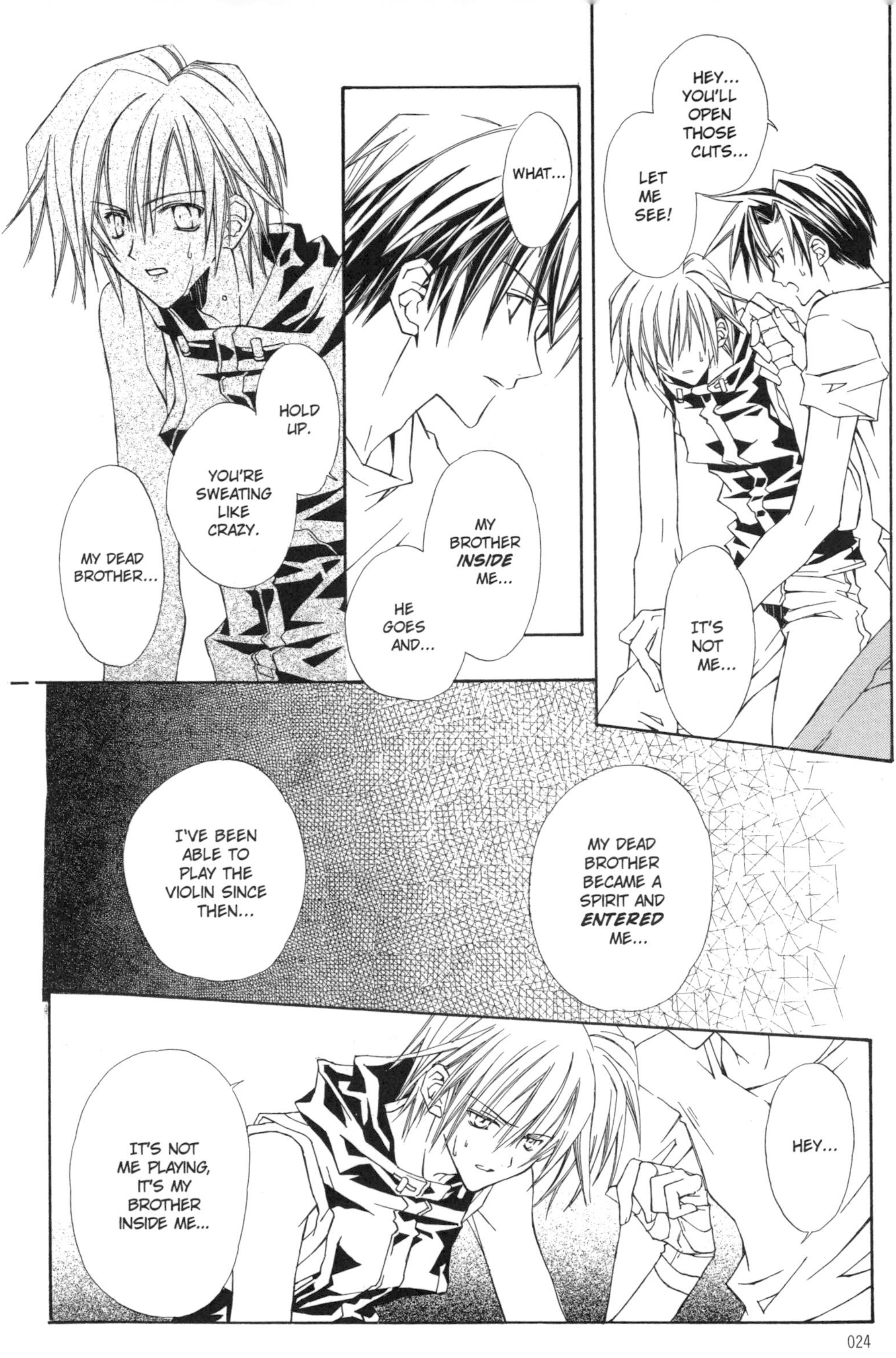
HEY... YOU'LL OPEN THOSE CUTS...
LET ME SEE!
IT'S NOT ME...
WHAT...
MY BROTHER *INSIDE* ME...
HE GOES AND...
HOLD UP.
YOU'RE SWEATING LIKE CRAZY.
MY DEAD BROTHER...
MY DEAD BROTHER BECAME A SPIRIT AND *ENTERED* ME...
I'VE BEEN ABLE TO PLAY THE VIOLIN SINCE THEN...
HEY...
IT'S NOT ME PLAYING, IT'S MY BROTHER INSIDE ME...

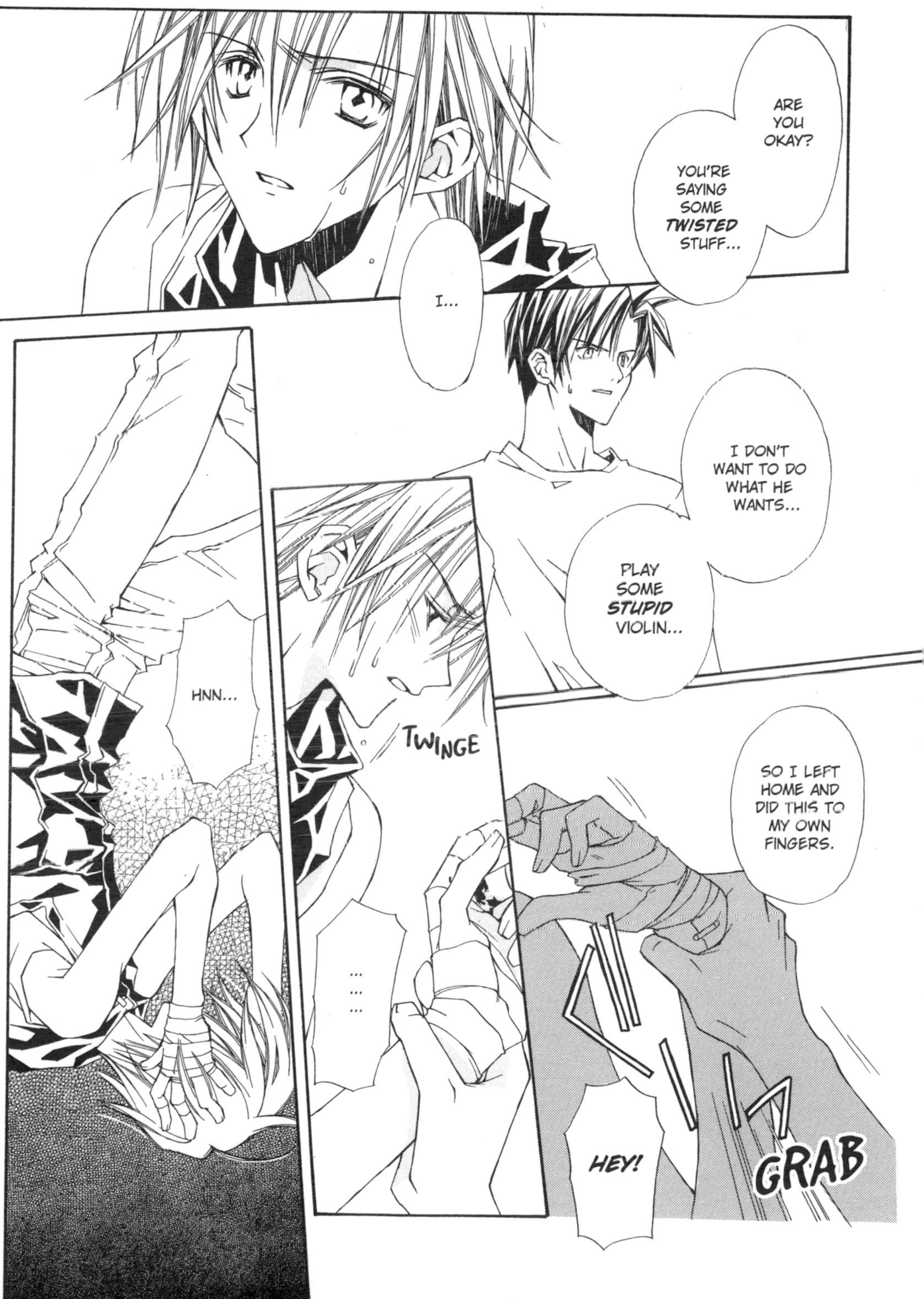
ARE YOU OKAY?
YOU'RE SAYING SOME TWISTED STUFF...
I...
I DON'T WANT TO DO WHAT HE WANTS...
PLAY SOME STUPID VIOLIN...
SO I LEFT HOME AND DID THIS TO MY OWN FINGERS.
GRAB
HEY!
TWINGE
...
...
...
HNN...

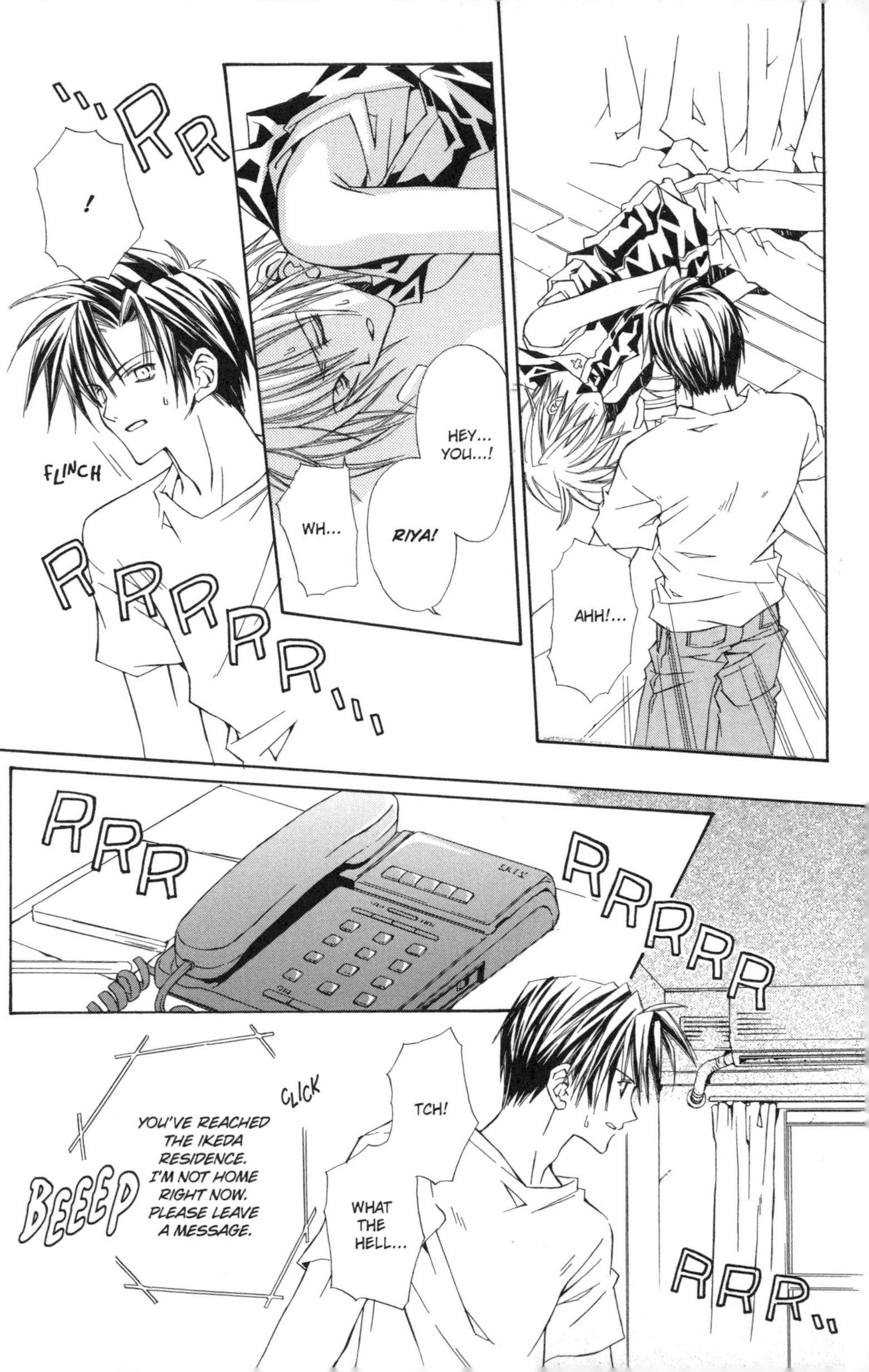
AHH!...
HEY... YOU...!
RIYA!
WH...
...RR
!
FLINCH
RRRRR...
RRRRRR
RRR
RRR..
TCH!
WHAT THE HELL...
CLICK
YOU'VE REACHED THE IKEDA RESIDENCE. I'M NOT HOME RIGHT NOW. PLEASE LEAVE A MESSAGE.
BEEEP

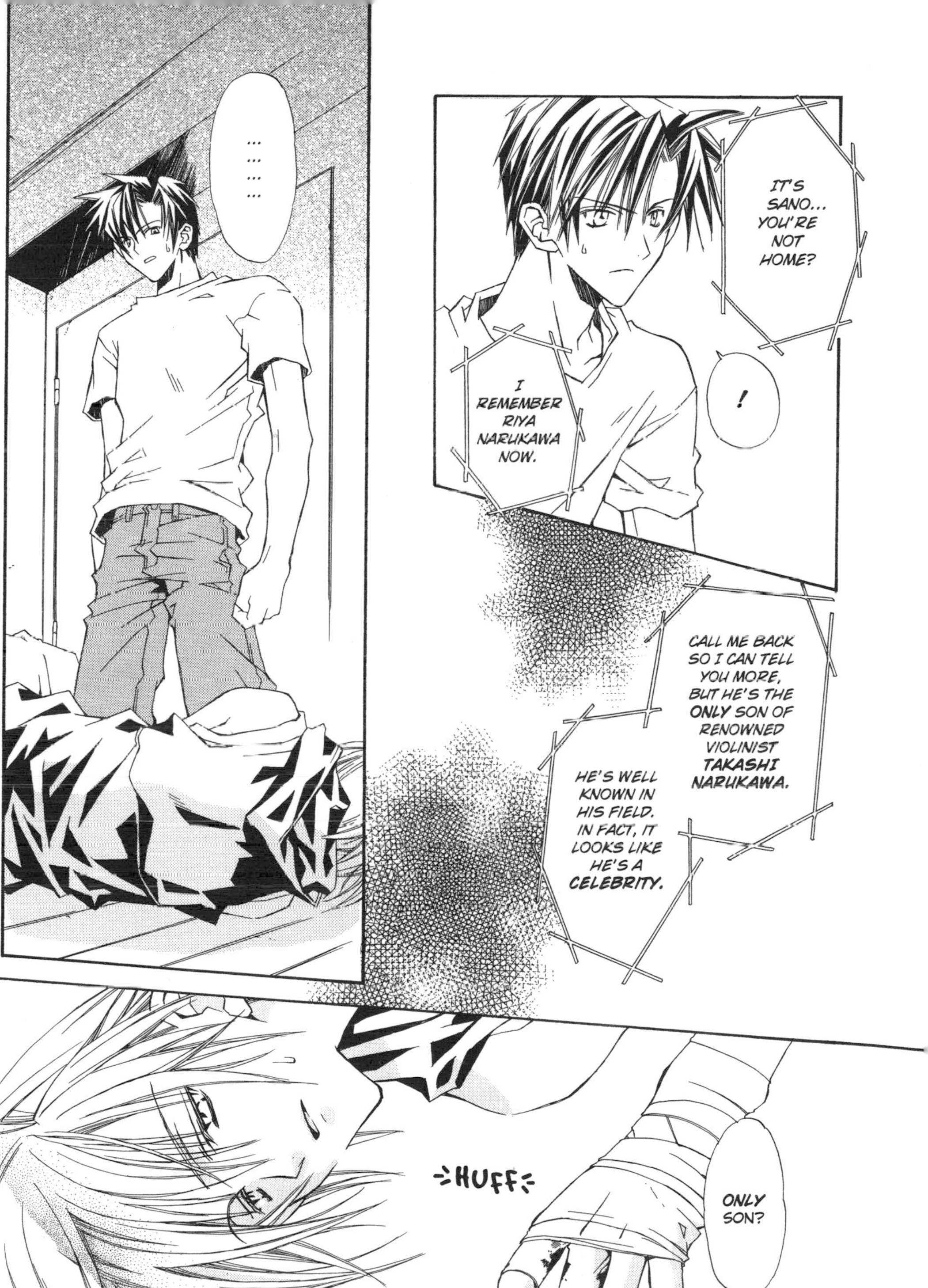
IT'S SANO... YOU'RE NOT HOME?
I REMEMBER RIYA NARUKAWA NOW.
!
CALL ME BACK SO I CAN TELL YOU MORE, BUT HE'S THE **ONLY** SON OF RENOWNED VIOLINIST **TAKASHI NARUKAWA.**
HE'S WELL KNOWN IN HIS FIELD. IN FACT, IT LOOKS LIKE HE'S A **CELEBRITY.**
....
ONLY SON?
HUFF

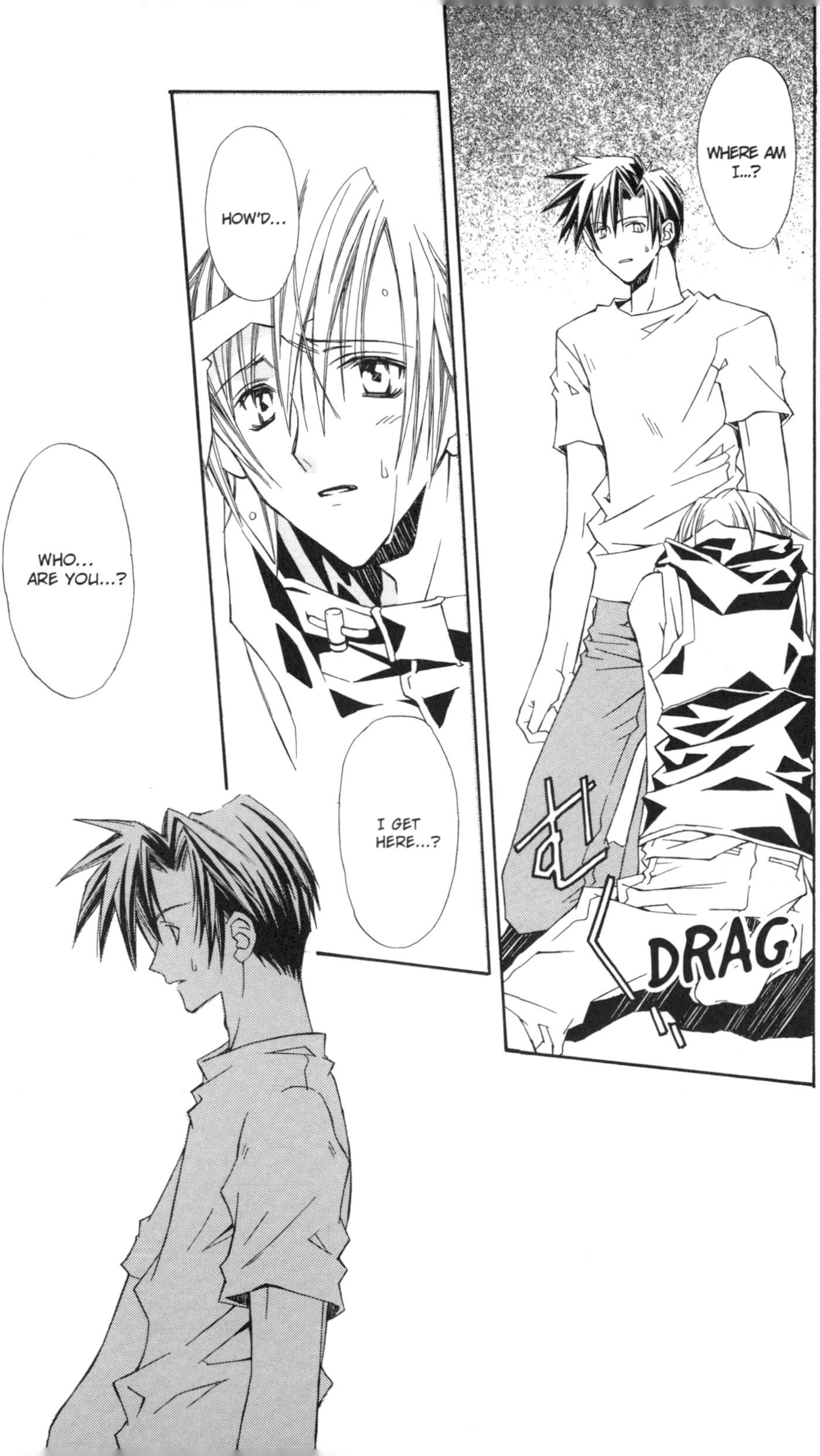
WHERE AM I...?
DRAG
HOW'D...
I GET HERE...?
WHO... ARE YOU...?

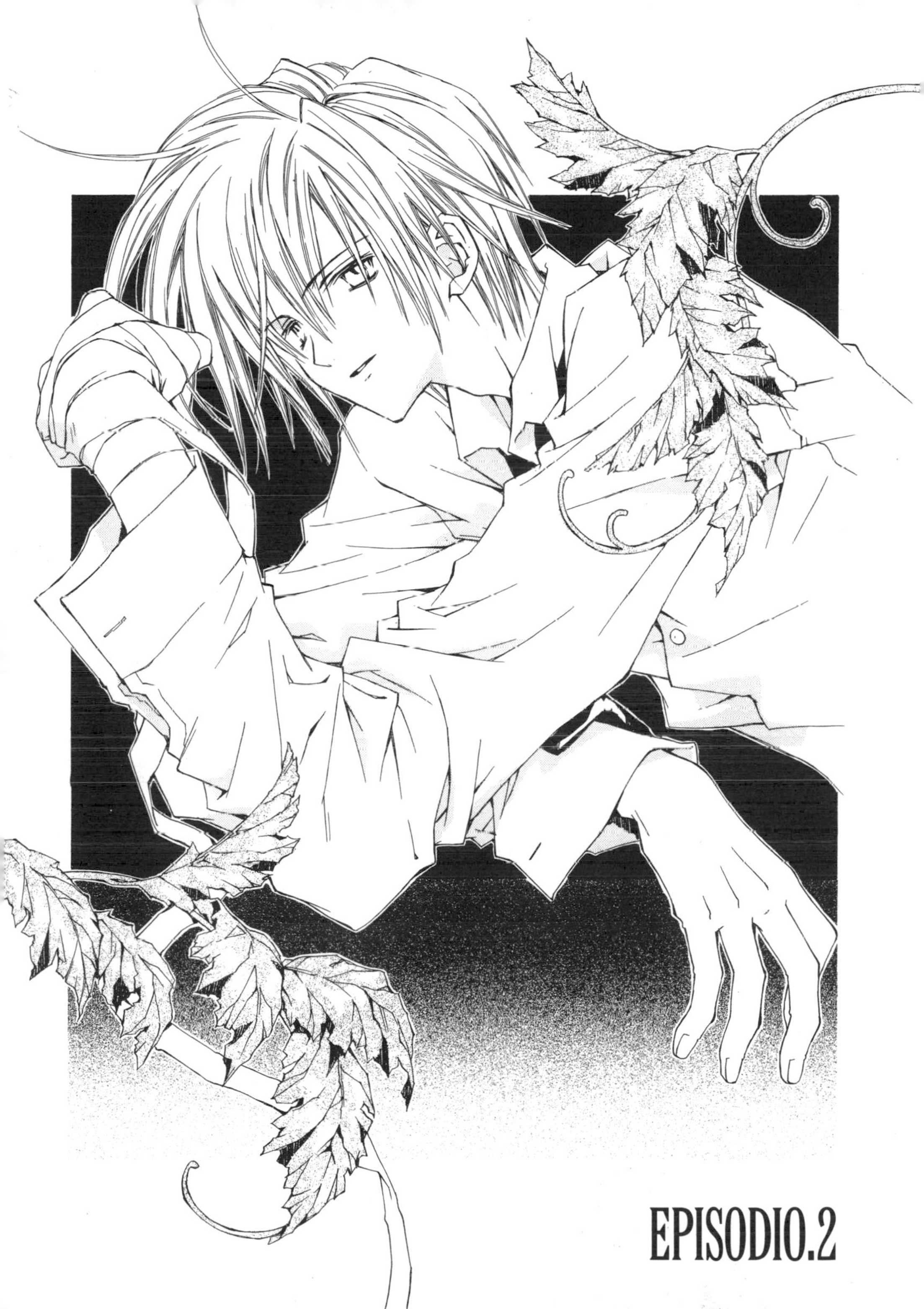

EPISODIO.2

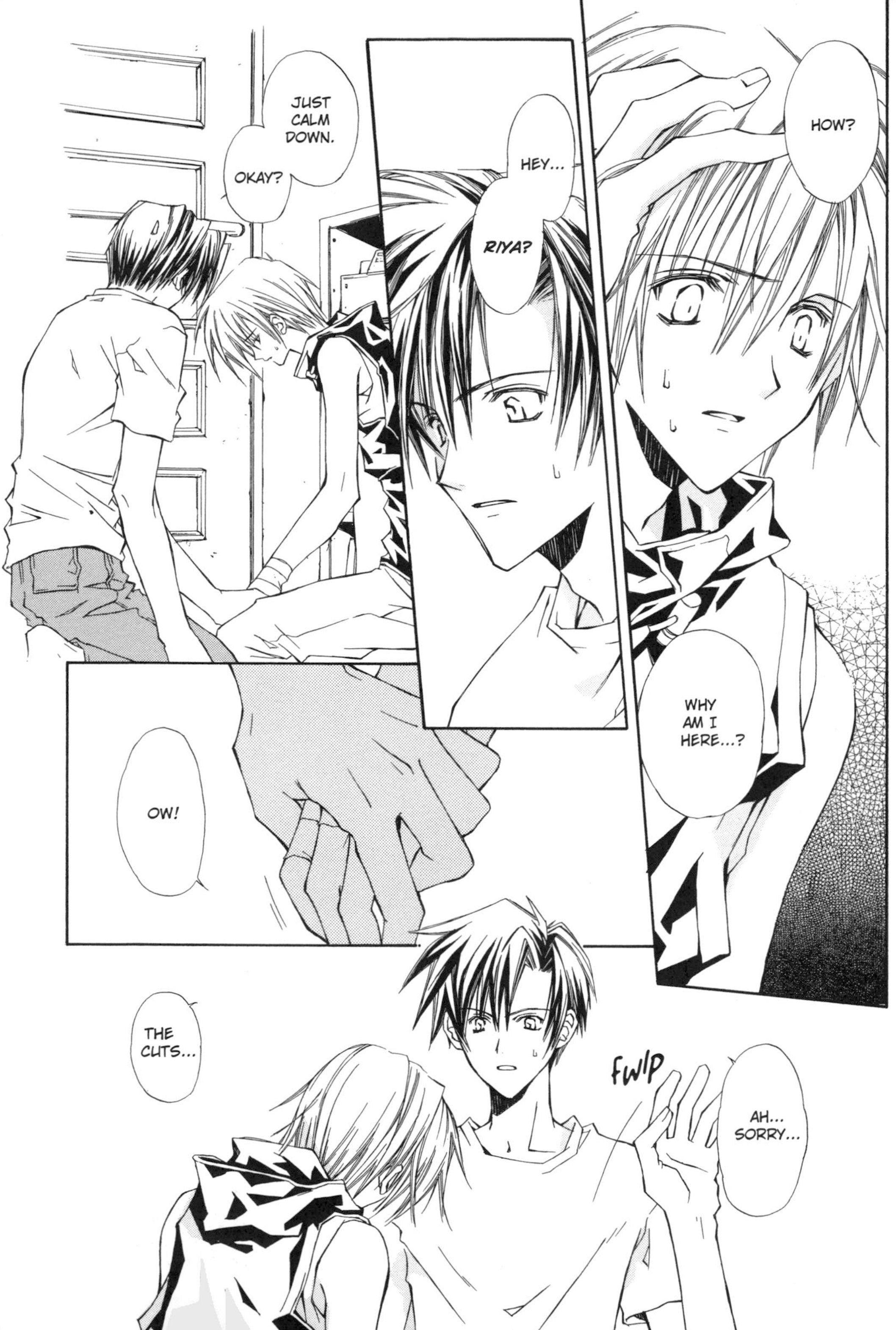
HOW?
WHY AM I HERE...?
HEY...
RIYA?
JUST CALM DOWN.
OKAY?
OW!
THE CUTS...
FWIP
AH... SORRY...

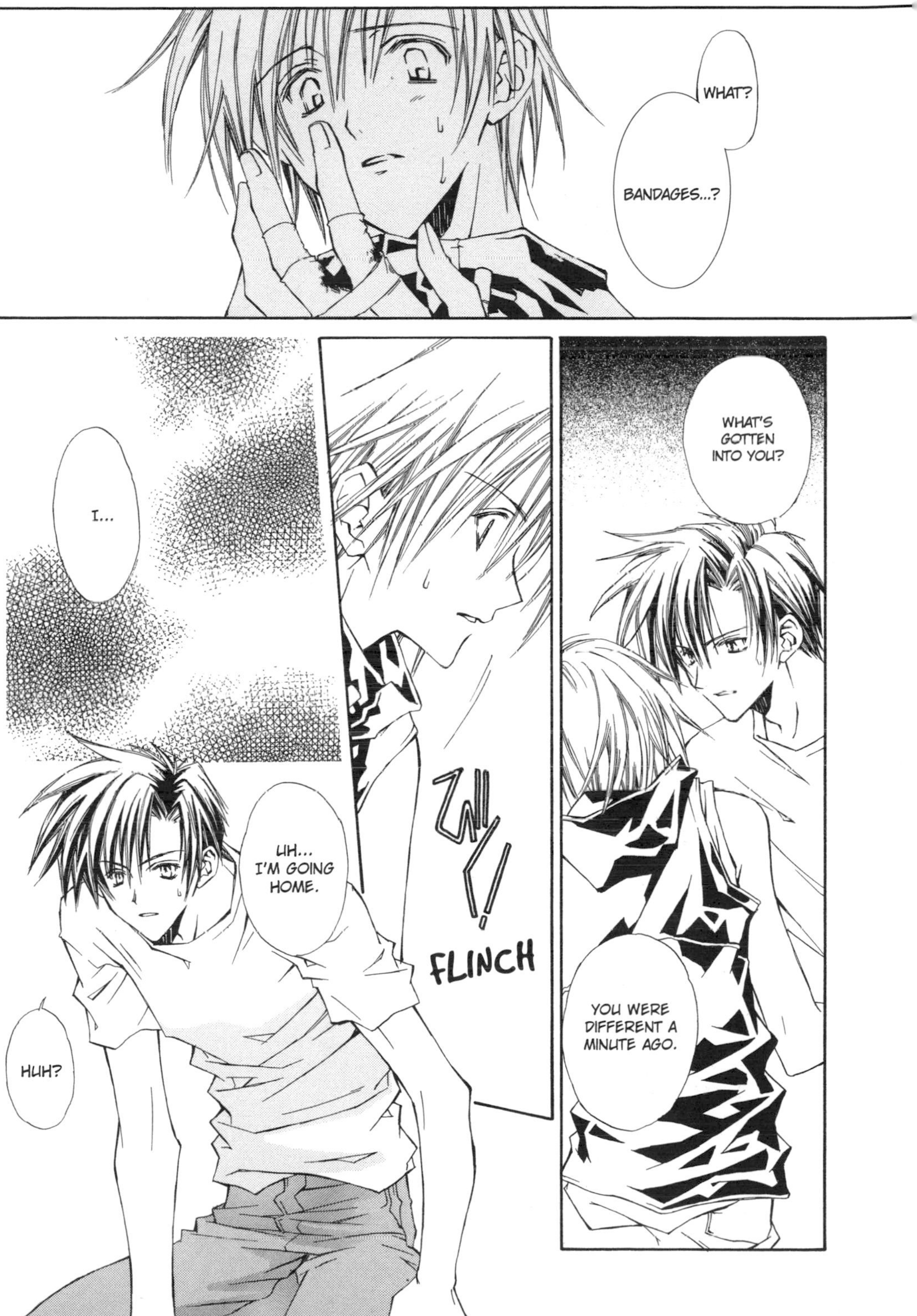
WHAT?
BANDAGES...?
WHAT'S GOTTEN INTO YOU?
YOU WERE DIFFERENT A MINUTE AGO.
FLINCH
I...
UH... I'M GOING HOME.
HUH?

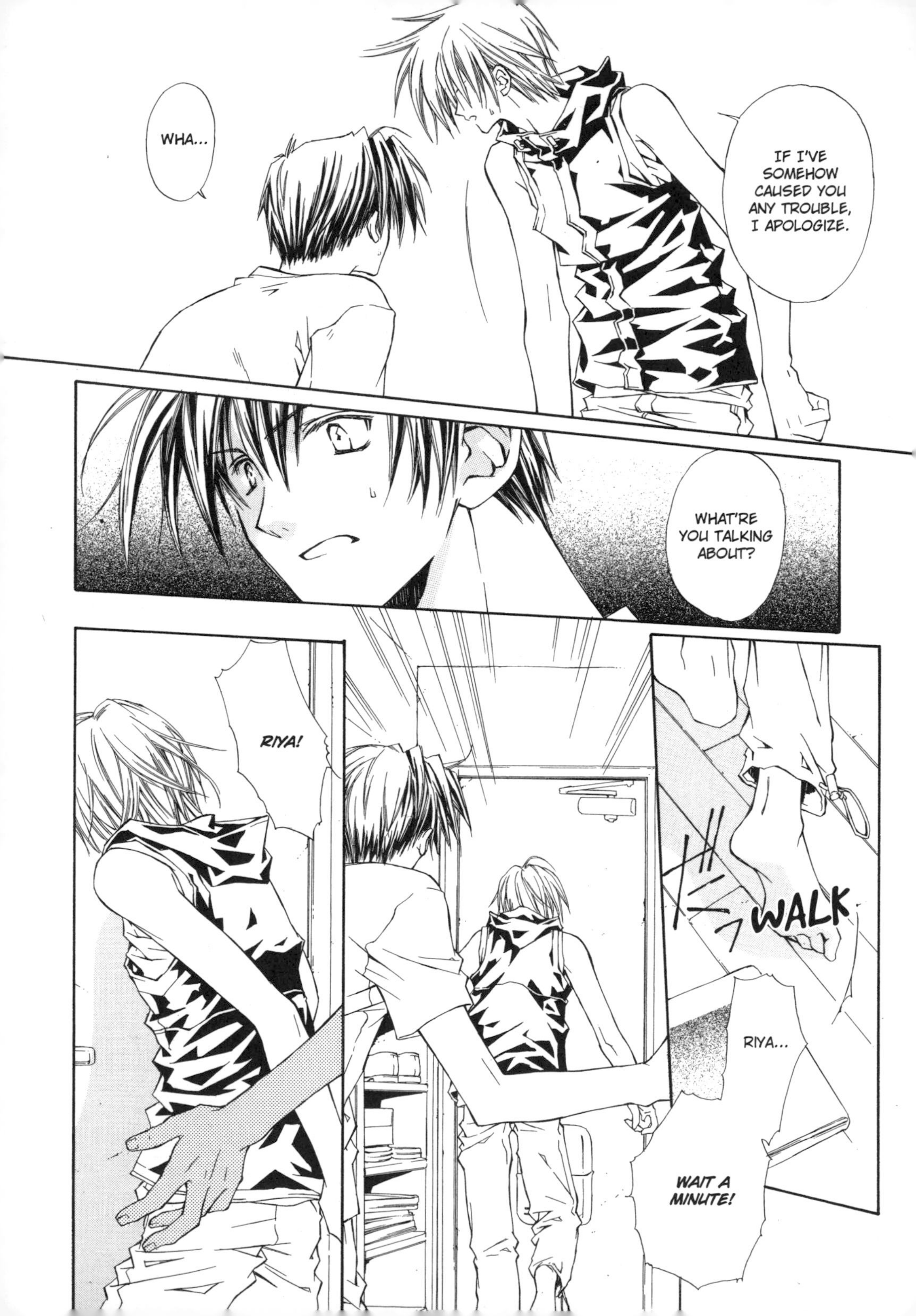
IF I'VE SOMEHOW CAUSED YOU ANY TROUBLE, I APOLOGIZE.
WHA...
WHAT'RE YOU TALKING ABOUT?
WALK
RIYA...
WAIT A MINUTE!
RIYA!

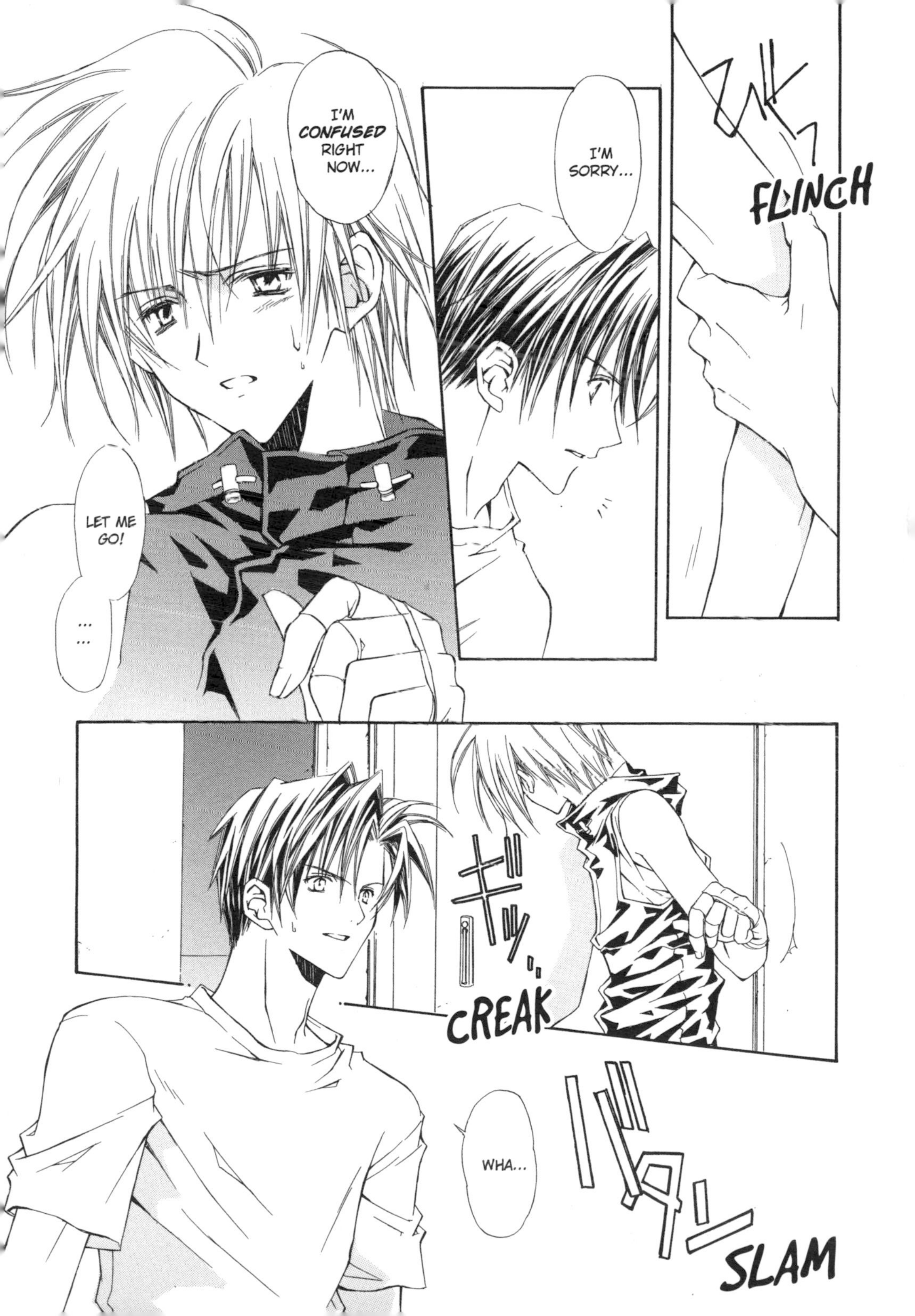

FLINCH
I'M SORRY...
I'M CONFUSED RIGHT NOW...
LET ME GO!
... ...
CREAK
SLAM
WHA...

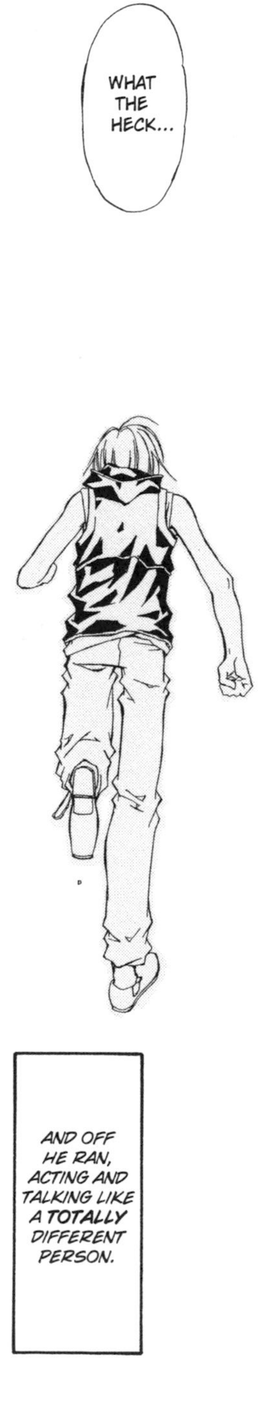
WHAT THE HECK...
AND OFF HE RAN, ACTING AND TALKING LIKE A **TOTALLY** DIFFERENT PERSON.

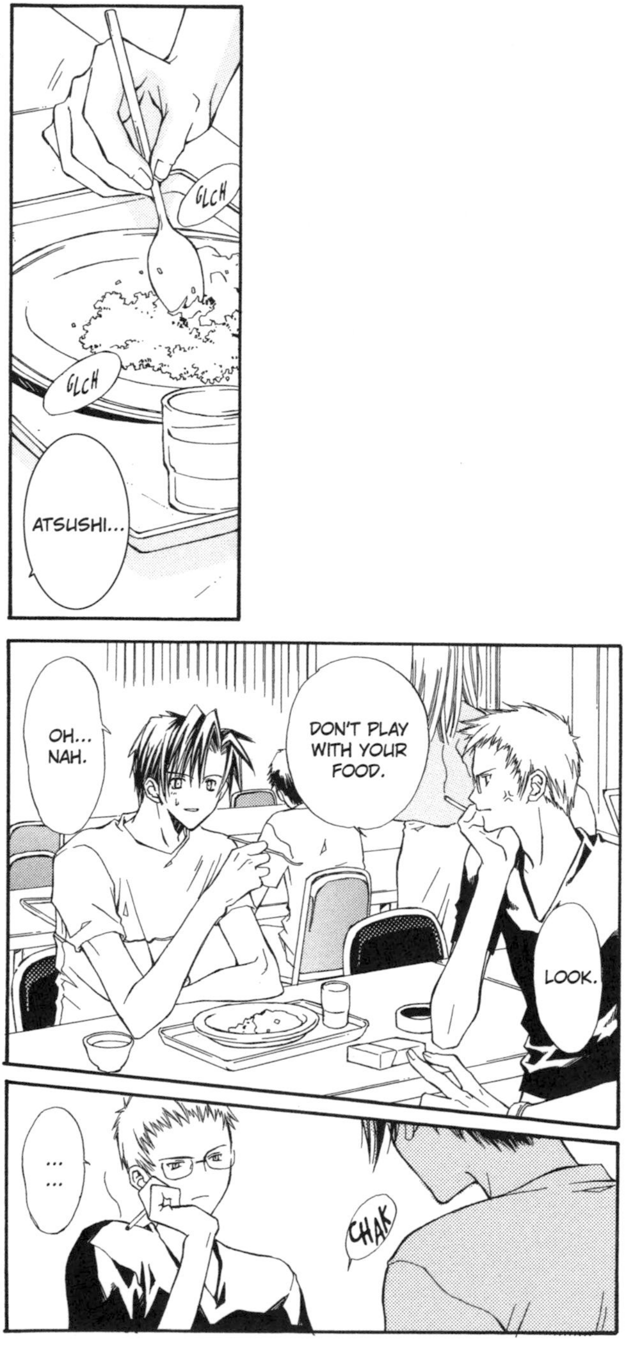
GLCH
GLCH
ATSUSHI...
DON'T PLAY WITH YOUR FOOD.
OH... NAH.
LOOK.
CHAK
... ...

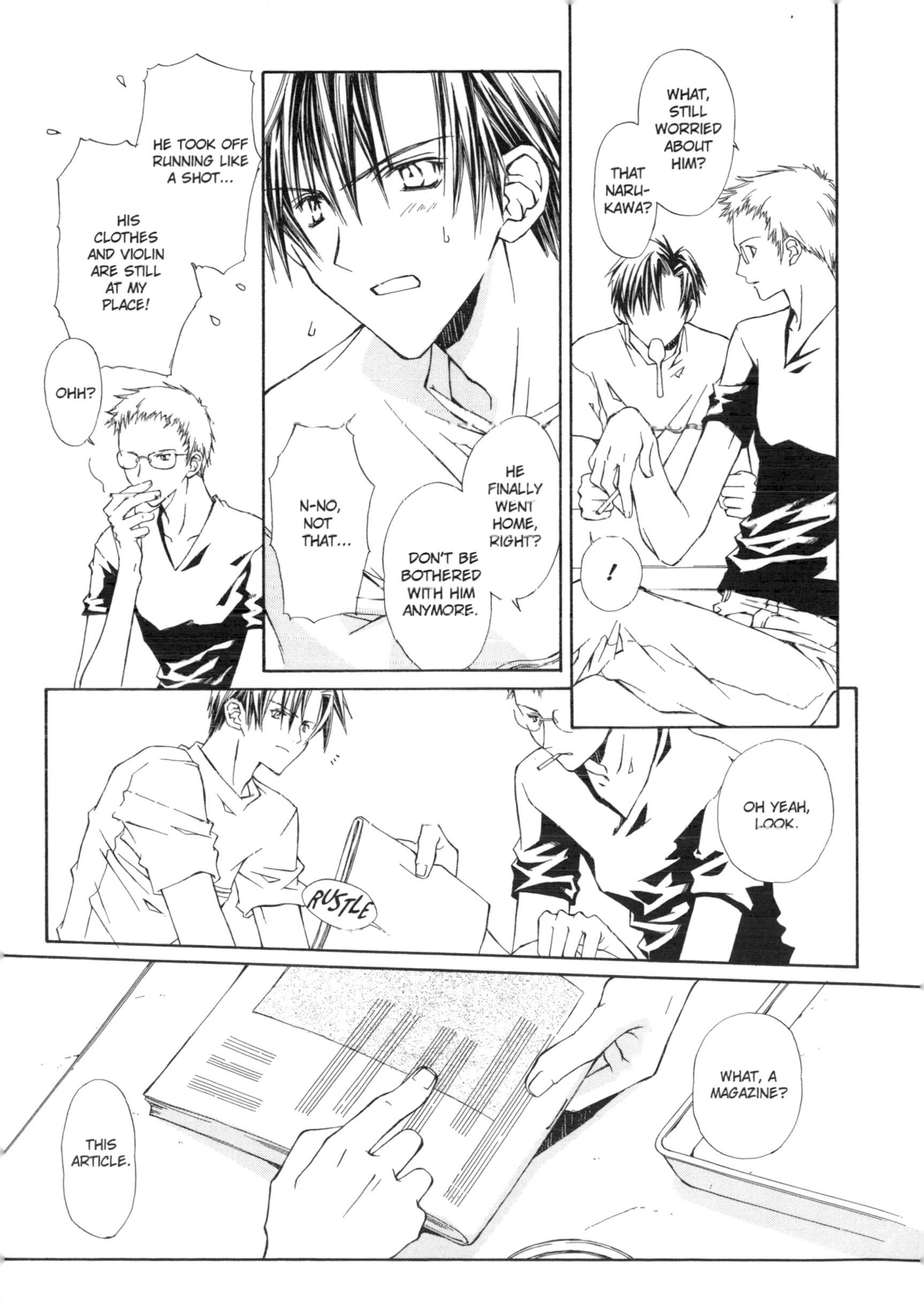
WHAT, STILL WORRIED ABOUT HIM?
THAT NARU-KAWA?
!
HE FINALLY WENT HOME, RIGHT?
DON'T BE BOTHERED WITH HIM ANYMORE.
N-NO, NOT THAT...
HE TOOK OFF RUNNING LIKE A SHOT...
HIS CLOTHES AND VIOLIN ARE STILL AT MY PLACE!
OHH?
OH YEAH, LOOK.
RUSTLE
WHAT, A MAGAZINE?
THIS ARTICLE.

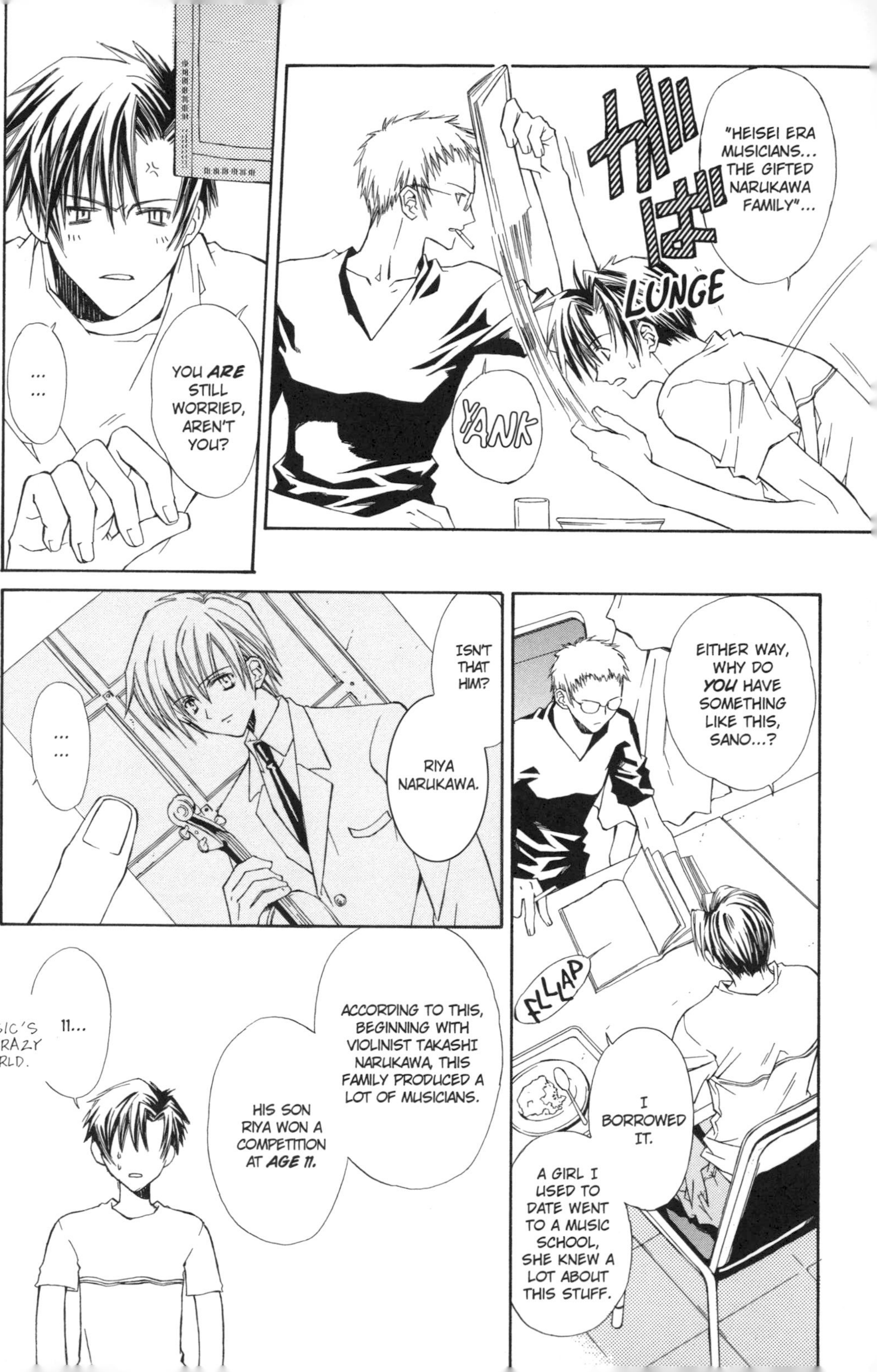
"HEISEI ERA MUSICIANS... THE GIFTED NARUKAWA FAMILY"...
LUNGE
YANK
YOU ARE STILL WORRIED, AREN'T YOU?
......
EITHER WAY, WHY DO YOU HAVE SOMETHING LIKE THIS, SANO...?
FLLLAP
I BORROWED IT.
A GIRL I USED TO DATE WENT TO A MUSIC SCHOOL, SHE KNEW A LOT ABOUT THIS STUFF.
ISN'T THAT HIM?
RIYA NARUKAWA.
......
ACCORDING TO THIS, BEGINNING WITH VIOLINIST TAKASHI NARUKAWA, THIS FAMILY PRODUCED A LOT OF MUSICIANS.
HIS SON RIYA WON A COMPETITION AT AGE 11.
11...
MUSIC'S A CRAZY WORLD.

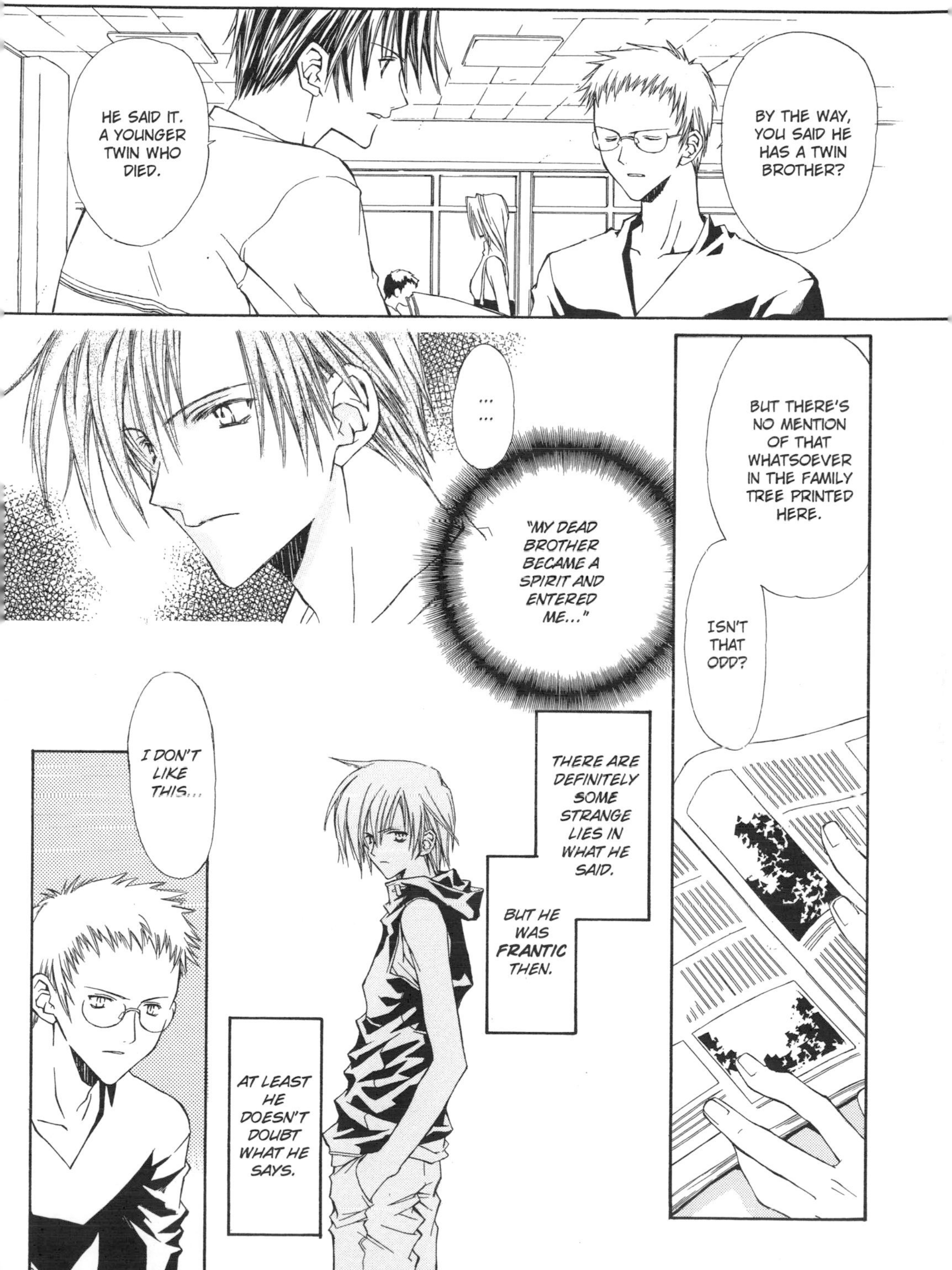
BY THE WAY, YOU SAID HE HAS A TWIN BROTHER?
HE SAID IT. A YOUNGER TWIN WHO DIED.
BUT THERE'S NO MENTION OF THAT WHATSOEVER IN THE FAMILY TREE PRINTED HERE.
ISN'T THAT ODD?
......
"MY DEAD BROTHER BECAME A SPIRIT AND ENTERED ME..."
THERE ARE DEFINITELY SOME STRANGE LIES IN WHAT HE SAID.
BUT HE WAS FRANTIC THEN.
I DON'T LIKE THIS...
AT LEAST HE DOESN'T DOUBT WHAT HE SAYS.

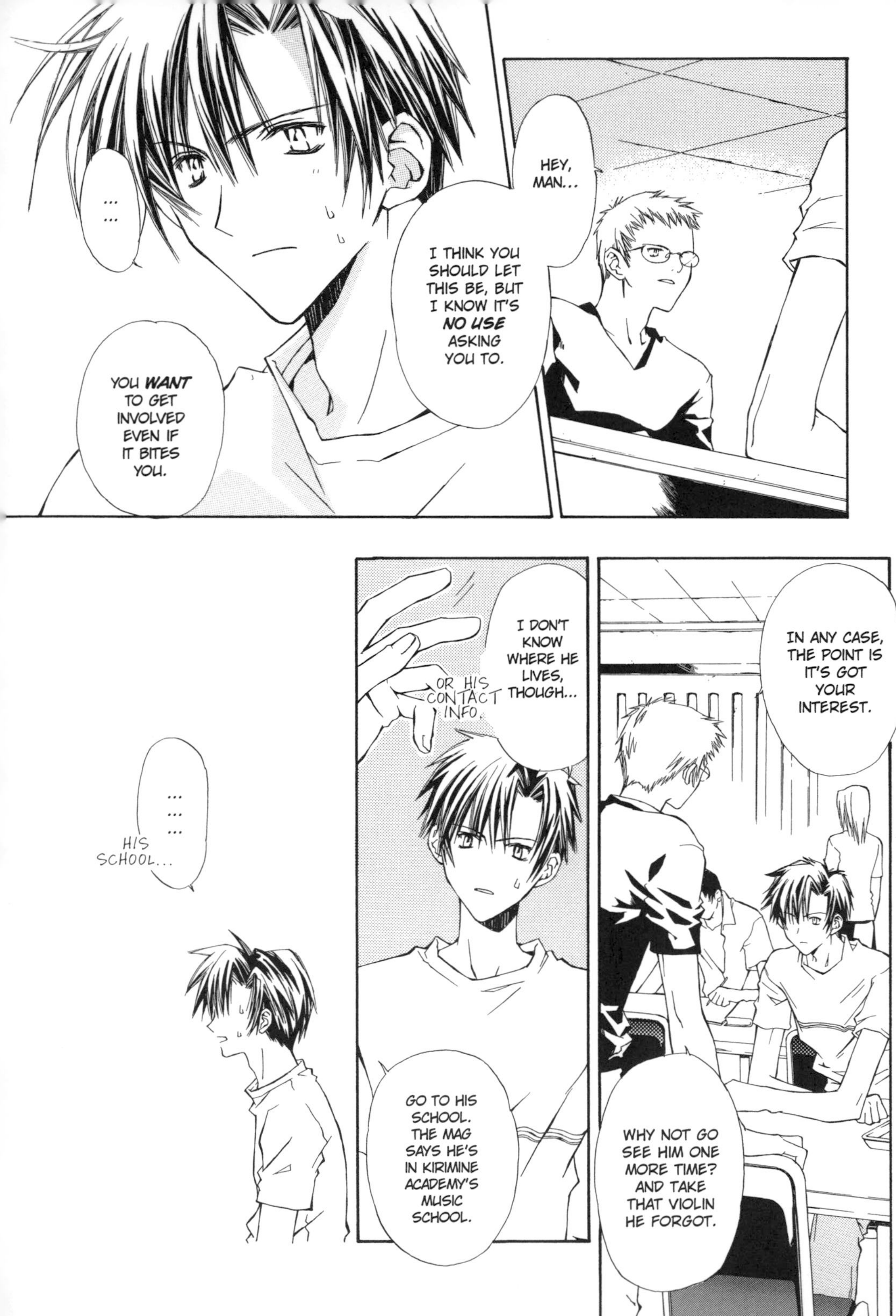

HEY, MAN...
I THINK YOU SHOULD LET THIS BE, BUT I KNOW IT'S **NO USE** ASKING YOU TO.
... ...
YOU **WANT** TO GET INVOLVED EVEN IF IT BITES YOU.
IN ANY CASE, THE POINT IS IT'S GOT YOUR INTEREST.
WHY NOT GO SEE HIM ONE MORE TIME? AND TAKE THAT VIOLIN HE FORGOT.
I DON'T KNOW WHERE HE LIVES, THOUGH...
OR HIS CONTACT INFO.
GO TO HIS SCHOOL. THE MAG SAYS HE'S IN KIRIMINE ACADEMY'S MUSIC SCHOOL.
... ...
HIS SCHOOL...

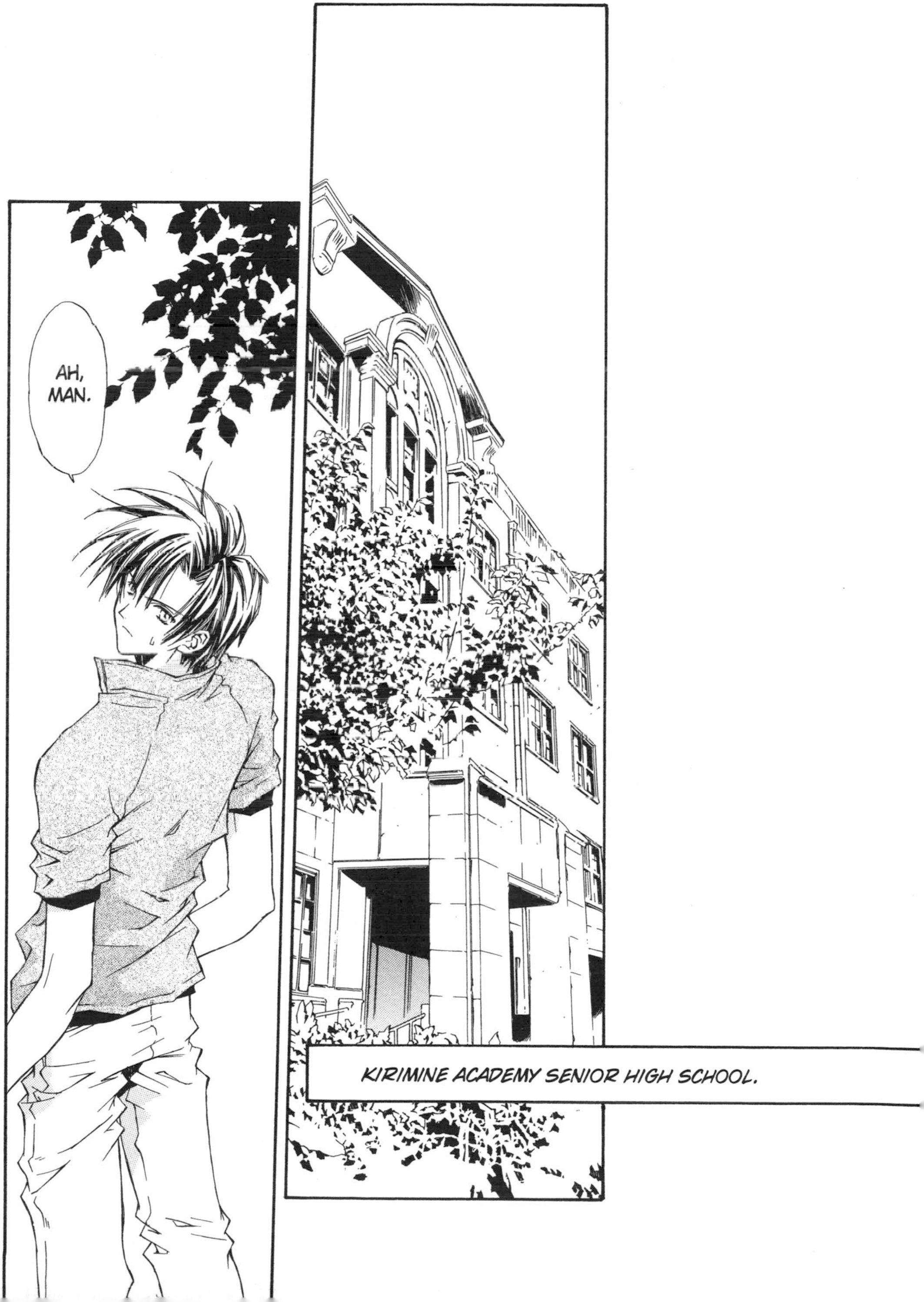
KIRIMINE ACADEMY SENIOR HIGH SCHOOL.
AH, MAN.

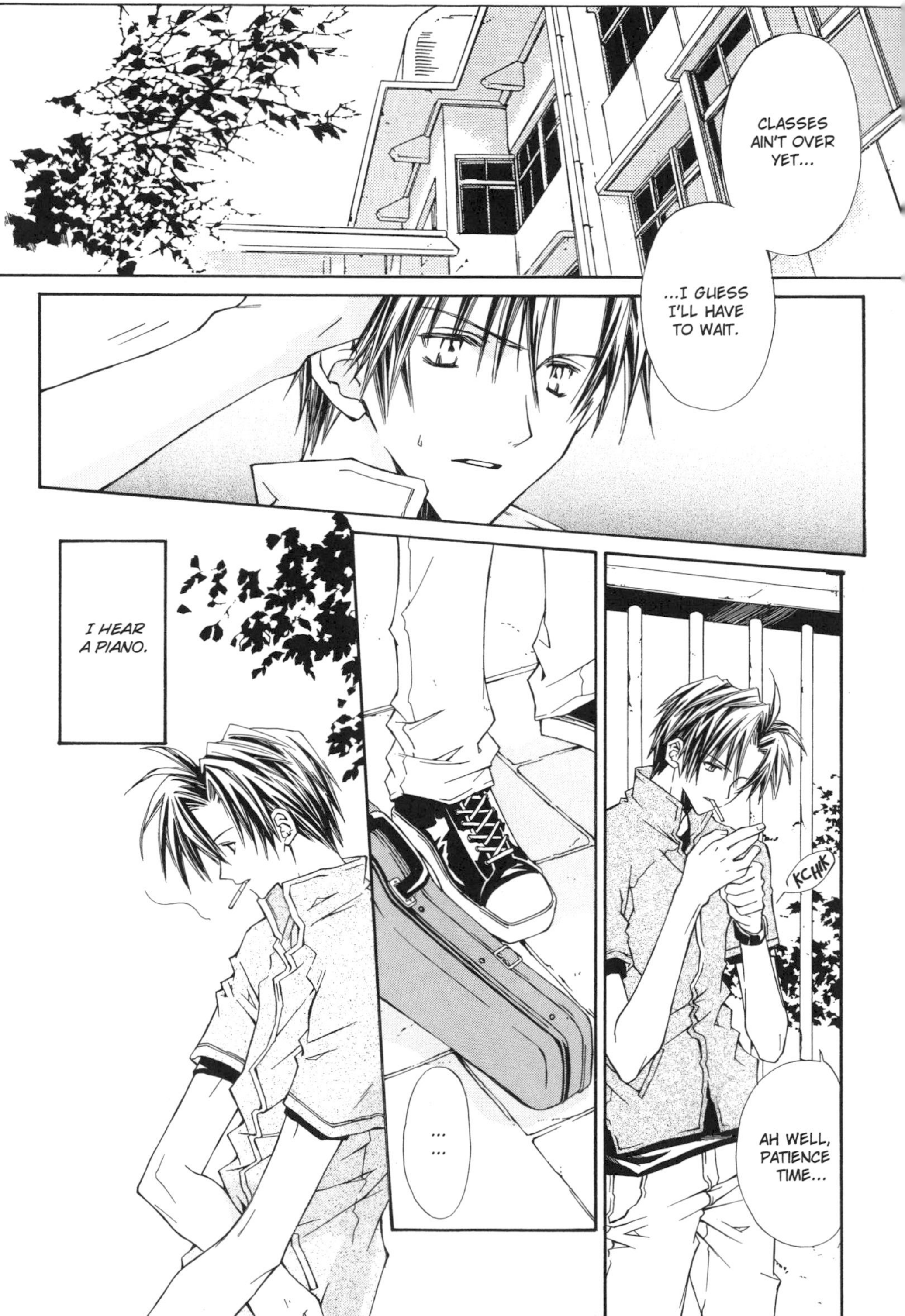
CLASSES AIN'T OVER YET...
...I GUESS I'LL HAVE TO WAIT.
KCHIK
AH WELL, PATIENCE TIME...
... ...
I HEAR A PIANO.

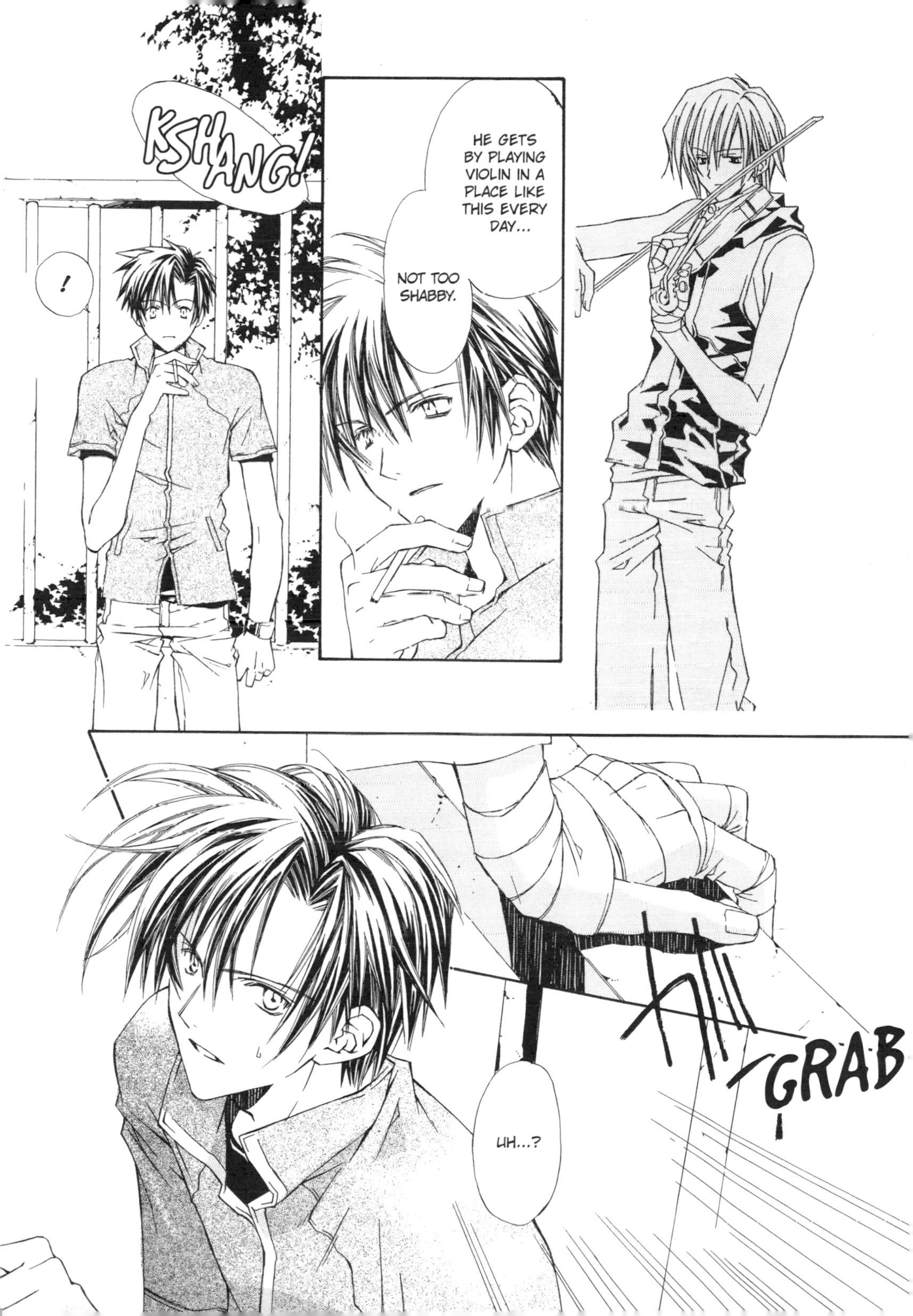
HE GETS BY PLAYING VIOLIN IN A PLACE LIKE THIS EVERY DAY...
NOT TOO SHABBY.
KSHANG!
!
GRAB
UH...?

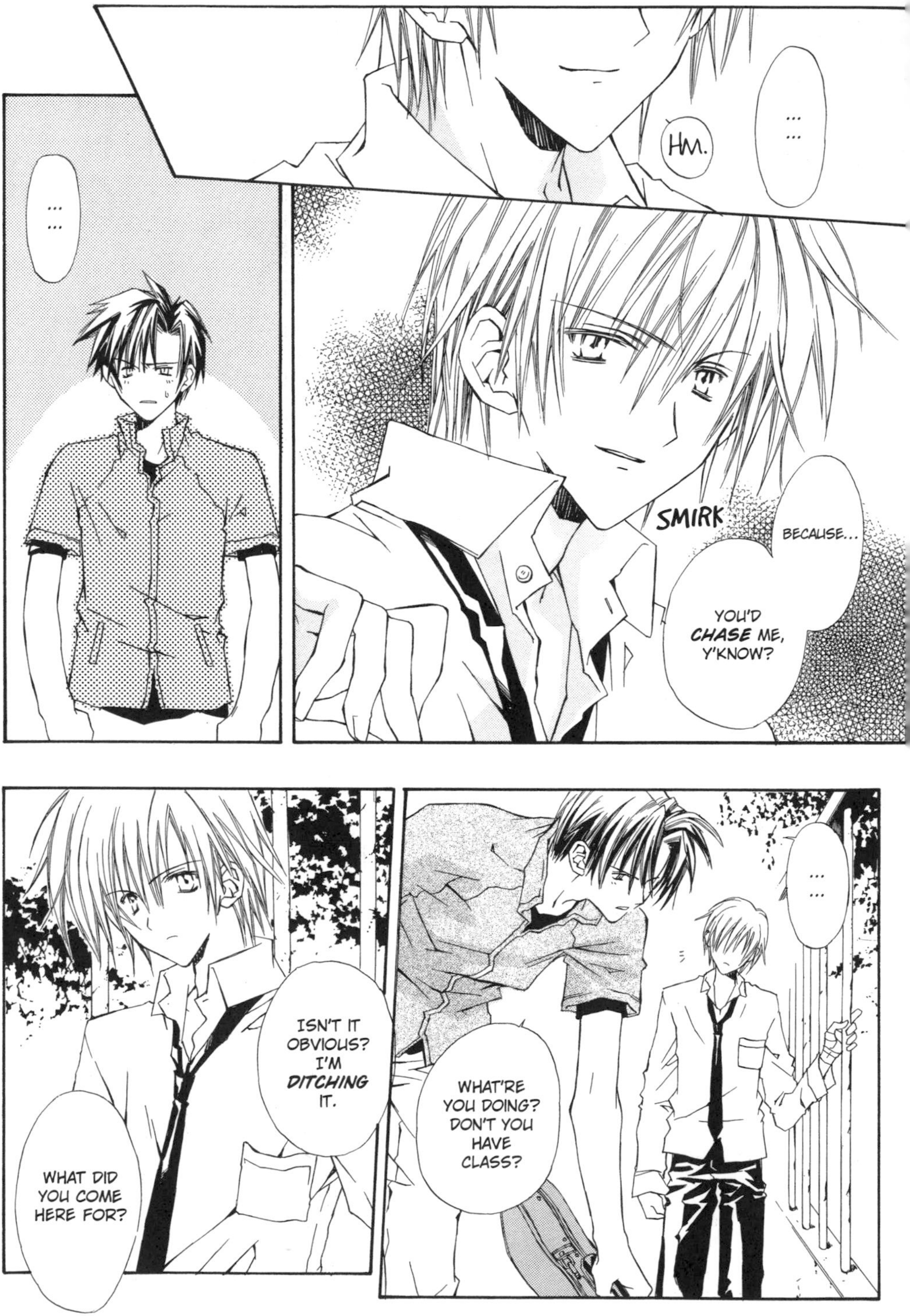
...
...
HM.
SMIRK
BECAUSE...
YOU'D CHASE ME, Y'KNOW?
...
...
...
...
WHAT'RE YOU DOING? DON'T YOU HAVE CLASS?
ISN'T IT OBVIOUS? I'M DITCHING IT.
WHAT DID YOU COME HERE FOR?

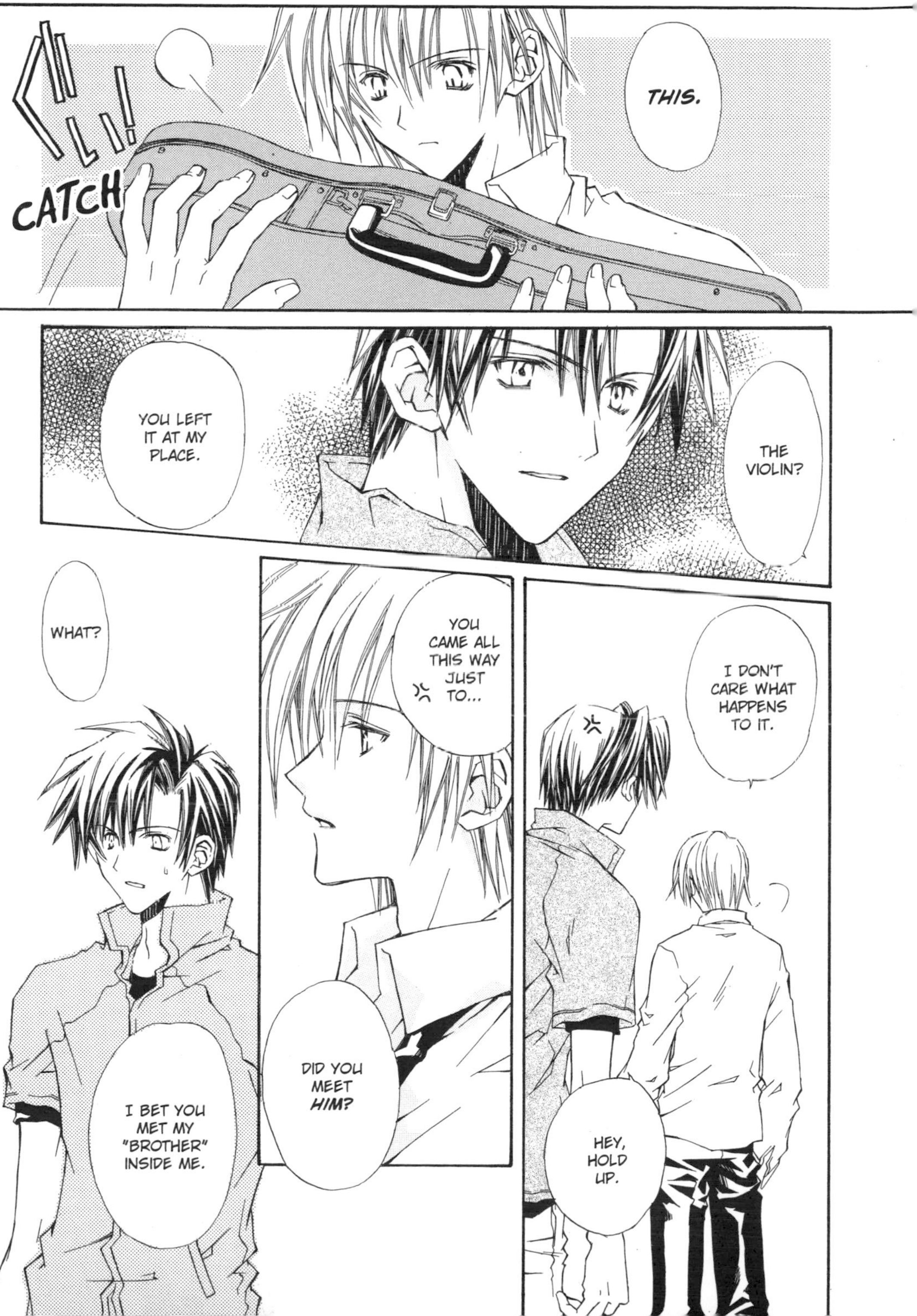
THIS.
CATCH
THE VIOLIN?
YOU LEFT IT AT MY PLACE.
I DON'T CARE WHAT HAPPENS TO IT.
HEY, HOLD UP.
YOU CAME ALL THIS WAY JUST TO...
DID YOU MEET *HIM*?
WHAT?
I BET YOU MET MY "BROTHER" INSIDE ME.

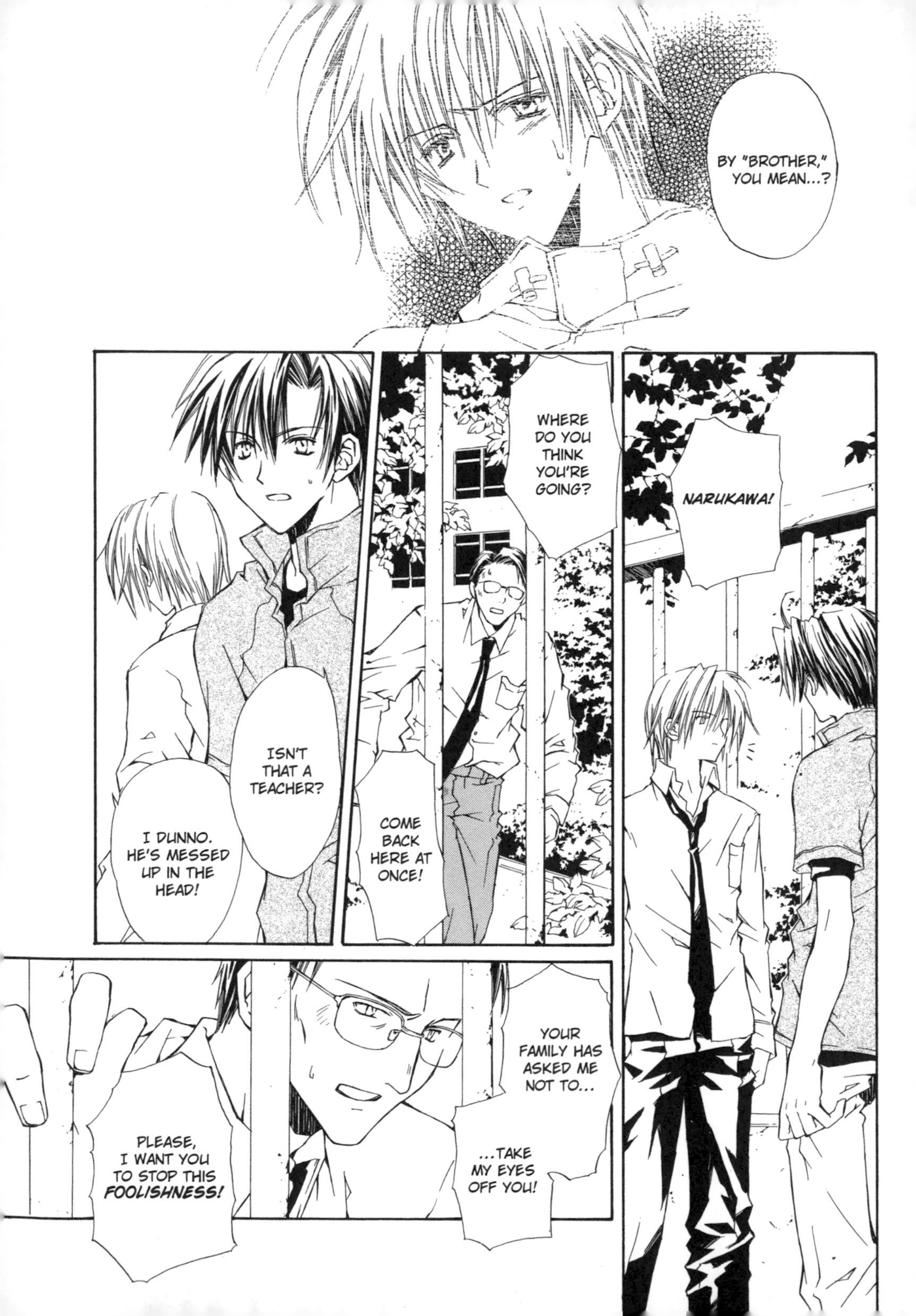
BY "BROTHER," YOU MEAN...?
NARUKAWA!
WHERE DO YOU THINK YOU'RE GOING?
COME BACK HERE AT ONCE!
ISN'T THAT A TEACHER?
I DUNNO. HE'S MESSED UP IN THE HEAD!
YOUR FAMILY HAS ASKED ME NOT TO...
...TAKE MY EYES OFF YOU!
PLEASE, I WANT YOU TO STOP THIS *FOOLISHNESS!*

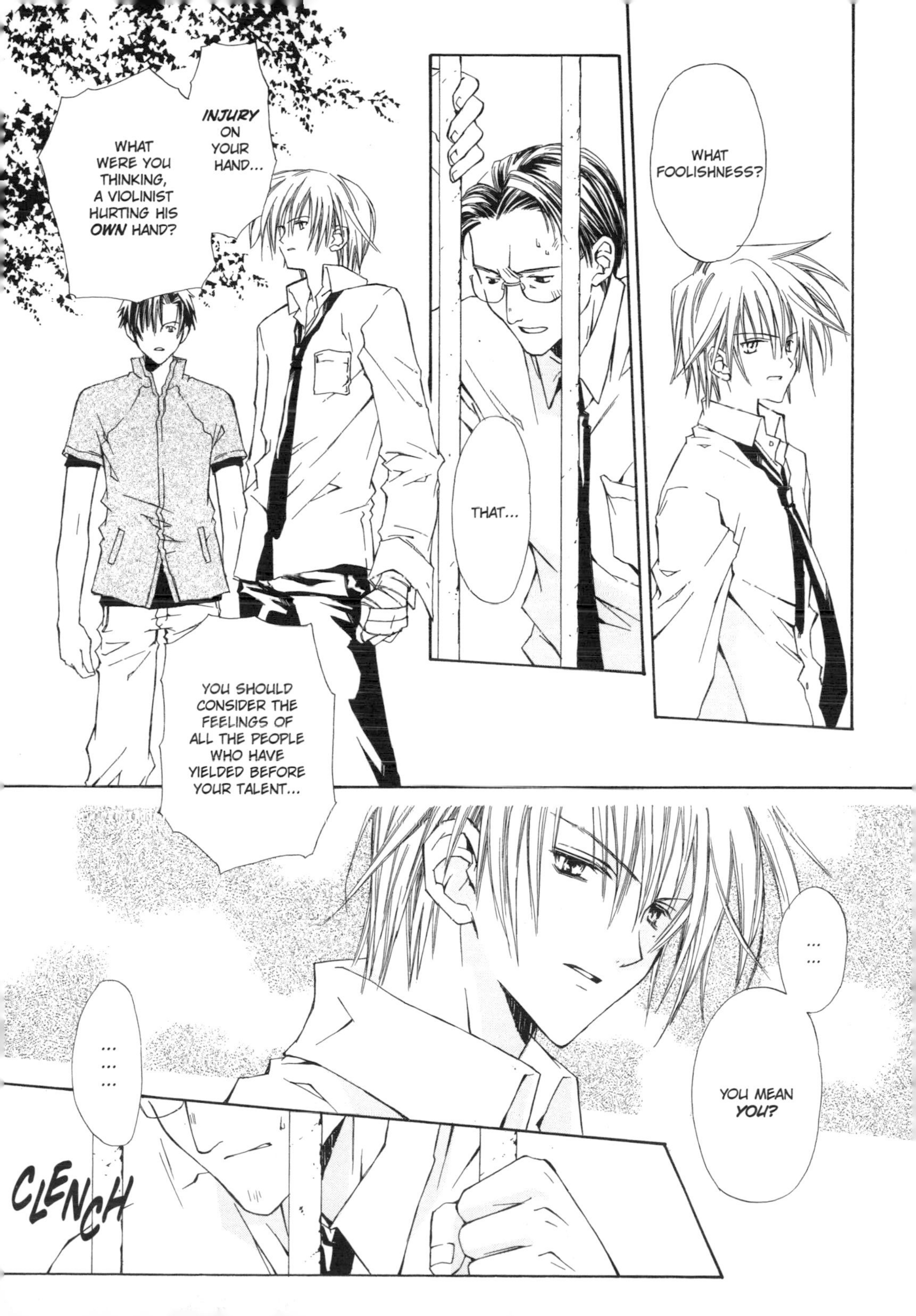
WHAT FOOLISHNESS?
THAT...
INJURY ON YOUR HAND...
WHAT WERE YOU THINKING, A VIOLINIST HURTING HIS OWN HAND?
YOU SHOULD CONSIDER THE FEELINGS OF ALL THE PEOPLE WHO HAVE YIELDED BEFORE YOUR TALENT...
... ...
YOU MEAN YOU?
... ...
CLENCH

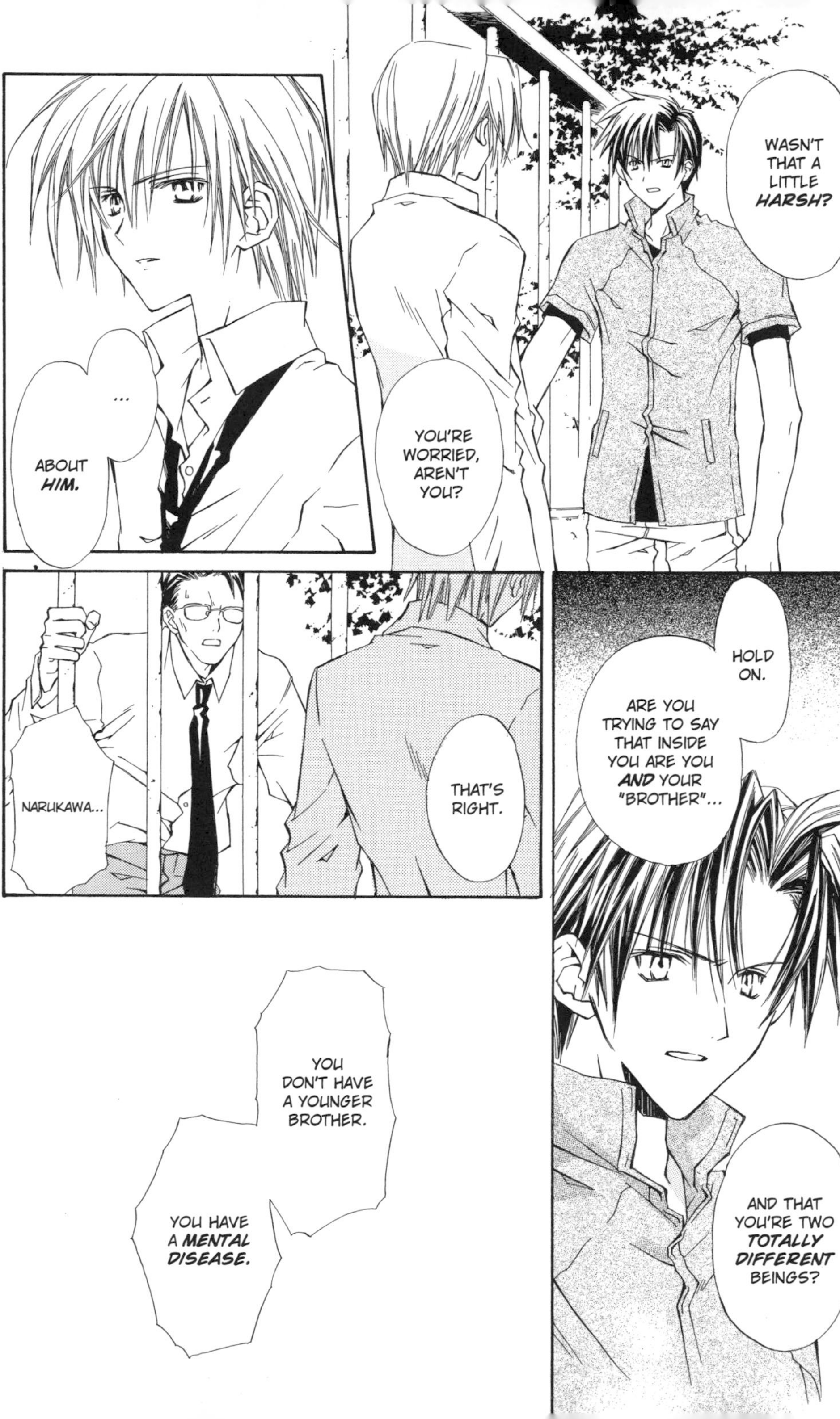
WASN'T THAT A LITTLE HARSH?
YOU'RE WORRIED, AREN'T YOU?
...
ABOUT HIM.
HOLD ON.
ARE YOU TRYING TO SAY THAT INSIDE YOU ARE YOU AND YOUR "BROTHER"...
AND THAT YOU'RE TWO TOTALLY DIFFERENT BEINGS?
THAT'S RIGHT.
NARUKAWA...
YOU DON'T HAVE A YOUNGER BROTHER.
YOU HAVE A MENTAL DISEASE.

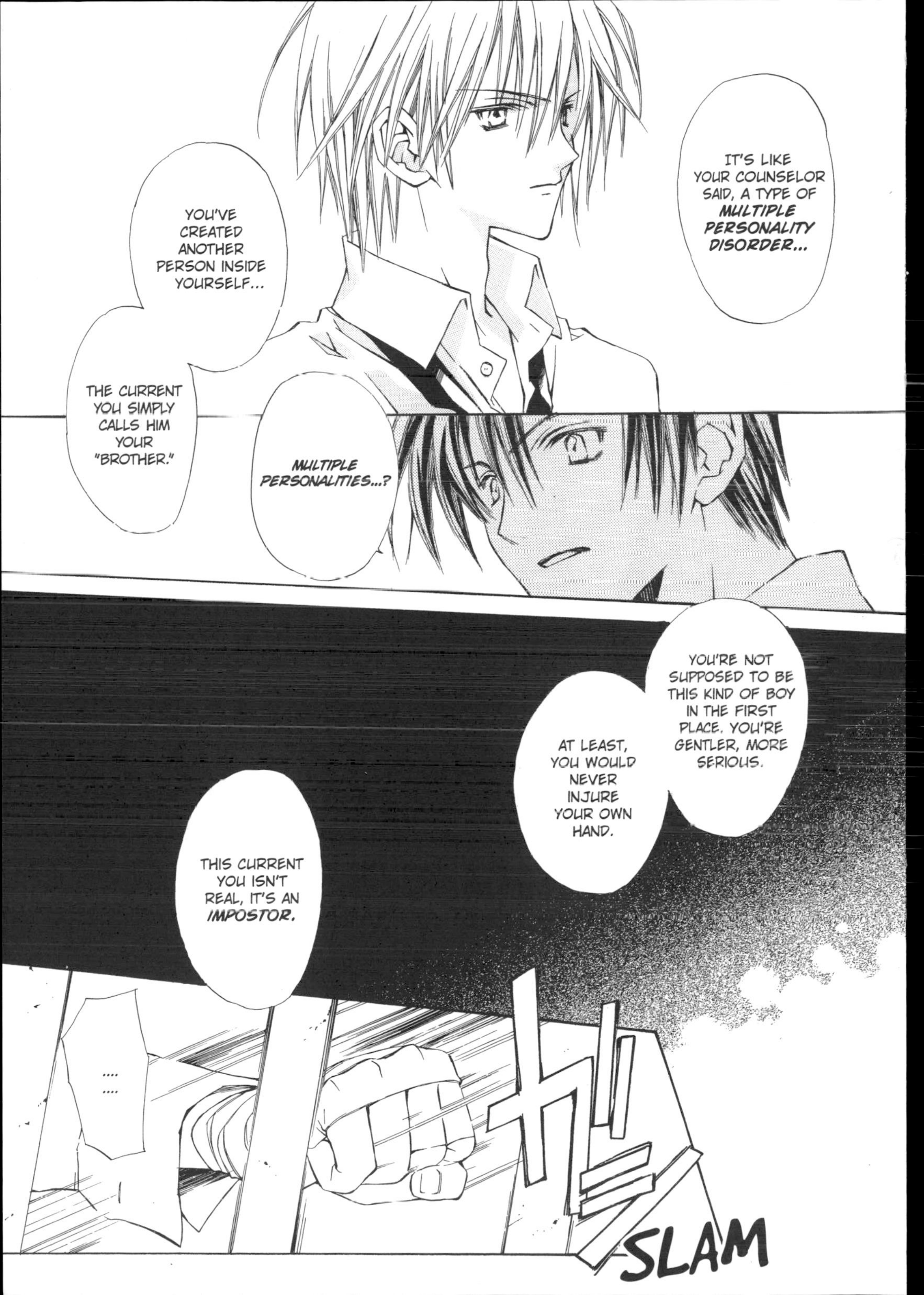
IT'S LIKE YOUR COUNSELOR SAID, A TYPE OF MULTIPLE PERSONALITY DISORDER...
YOU'VE CREATED ANOTHER PERSON INSIDE YOURSELF...
THE CURRENT YOU SIMPLY CALLS HIM YOUR "BROTHER."
MULTIPLE PERSONALITIES...?
YOU'RE NOT SUPPOSED TO BE THIS KIND OF BOY IN THE FIRST PLACE. YOU'RE GENTLER, MORE SERIOUS.
AT LEAST, YOU WOULD NEVER INJURE YOUR OWN HAND.
THIS CURRENT YOU ISN'T REAL, IT'S AN IMPOSTOR.
....
....
SLAM

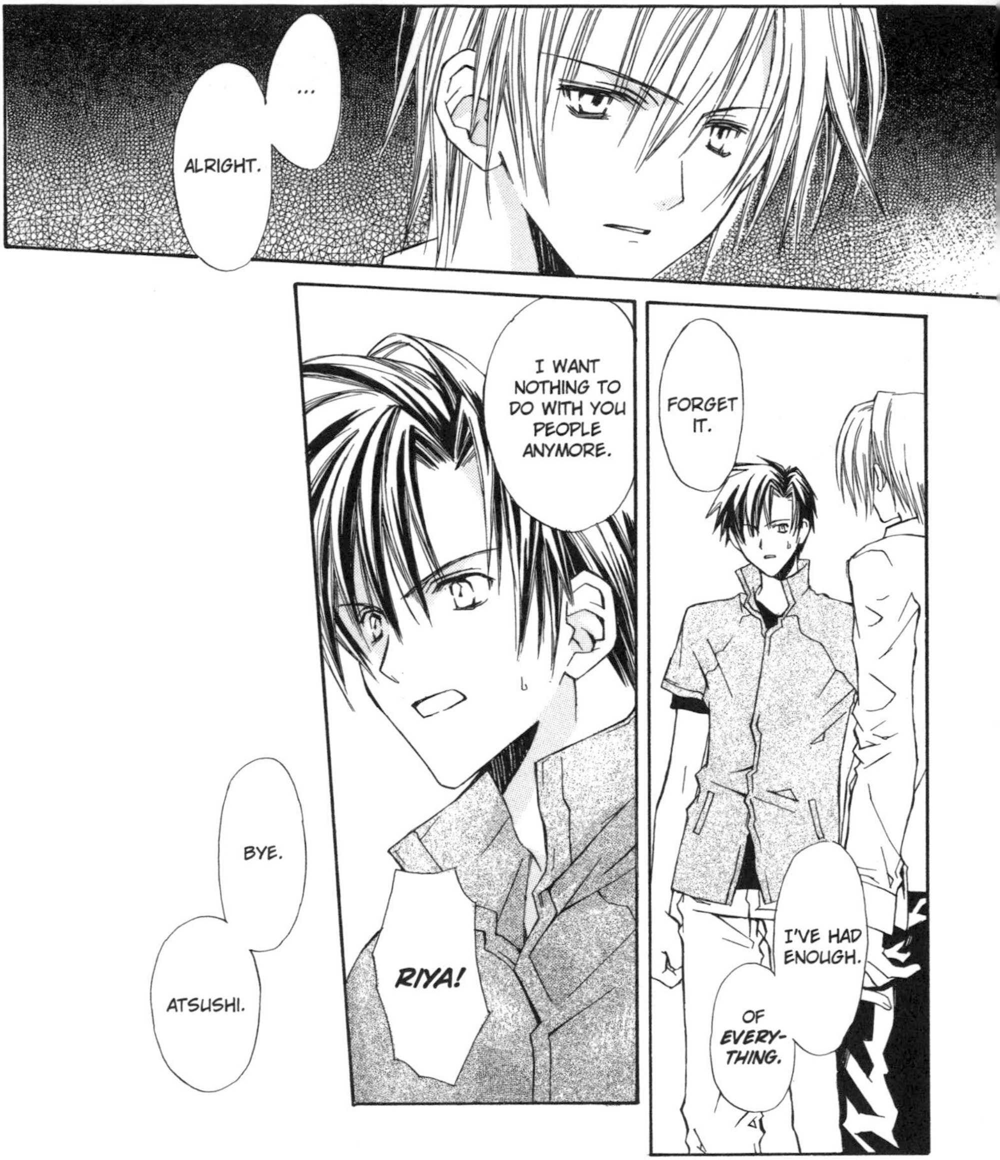
...
ALRIGHT.
FORGET IT.
I'VE HAD ENOUGH.
OF EVERYTHING.
I WANT NOTHING TO DO WITH YOU PEOPLE ANYMORE.
RIYA!
BYE.
ATSUSHI.

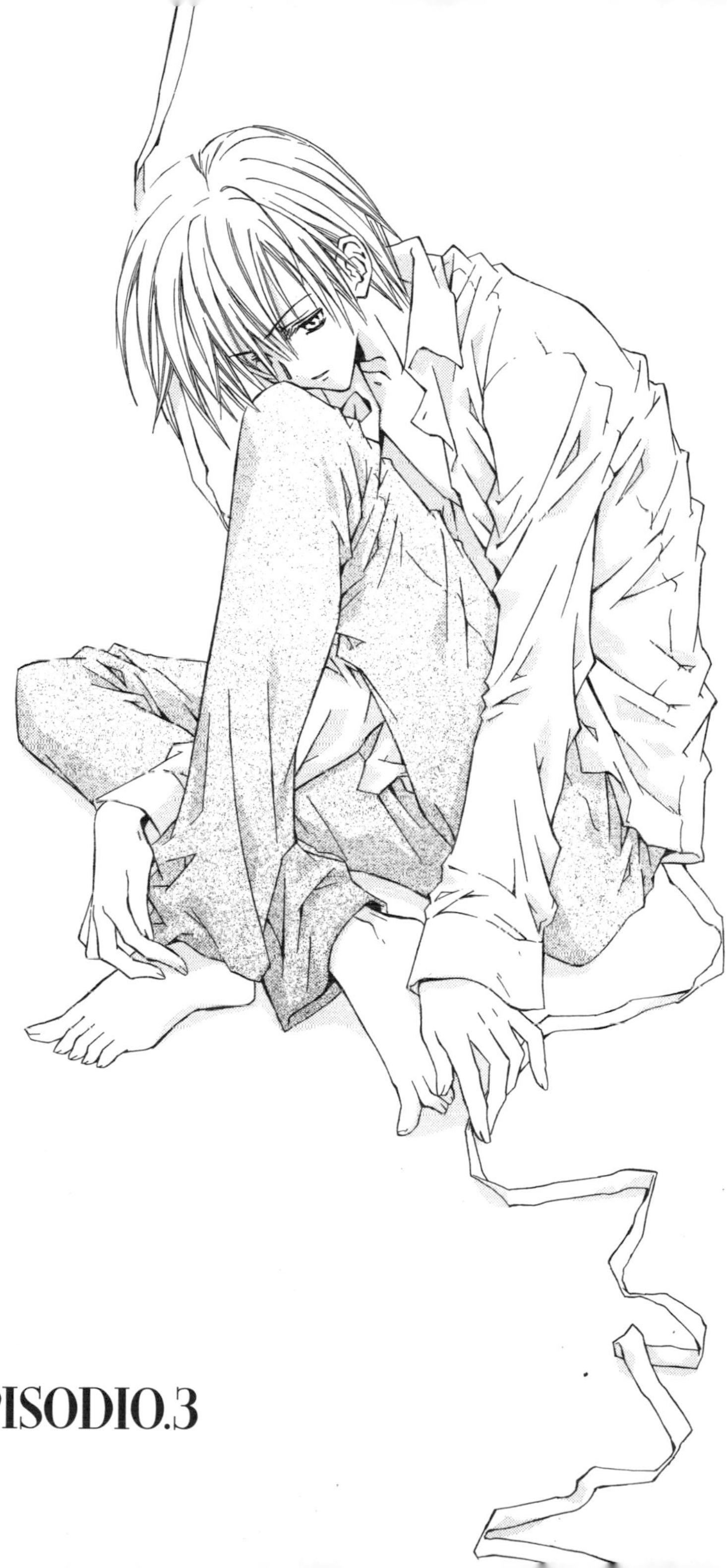

EPISODIO.3

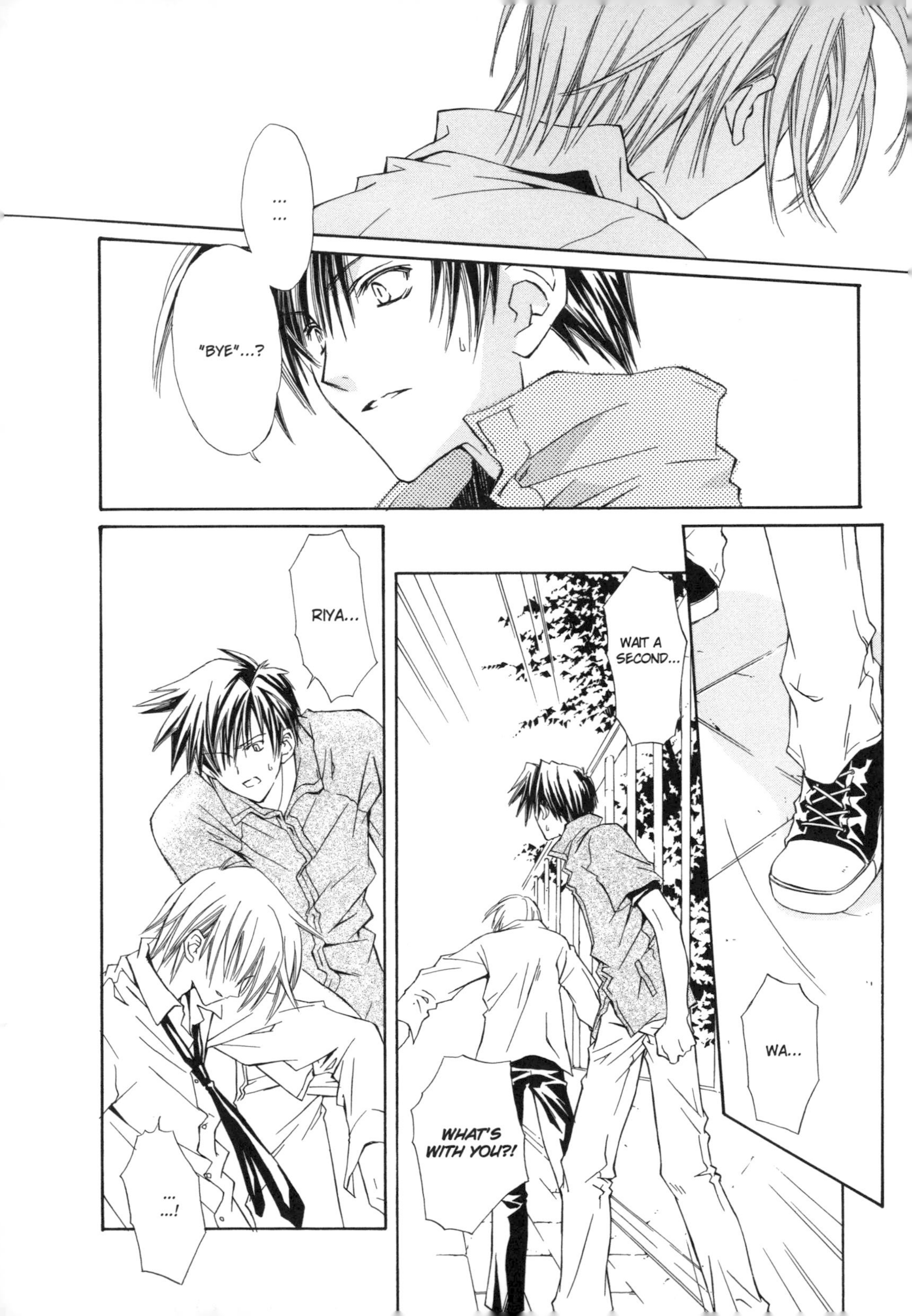
......
"BYE"...?
WA...
WAIT A SECOND...
WHAT'S WITH YOU?!
RIYA...
...
...!

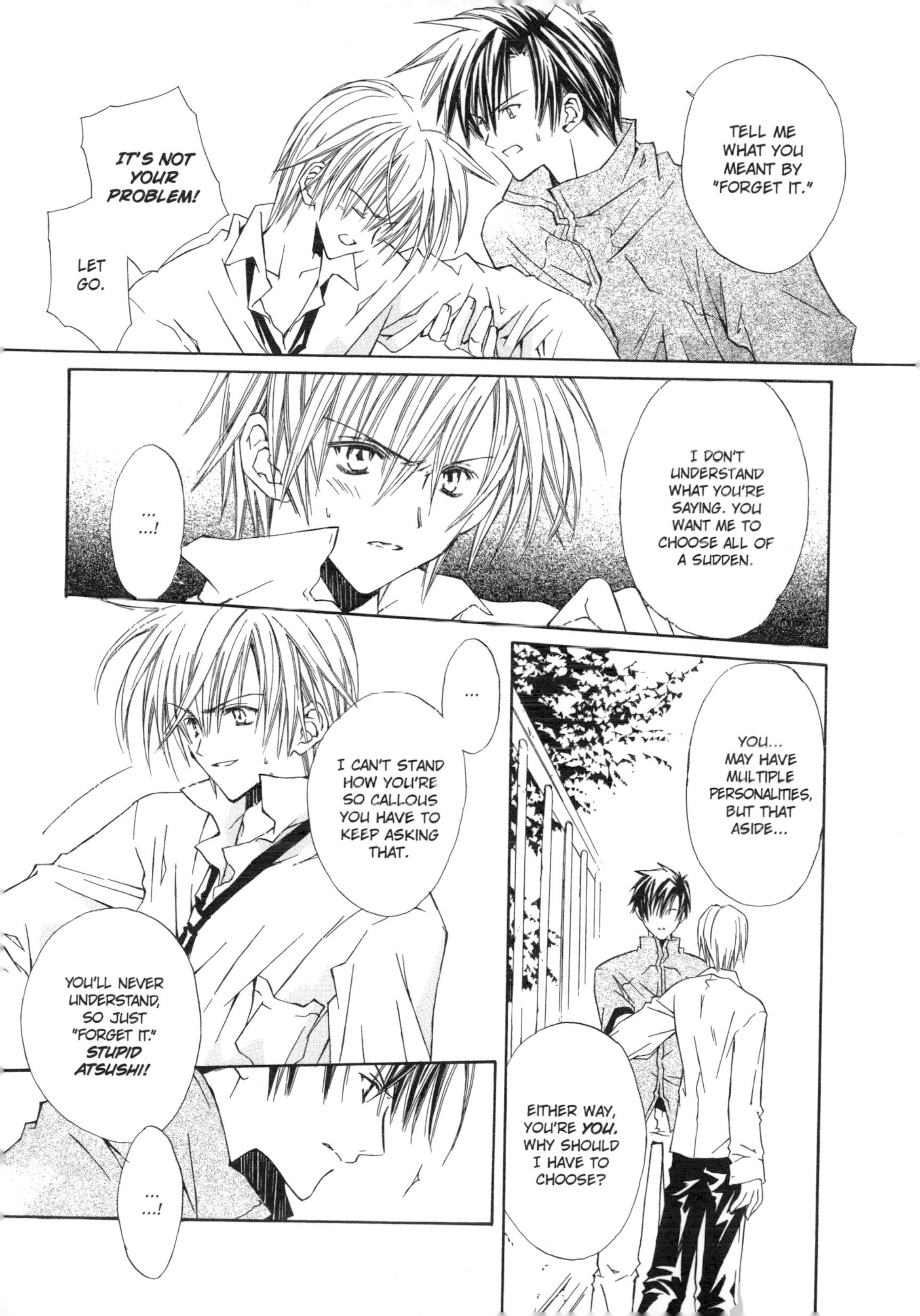
TELL ME WHAT YOU MEANT BY "FORGET IT."
IT'S NOT YOUR PROBLEM!
LET GO.
I DON'T UNDERSTAND WHAT YOU'RE SAYING. YOU WANT ME TO CHOOSE ALL OF A SUDDEN.
... ...!
YOU... MAY HAVE MULTIPLE PERSONALITIES, BUT THAT ASIDE...
EITHER WAY, YOU'RE YOU. WHY SHOULD I HAVE TO CHOOSE?
...
I CAN'T STAND HOW YOU'RE SO CALLOUS YOU HAVE TO KEEP ASKING THAT.
YOU'LL NEVER UNDERSTAND, SO JUST "FORGET IT." STUPID ATSUSHI!
... ...!

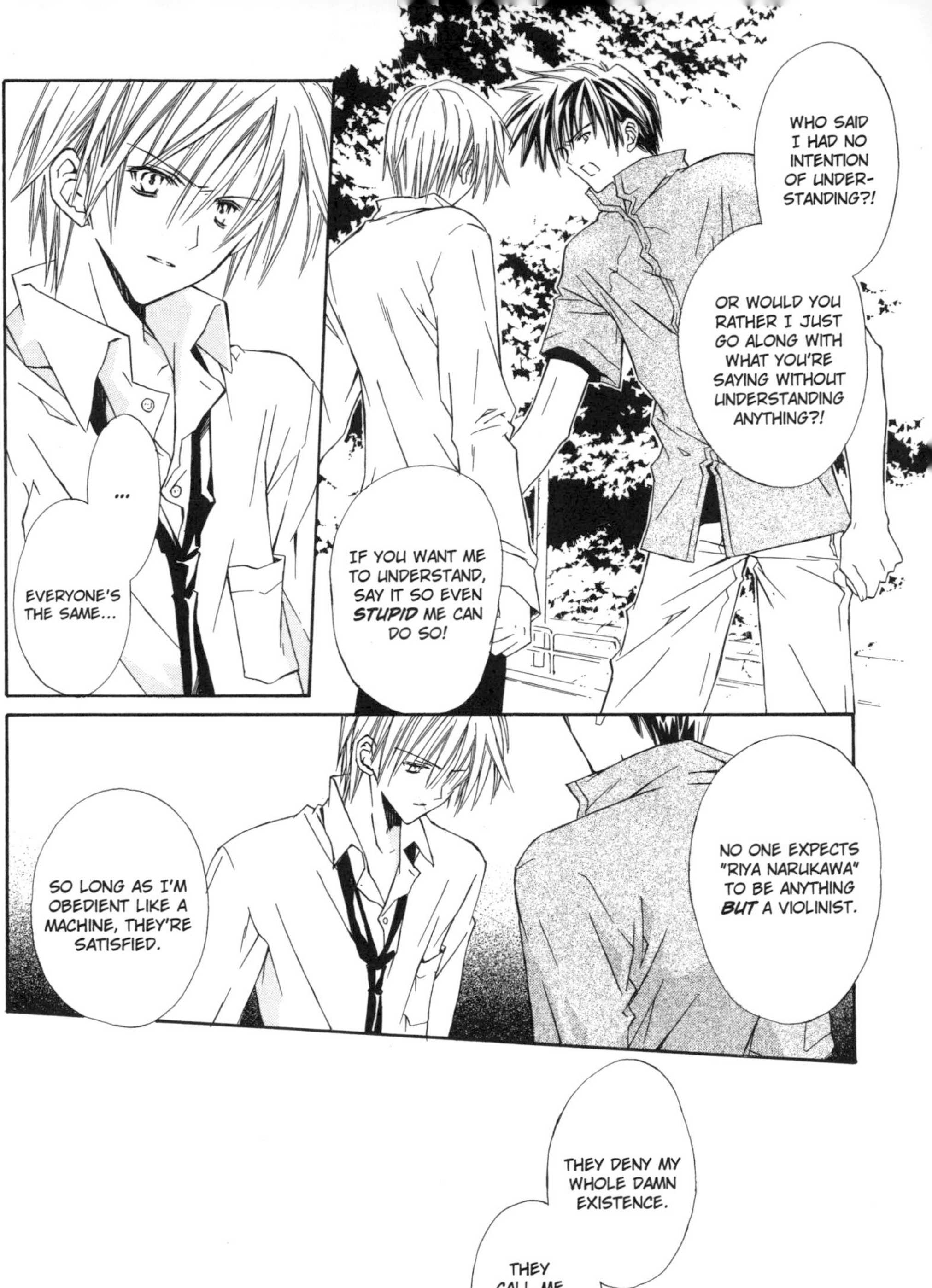
WHO SAID I HAD NO INTENTION OF UNDER-STANDING?!
OR WOULD YOU RATHER I JUST GO ALONG WITH WHAT YOU'RE SAYING WITHOUT UNDERSTANDING ANYTHING?!
IF YOU WANT ME TO UNDERSTAND, SAY IT SO EVEN *STUPID* ME CAN DO SO!
...
EVERYONE'S THE SAME...
NO ONE EXPECTS "RIYA NARUKAWA" TO BE ANYTHING *BUT* A VIOLINIST.
SO LONG AS I'M OBEDIENT LIKE A MACHINE, THEY'RE SATISFIED.
THEY DENY MY WHOLE DAMN EXISTENCE.
THEY CALL ME "IMPOSTOR"...!

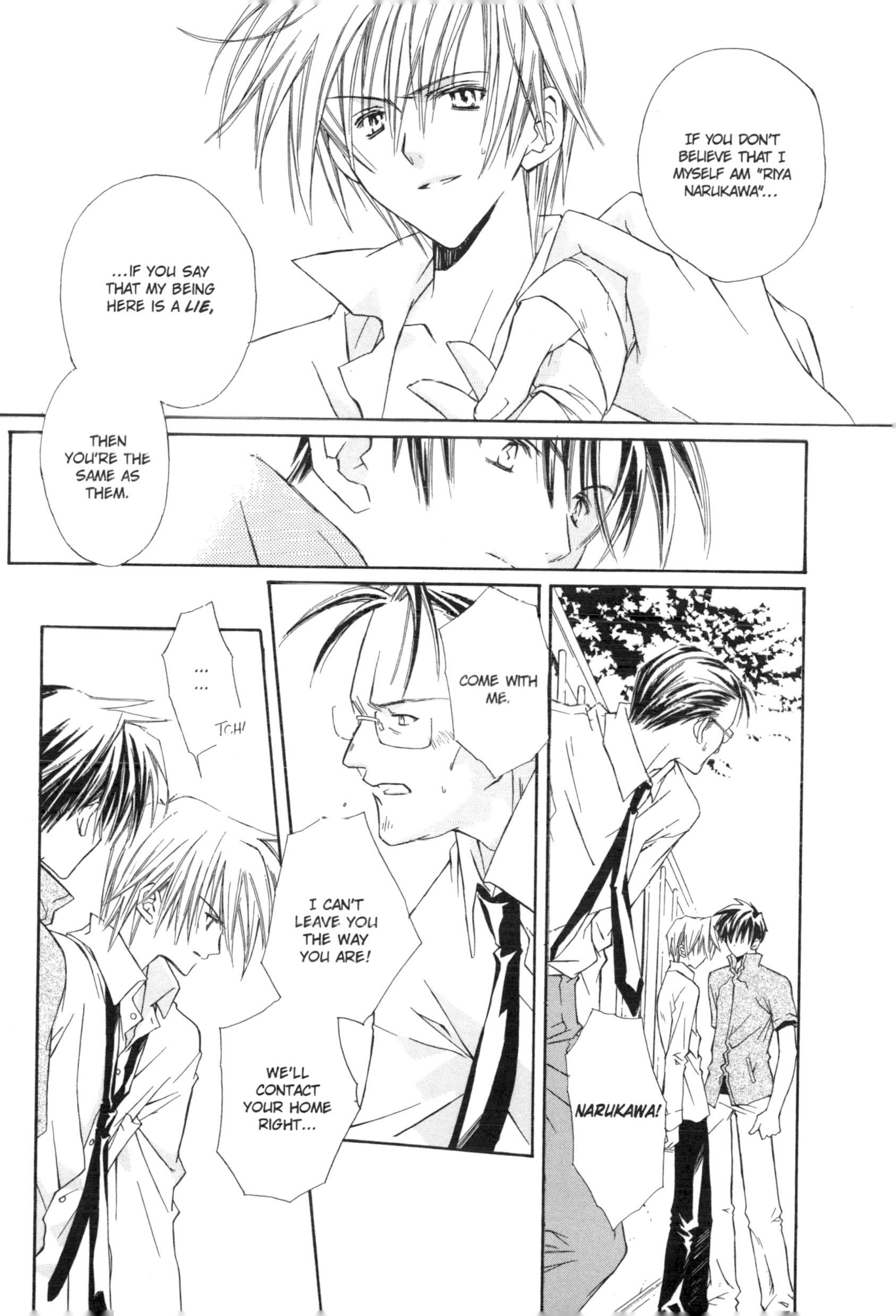
IF YOU DON'T BELIEVE THAT I MYSELF AM "RIYA NARUKAWA"...
...IF YOU SAY THAT MY BEING HERE IS A *LIE,*
THEN YOU'RE THE SAME AS THEM.
NARUKAWA!
COME WITH ME.
I CAN'T LEAVE YOU THE WAY YOU ARE!
WE'LL CONTACT YOUR HOME RIGHT...
......
TCH!

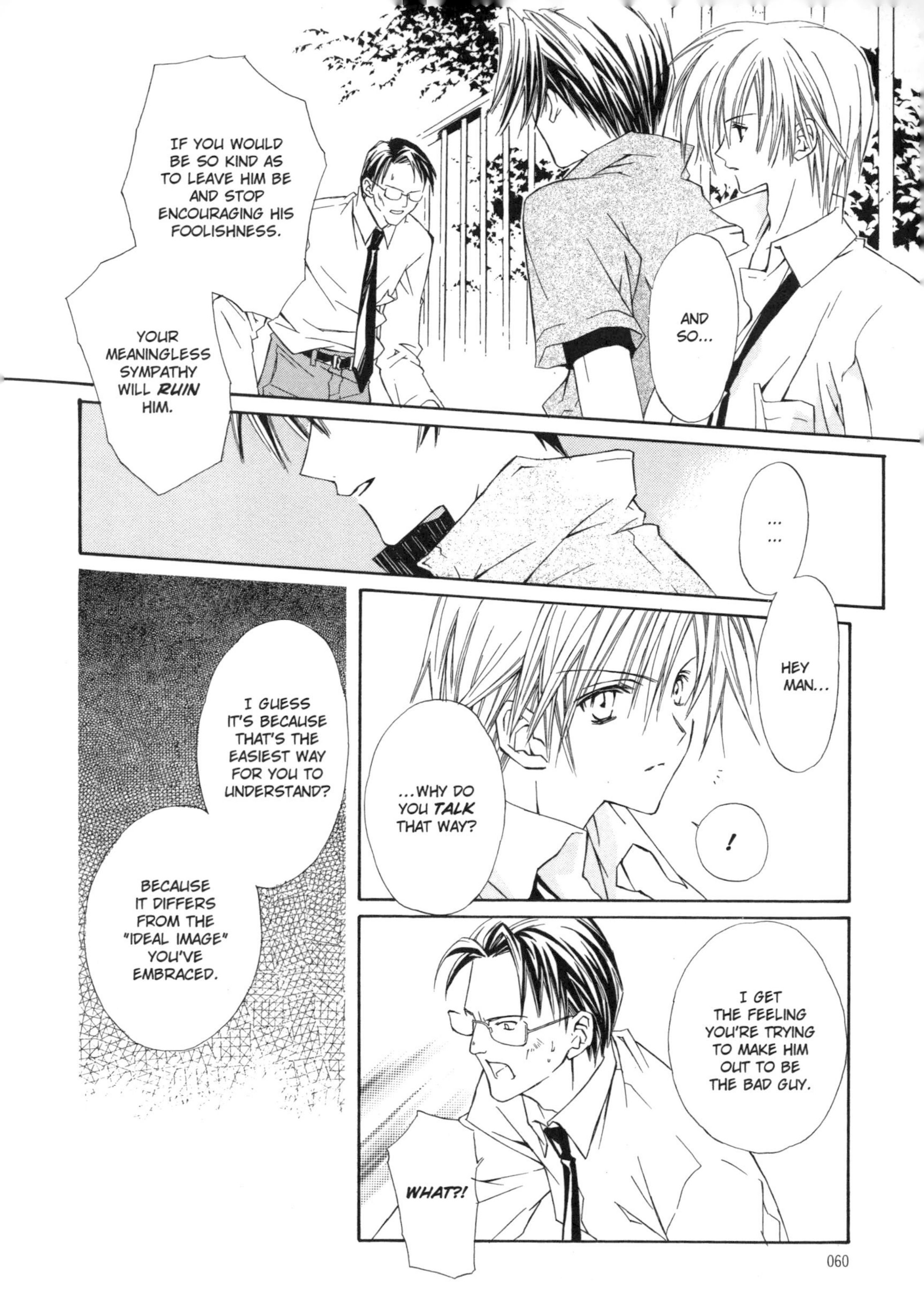
IF YOU WOULD BE SO KIND AS TO LEAVE HIM BE AND STOP ENCOURAGING HIS FOOLISHNESS.
YOUR MEANINGLESS SYMPATHY WILL *RUIN* HIM.
AND SO...
......
HEY MAN...
...WHY DO YOU *TALK* THAT WAY?
!
I GET THE FEELING YOU'RE TRYING TO MAKE HIM OUT TO BE THE BAD GUY.
WHAT?!
I GUESS IT'S BECAUSE THAT'S THE EASIEST WAY FOR YOU TO UNDERSTAND?
BECAUSE IT DIFFERS FROM THE "IDEAL IMAGE" YOU'VE EMBRACED.

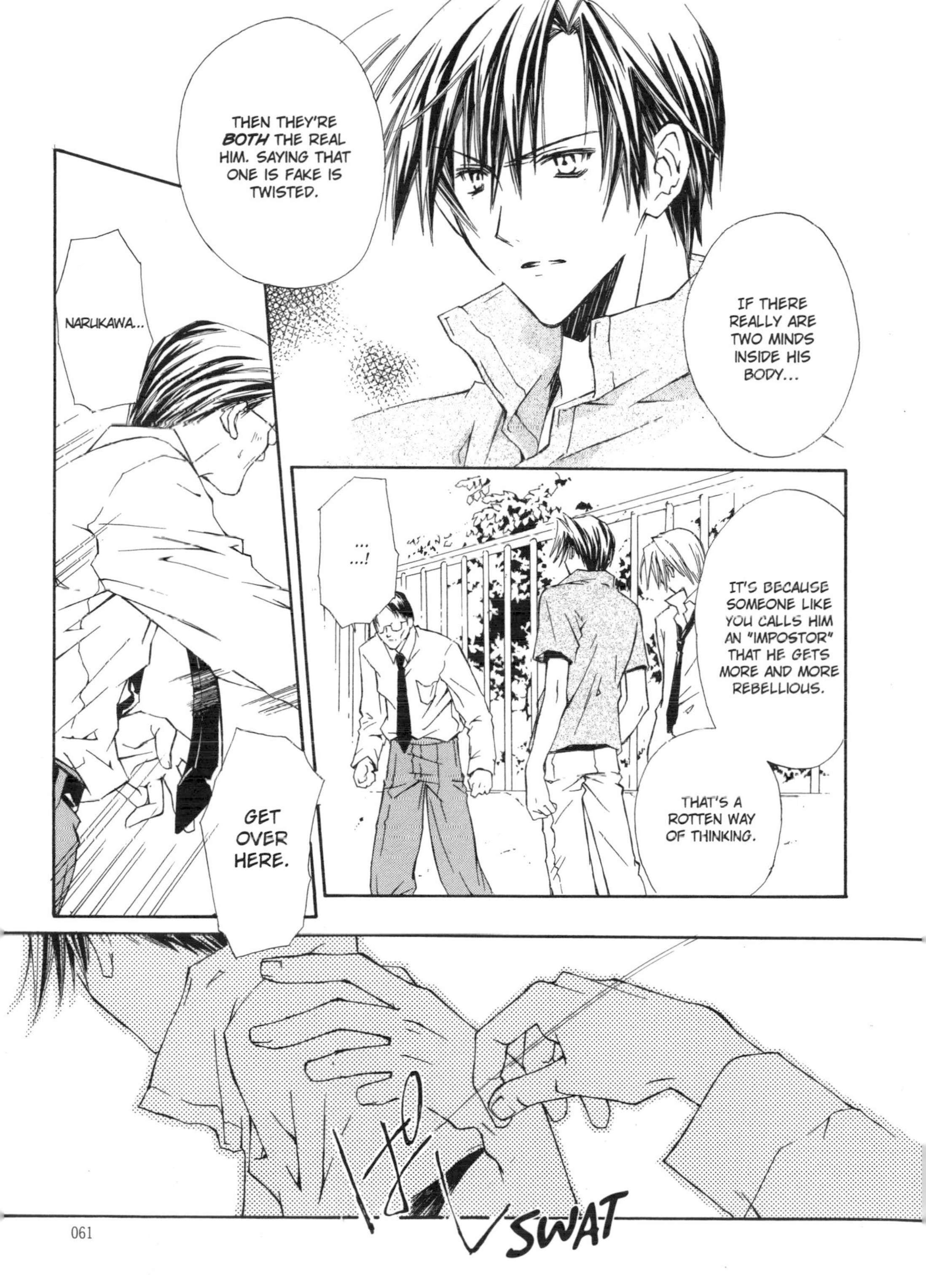
IF THERE REALLY ARE TWO MINDS INSIDE HIS BODY...
THEN THEY'RE *BOTH* THE REAL HIM. SAYING THAT ONE IS FAKE IS TWISTED.
IT'S BECAUSE SOMEONE LIKE YOU CALLS HIM AN "IMPOSTOR" THAT HE GETS MORE AND MORE REBELLIOUS.
THAT'S A ROTTEN WAY OF THINKING.
...
...!
NARUKAWA...
GET OVER HERE.
SWAT

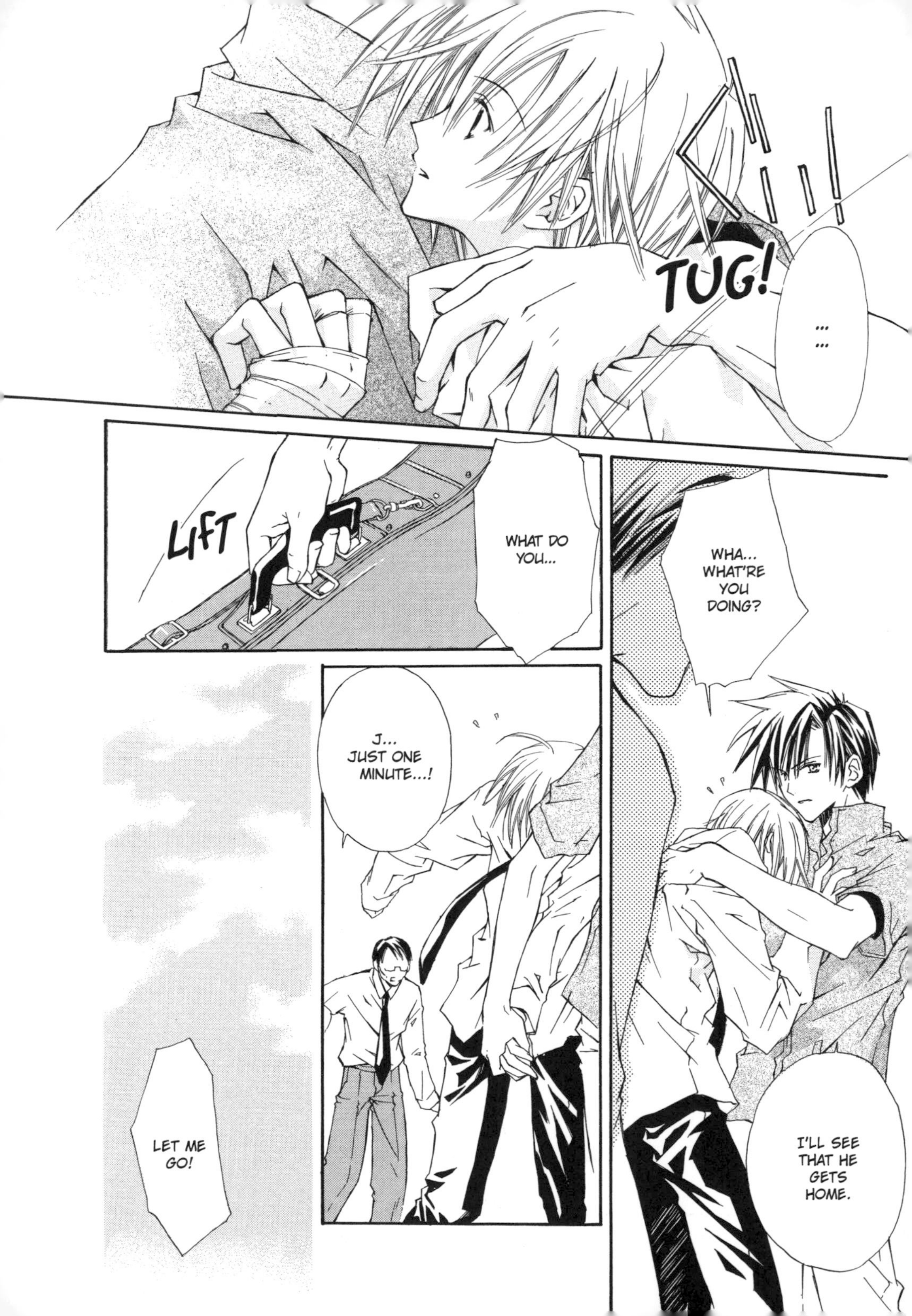
TUG!
... ...
LIFT
WHAT DO YOU...
WHA... WHAT'RE YOU DOING?
I'LL SEE THAT HE GETS HOME.
J... JUST ONE MINUTE...!
LET ME GO!

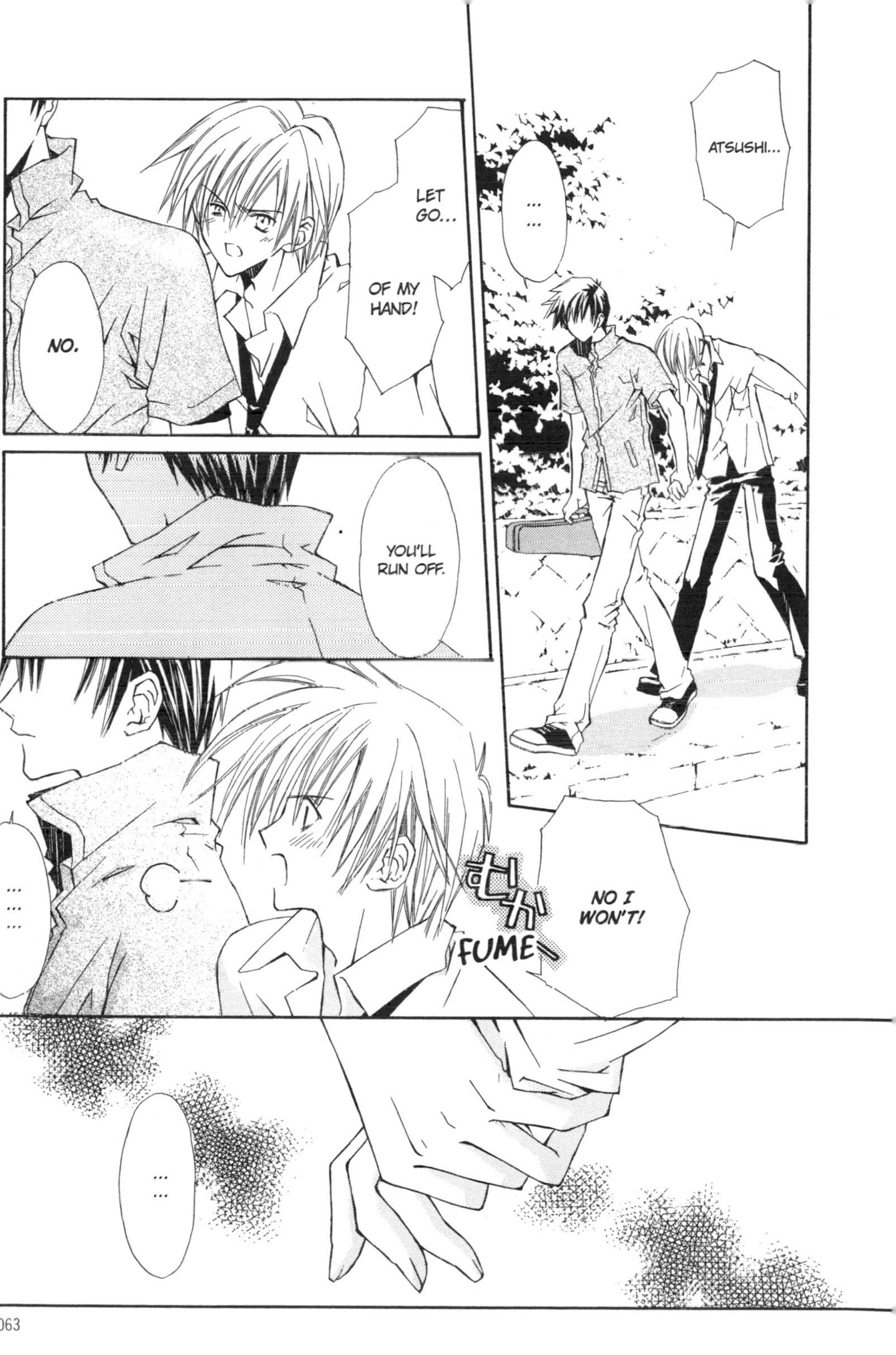

ATSUSHI...
... ...
LET GO... OF MY HAND!
NO.
YOU'LL RUN OFF.
NO I WON'T!
むか FUME
... ...
... ...

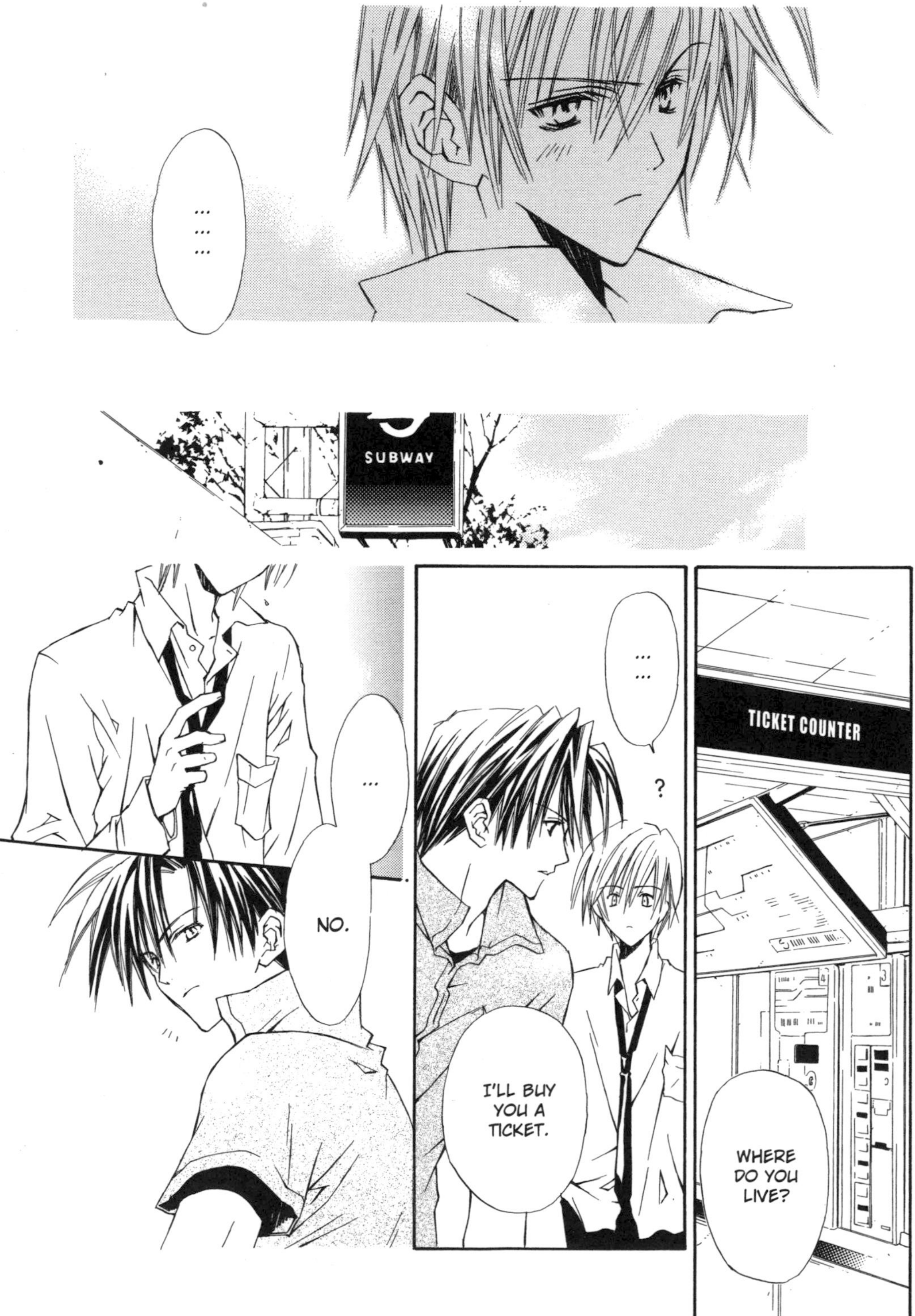
... ...
SUBWAY
TICKET COUNTER
WHERE DO YOU LIVE?
... ...
?
I'LL BUY YOU A TICKET.
...
NO.

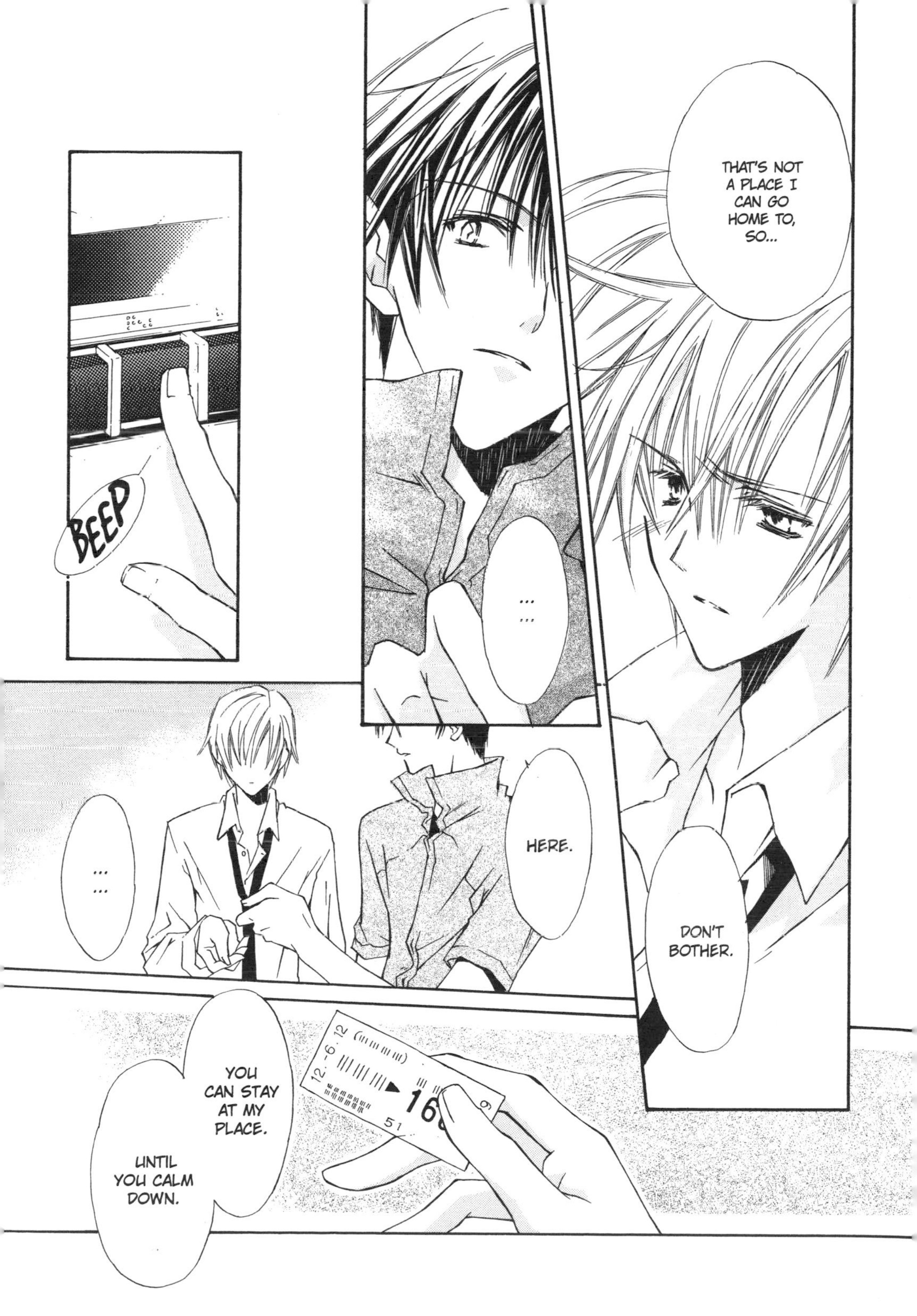
THAT'S NOT A PLACE I CAN GO HOME TO, SO...
DON'T BOTHER.
......
BEEP
HERE.
......
YOU CAN STAY AT MY PLACE.
UNTIL YOU CALM DOWN.

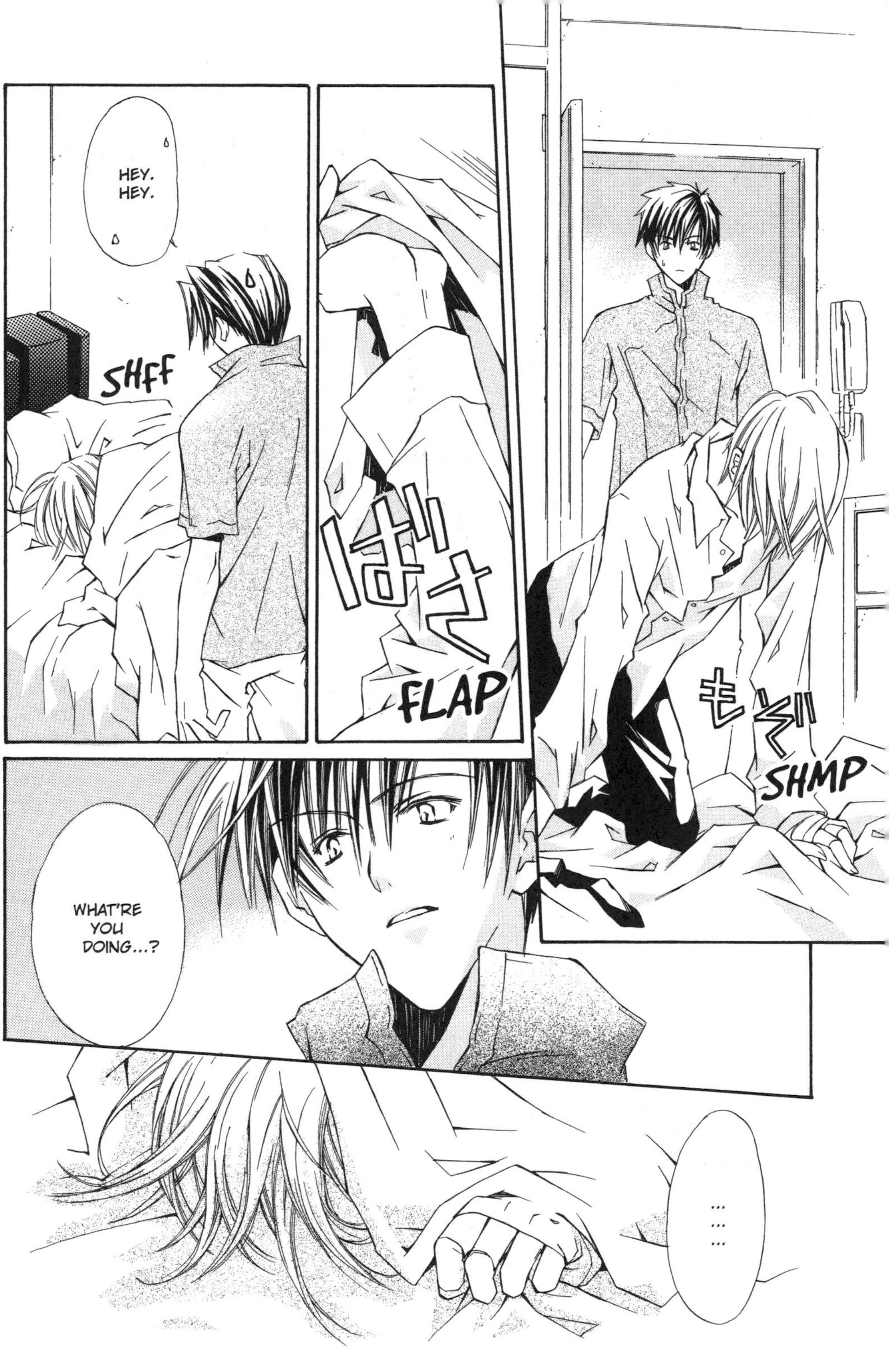
もぞ
SHMP
ばさ
FLAP
HEY. HEY.
SHFF
WHAT'RE YOU DOING...?
....

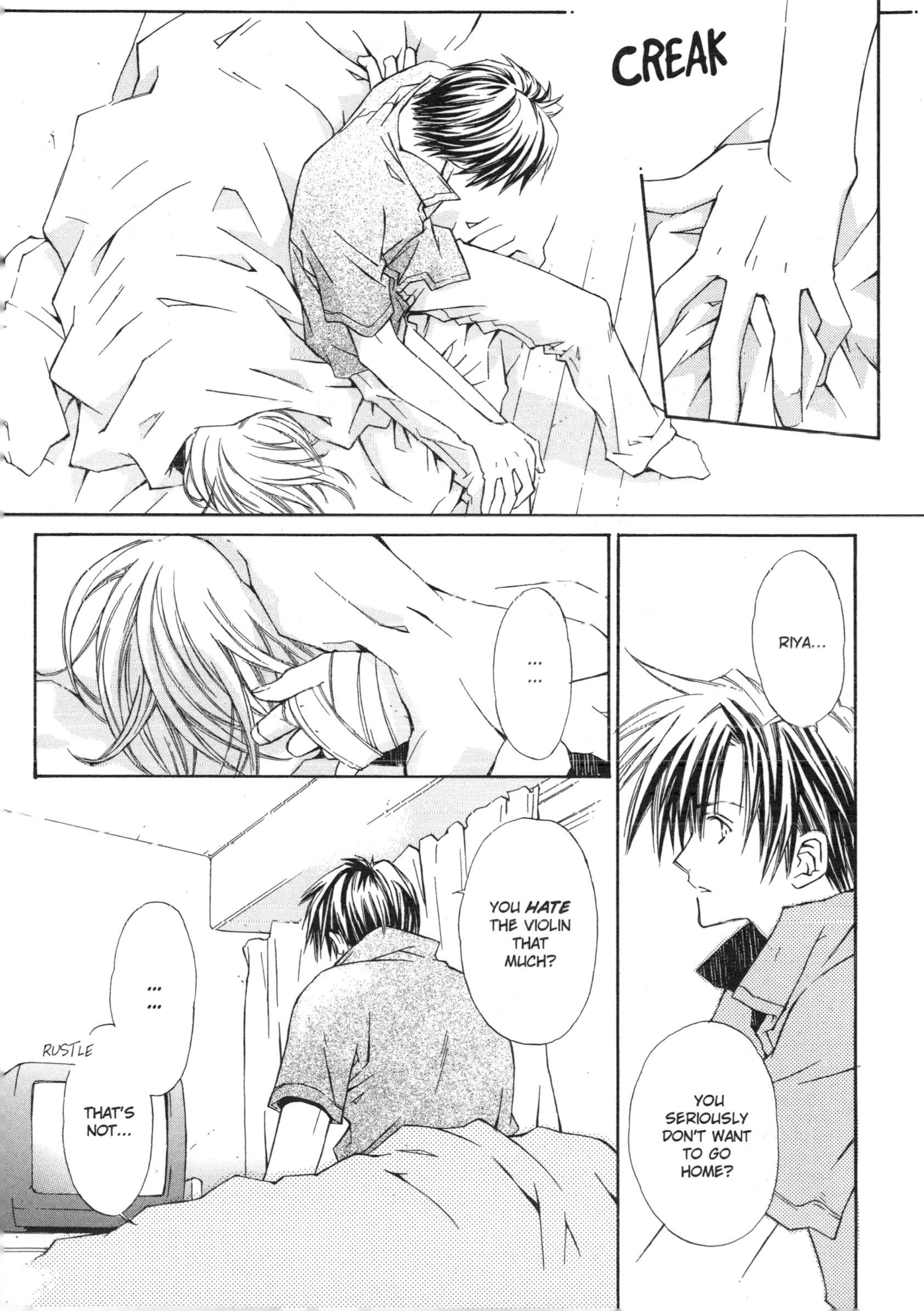
CREAK
RIYA...
YOU SERIOUSLY DON'T WANT TO GO HOME?
......
YOU *HATE* THE VIOLIN THAT MUCH?
......
RUSTLE
THAT'S NOT...

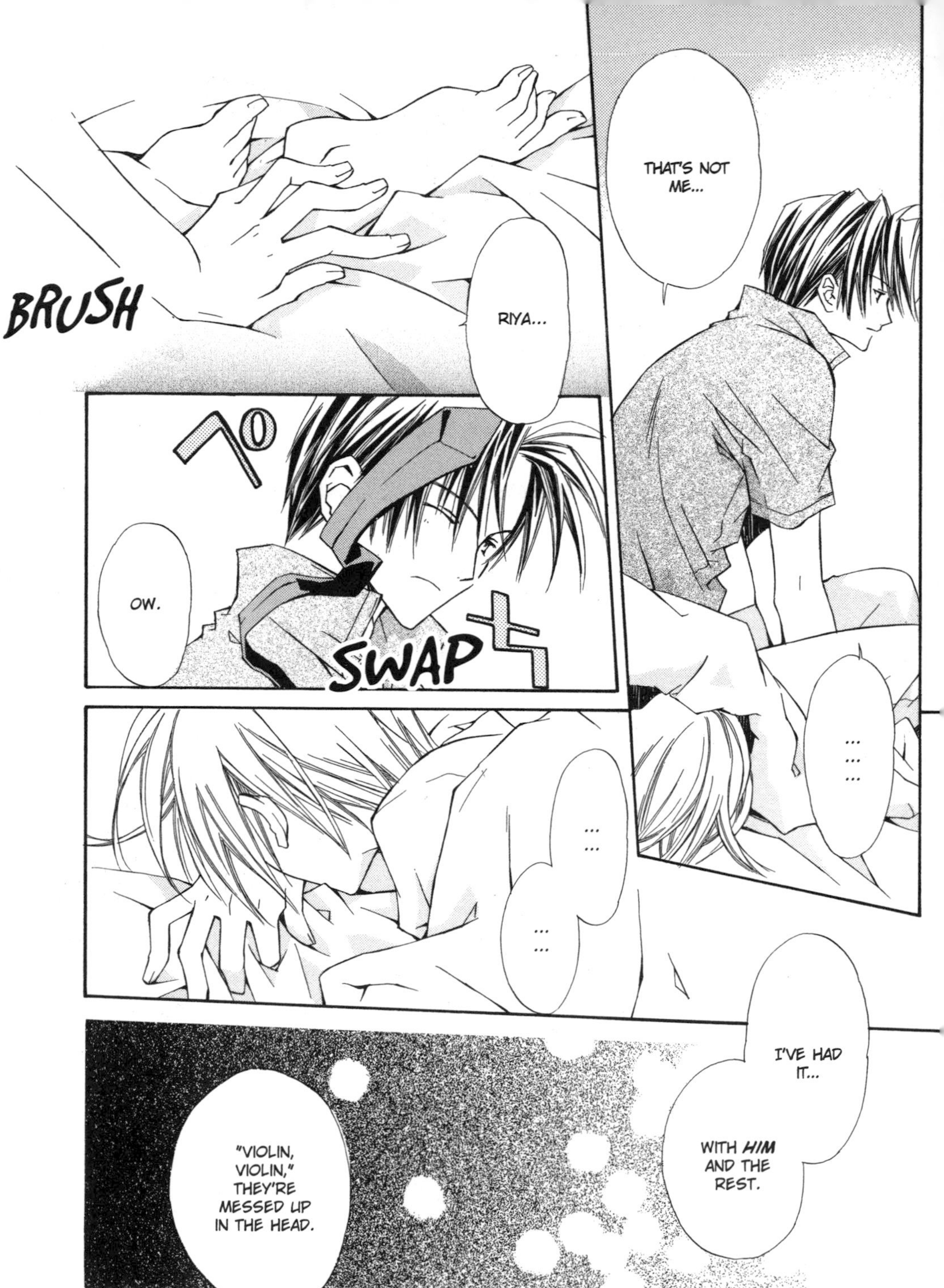
THAT'S NOT ME...
...
...
...
BRUSH
RIYA...
SWAP
OW.
...
...
...
...
I'VE HAD IT...
WITH *HIM* AND THE REST.
"VIOLIN, VIOLIN," THEY'RE MESSED UP IN THE HEAD.

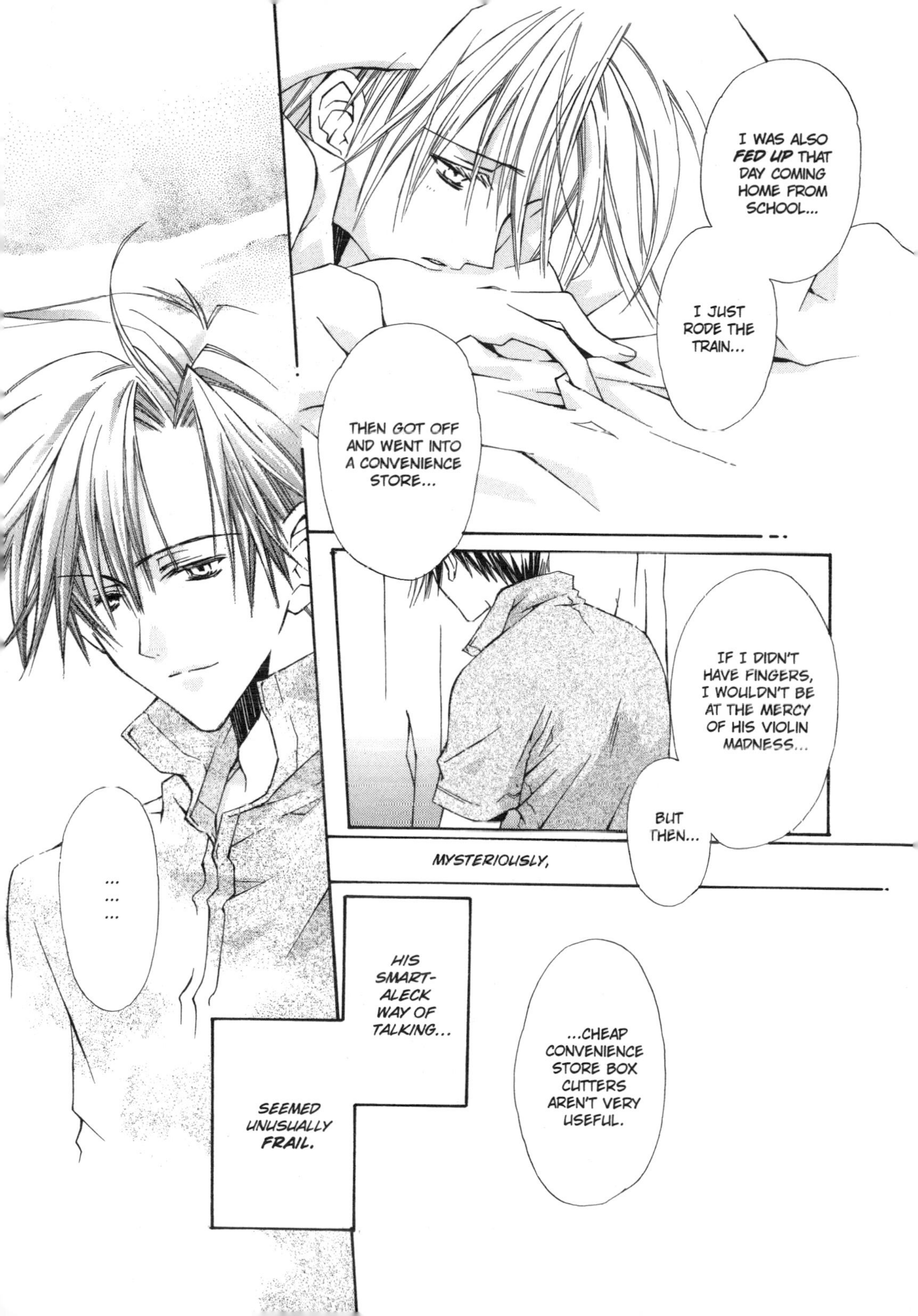
I WAS ALSO FED UP THAT DAY COMING HOME FROM SCHOOL...
I JUST RODE THE TRAIN...
THEN GOT OFF AND WENT INTO A CONVENIENCE STORE...
IF I DIDN'T HAVE FINGERS, I WOULDN'T BE AT THE MERCY OF HIS VIOLIN MADNESS...
BUT THEN...
MYSTERIOUSLY,
...CHEAP CONVENIENCE STORE BOX CUTTERS AREN'T VERY USEFUL.
HIS SMART-ALECK WAY OF TALKING...
SEEMED UNUSUALLY FRAIL.
... ...

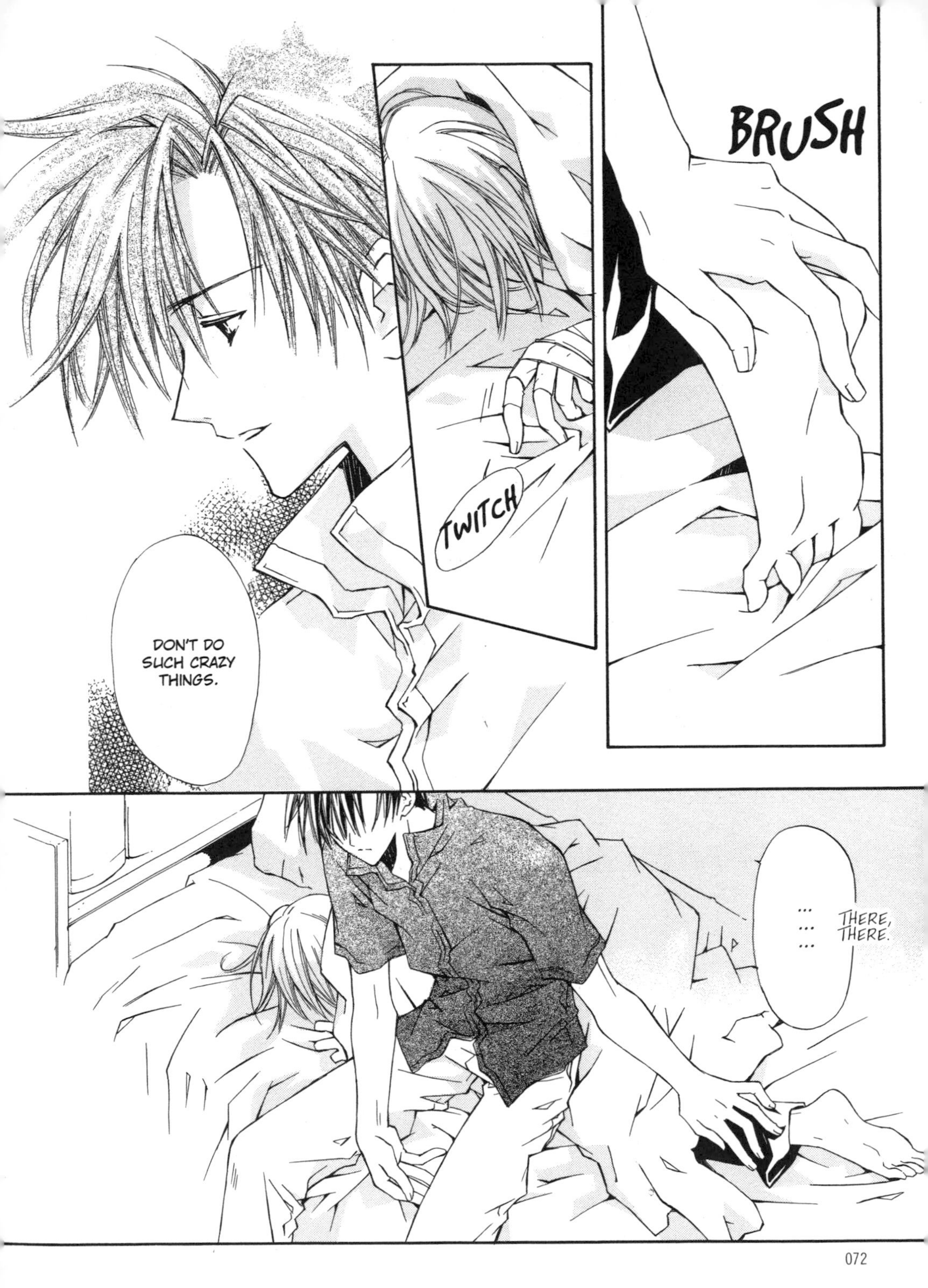
BRUSH
TWITCH
DON'T DO SUCH CRAZY THINGS.
...
...
...
THERE, THERE.

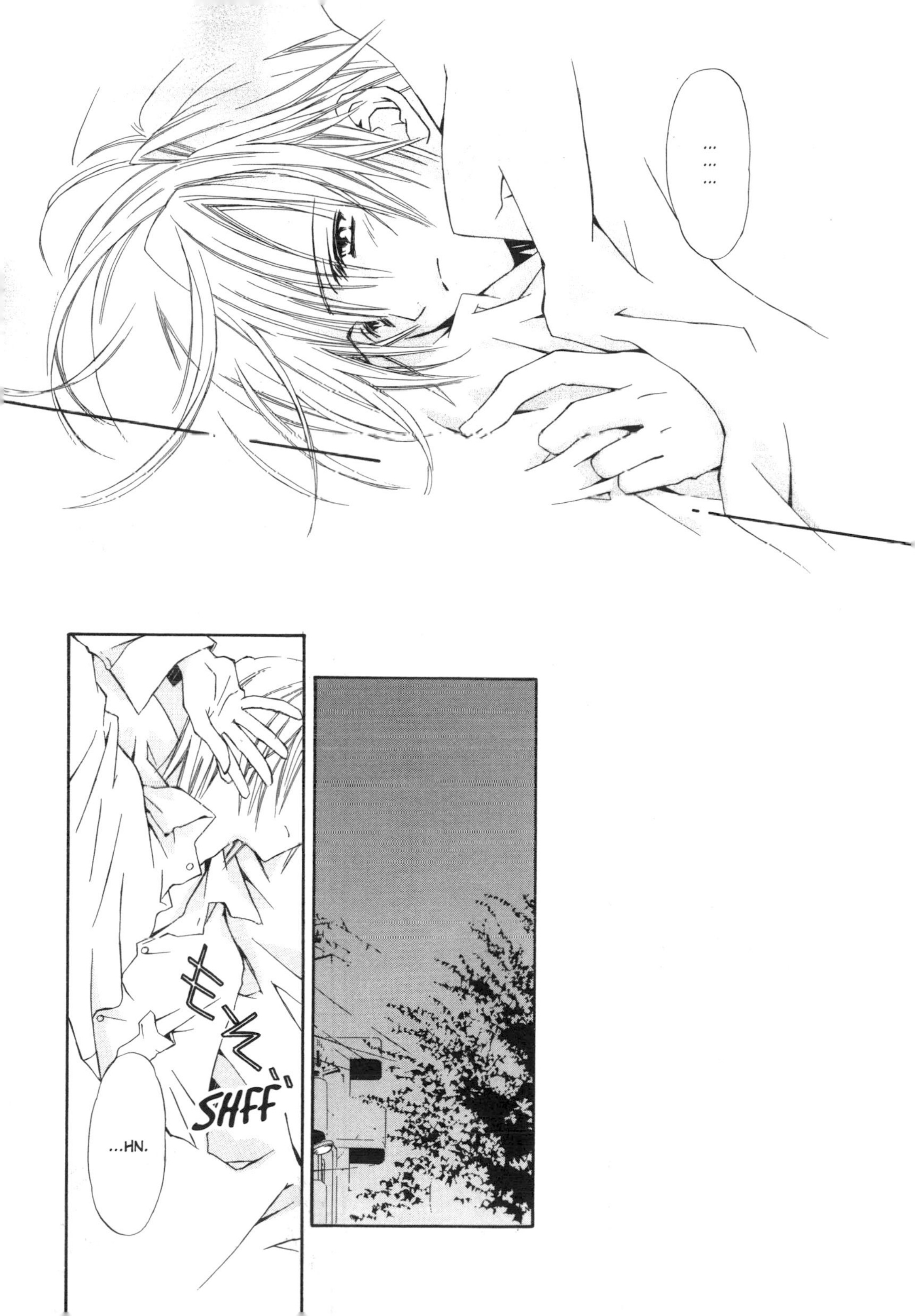
...
...
...
SHFF
...HN.

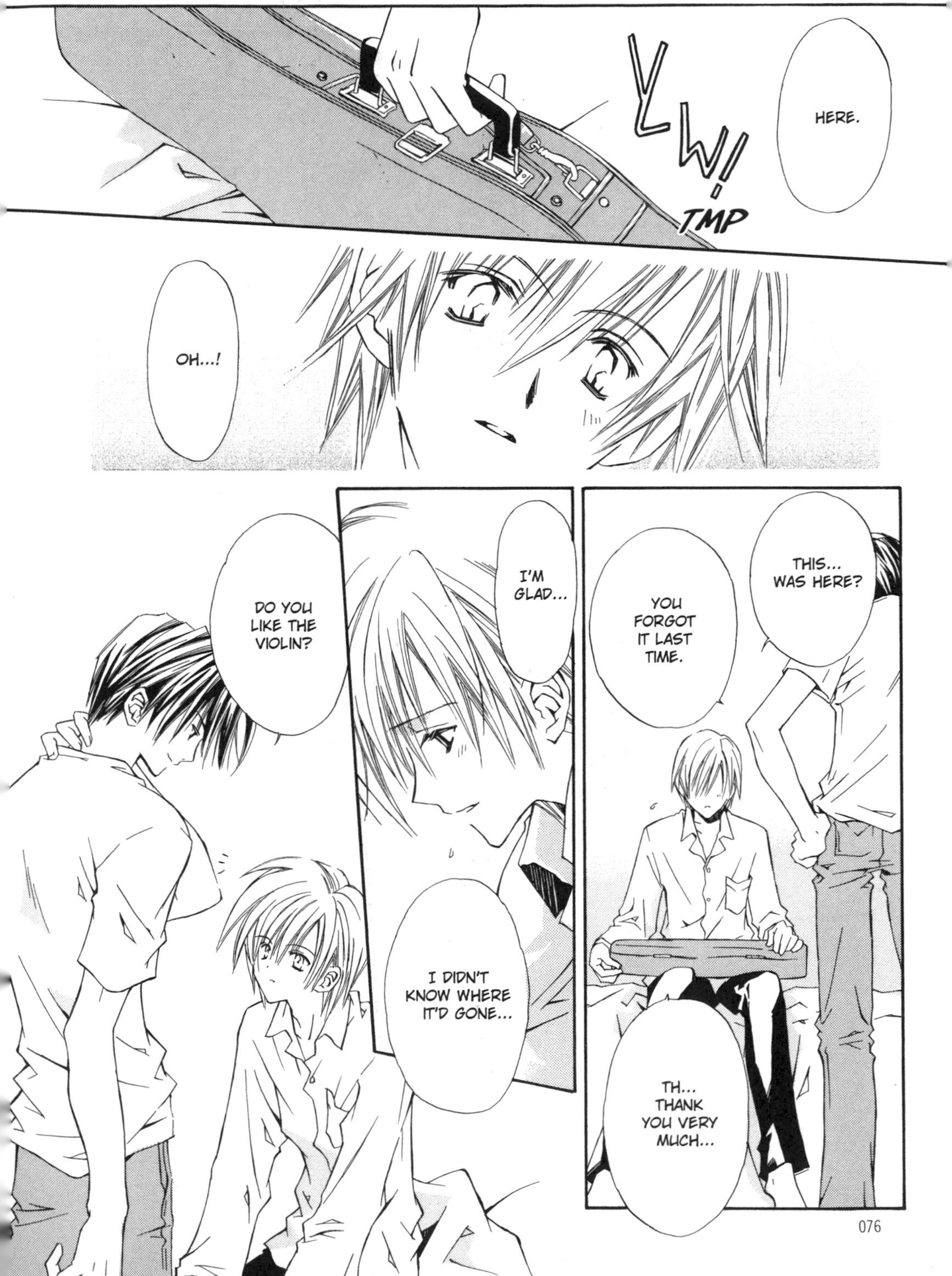
HERE.
YLW!
TMP
OH...!
THIS... WAS HERE?
YOU FORGOT IT LAST TIME.
TH... THANK YOU VERY MUCH...
I'M GLAD...
I DIDN'T KNOW WHERE IT'D GONE...
DO YOU LIKE THE VIOLIN?

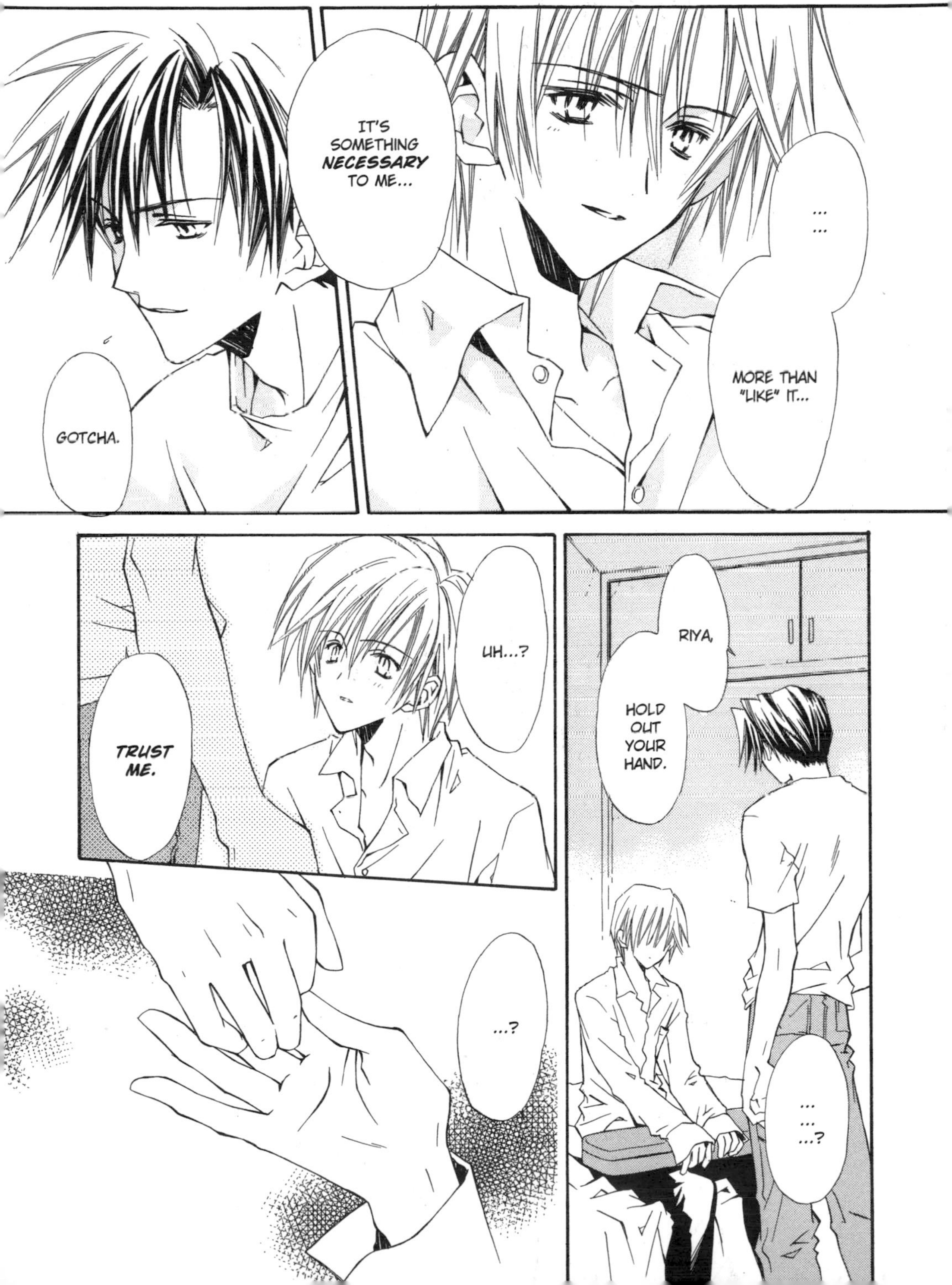

...
...
MORE THAN "LIKE" IT...
IT'S SOMETHING NECESSARY TO ME...
GOTCHA.
RIYA,
HOLD OUT YOUR HAND.
...
...
...?
UH...?
TRUST ME.
...?

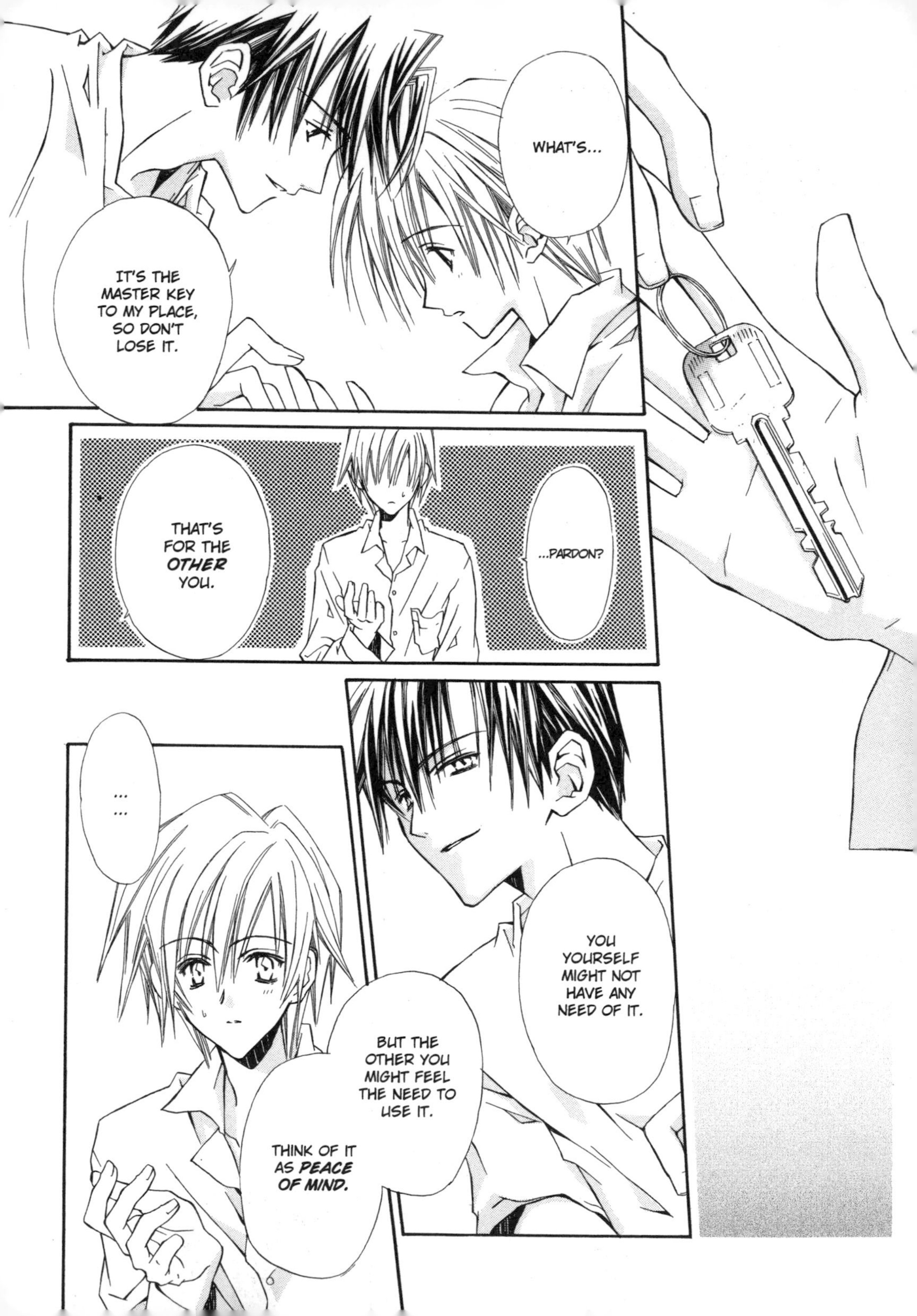
WHAT'S...
IT'S THE MASTER KEY TO MY PLACE, SO DON'T LOSE IT.
...PARDON?
THAT'S FOR THE *OTHER* YOU.
YOU YOURSELF MIGHT NOT HAVE ANY NEED OF IT.
BUT THE OTHER YOU MIGHT FEEL THE NEED TO USE IT.
THINK OF IT AS *PEACE OF MIND.*
... ...

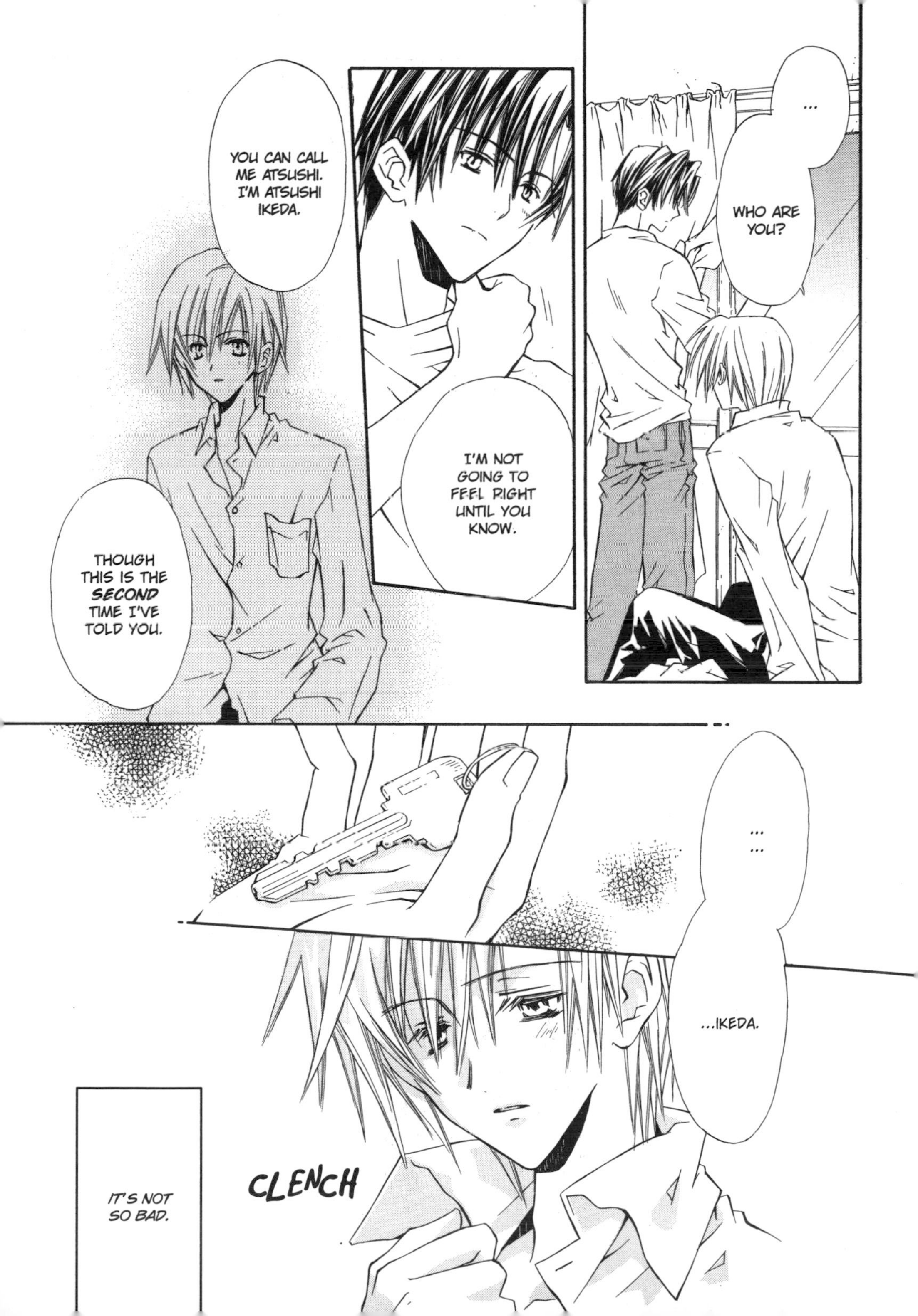
...
WHO ARE YOU?
I'M NOT GOING TO FEEL RIGHT UNTIL YOU KNOW.
YOU CAN CALL ME ATSUSHI. I'M ATSUSHI IKEDA.
THOUGH THIS IS THE ***SECOND*** TIME I'VE TOLD YOU.
... ...
...IKEDA.
CLENCH
IT'S NOT SO BAD.

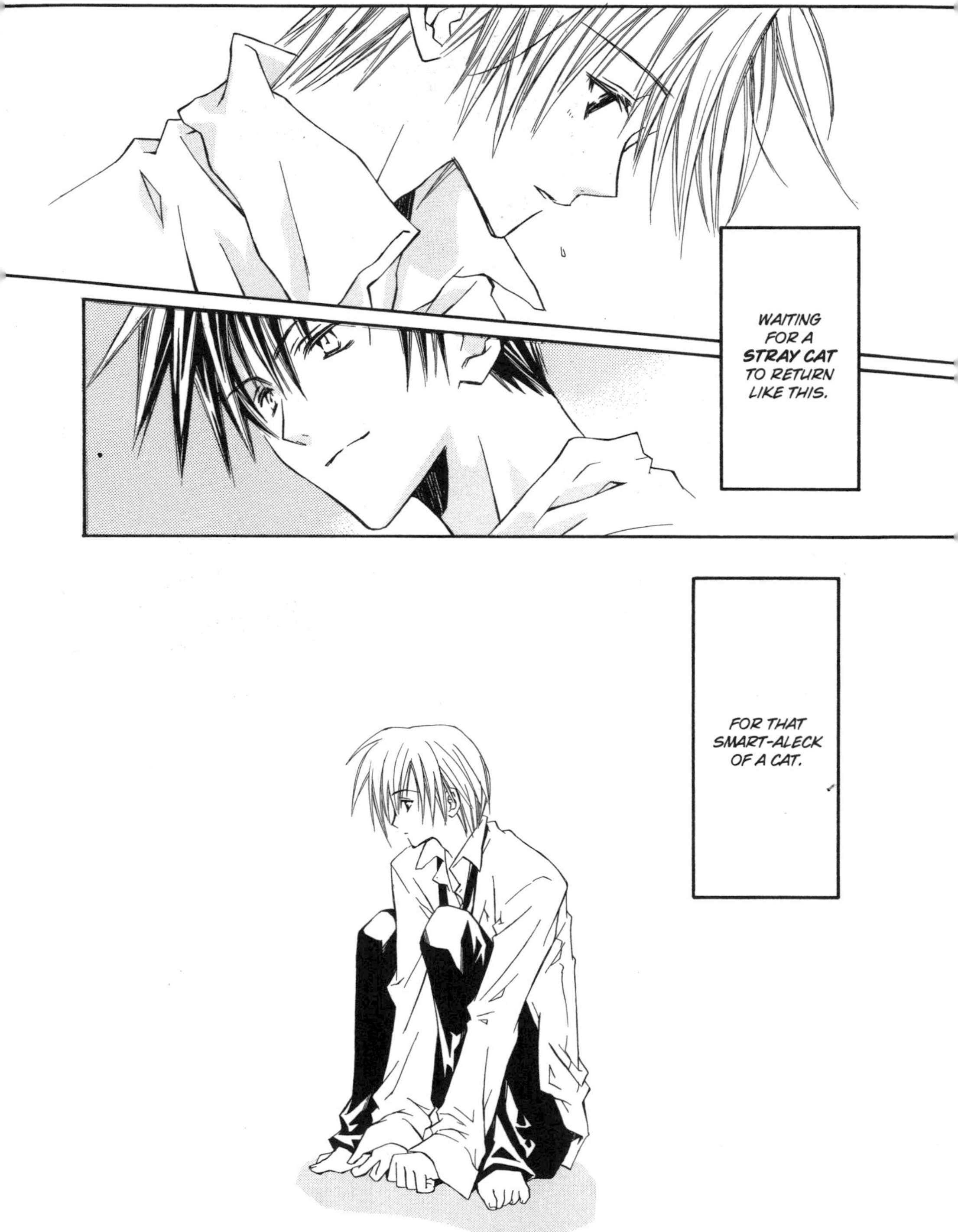
WAITING FOR A **STRAY CAT** TO RETURN LIKE THIS.
FOR THAT SMART-ALECK OF A CAT.

IL GATTO SUL G. (NERO) / FINO

Il gatto sul G.

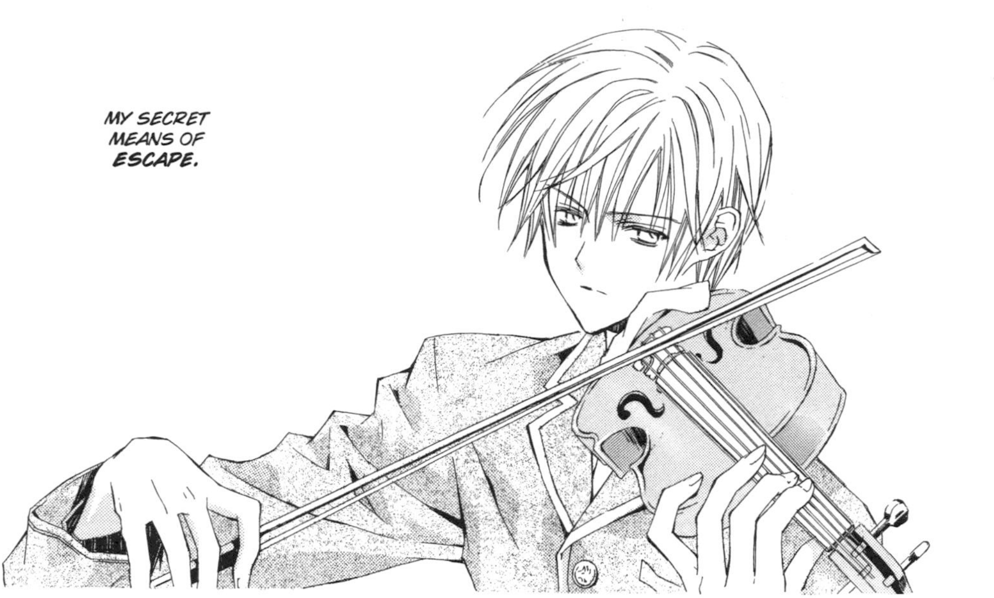
MY SECRET MEANS OF ESCAPE.

Il gatto sul G. THE PRACTICE ROOM

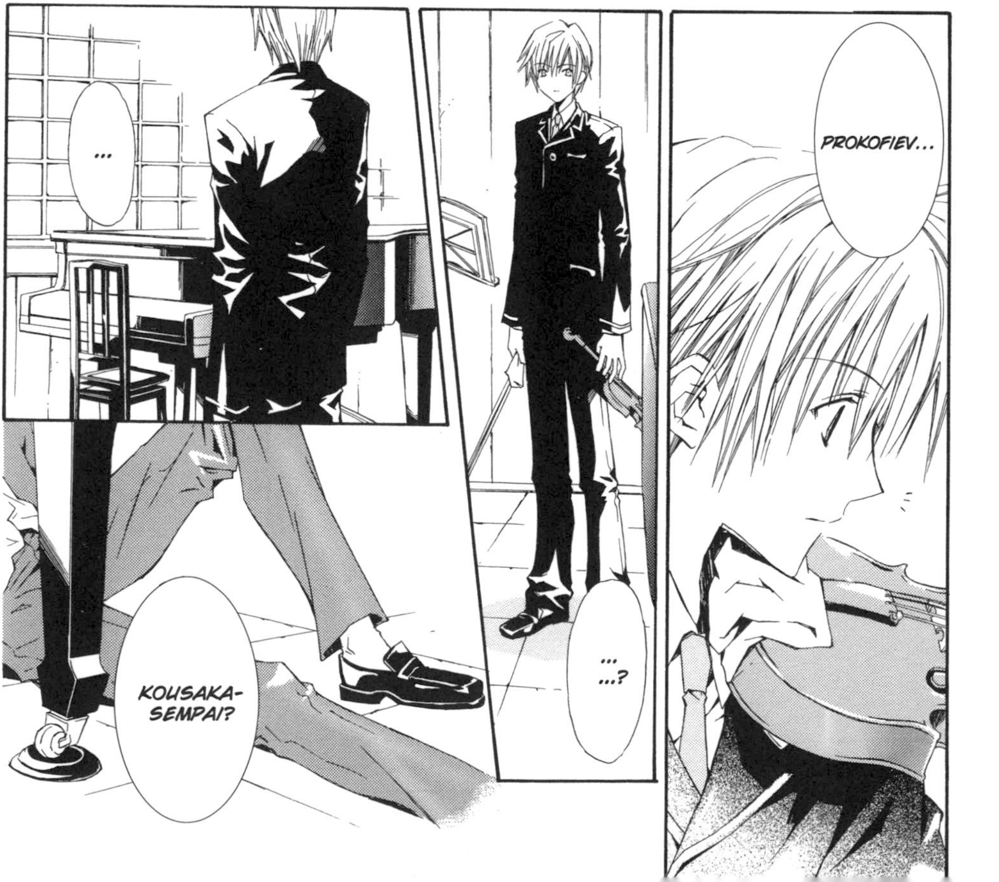
PROKOFIEV...
...
...?
...
KOUSAKA-SEMPAI?

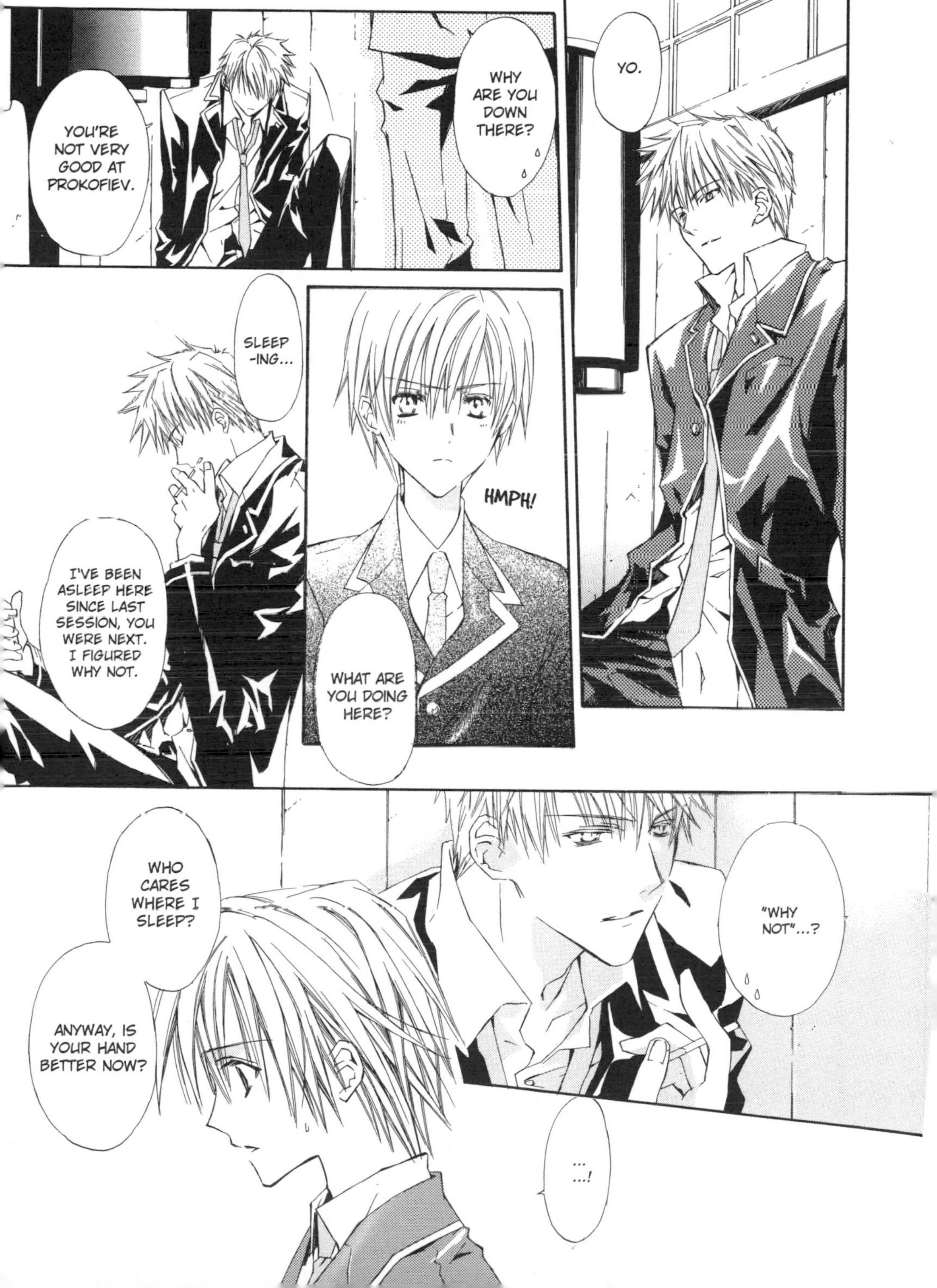

YO.
WHY ARE YOU DOWN THERE?
YOU'RE NOT VERY GOOD AT PROKOFIEV.
HMPH!
WHAT ARE YOU DOING HERE?
SLEEP -ING...
I'VE BEEN ASLEEP HERE SINCE LAST SESSION, YOU WERE NEXT. I FIGURED WHY NOT.
"WHY NOT"...?
WHO CARES WHERE I SLEEP?
ANYWAY, IS YOUR HAND BETTER NOW?
... ...!

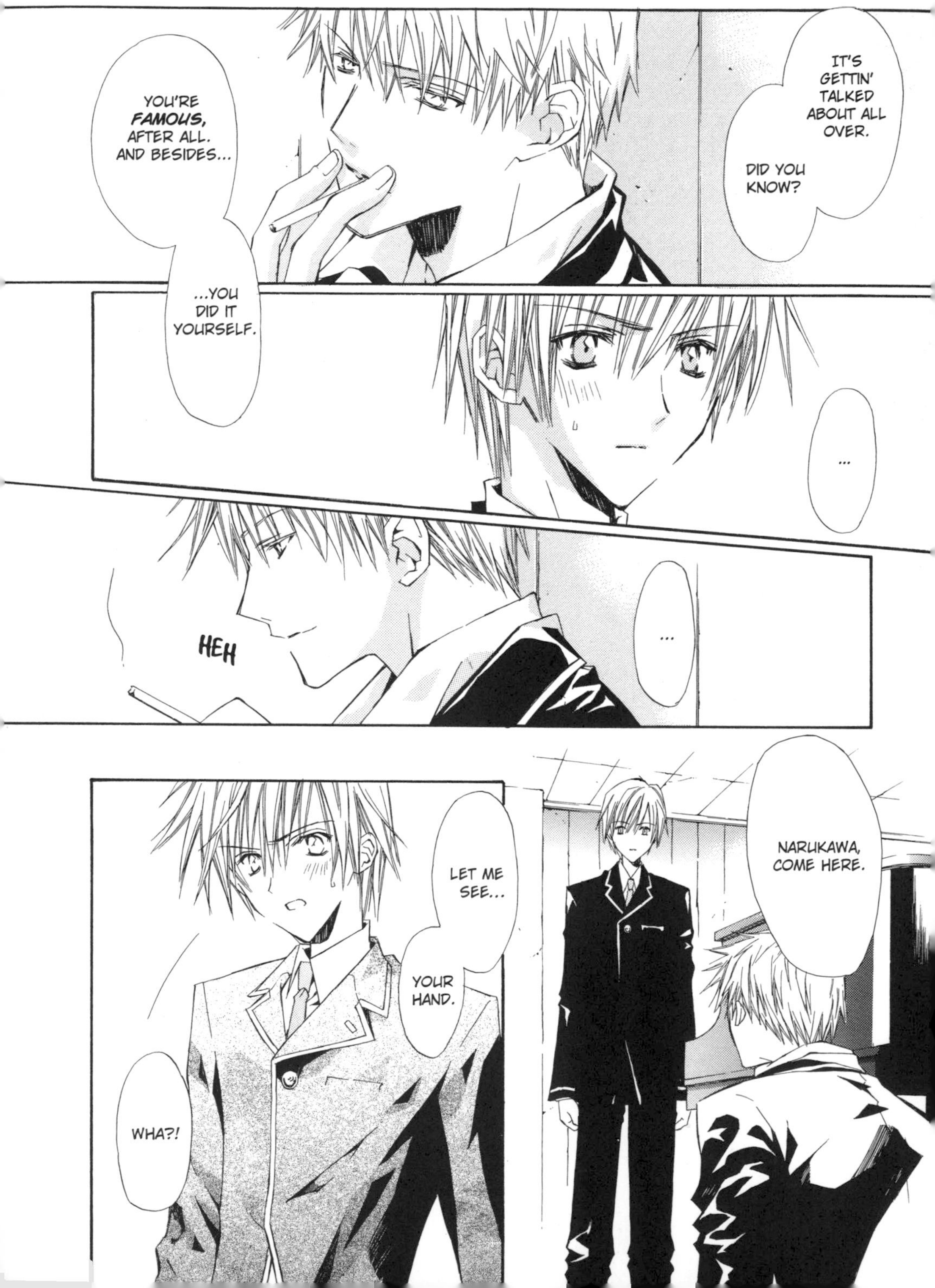
IT'S GETTIN' TALKED ABOUT ALL OVER.
DID YOU KNOW?
YOU'RE **FAMOUS,** AFTER ALL. AND BESIDES...
...YOU DID IT YOURSELF.
...
...
HEH
NARUKAWA, COME HERE.
LET ME SEE...
YOUR HAND.
WHA?!

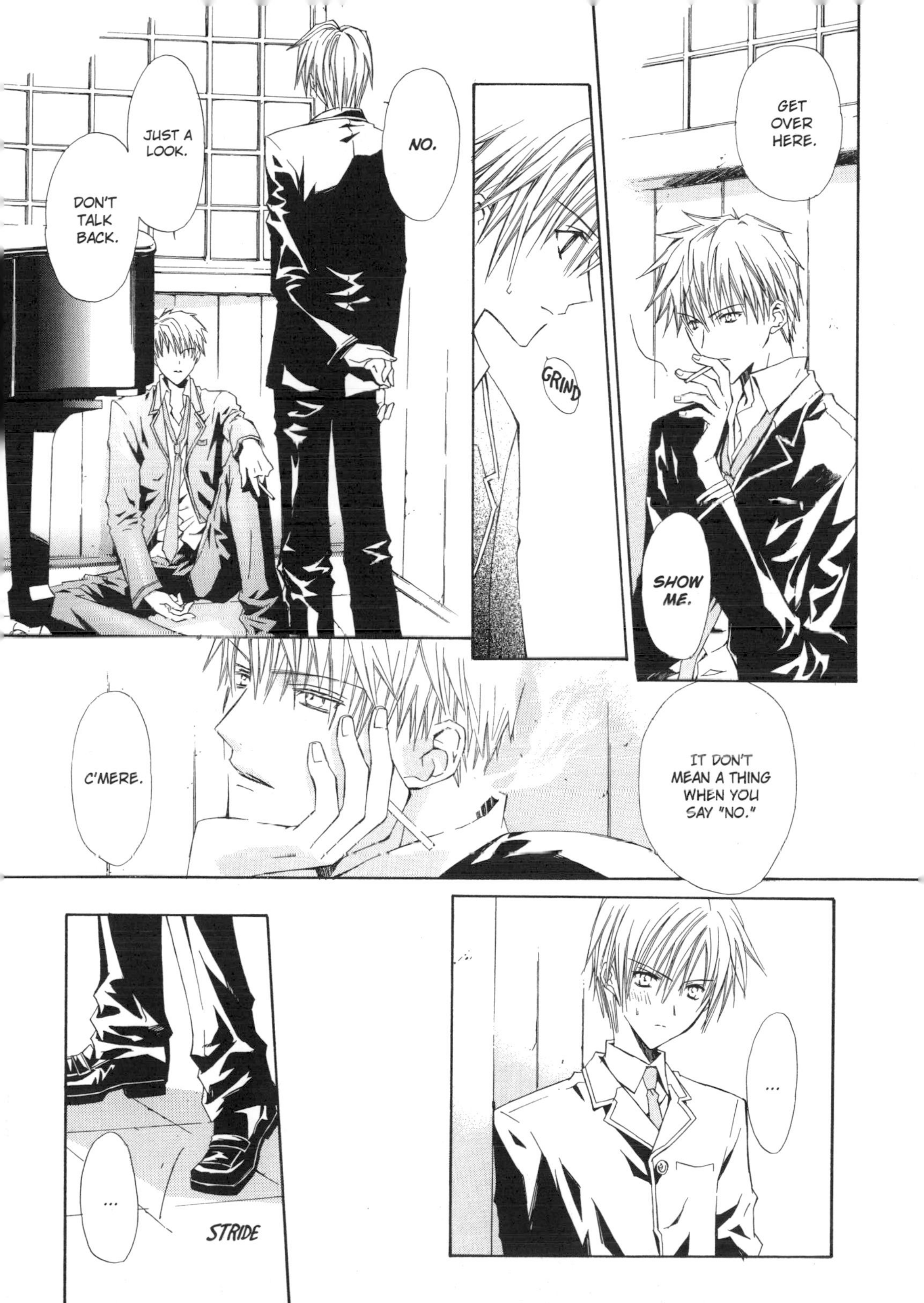
GET OVER HERE.
SHOW ME.
GRIND
NO.
JUST A LOOK.
DON'T TALK BACK.
IT DON'T MEAN A THING WHEN YOU SAY "NO."
C'MERE.
...
...
STRIDE

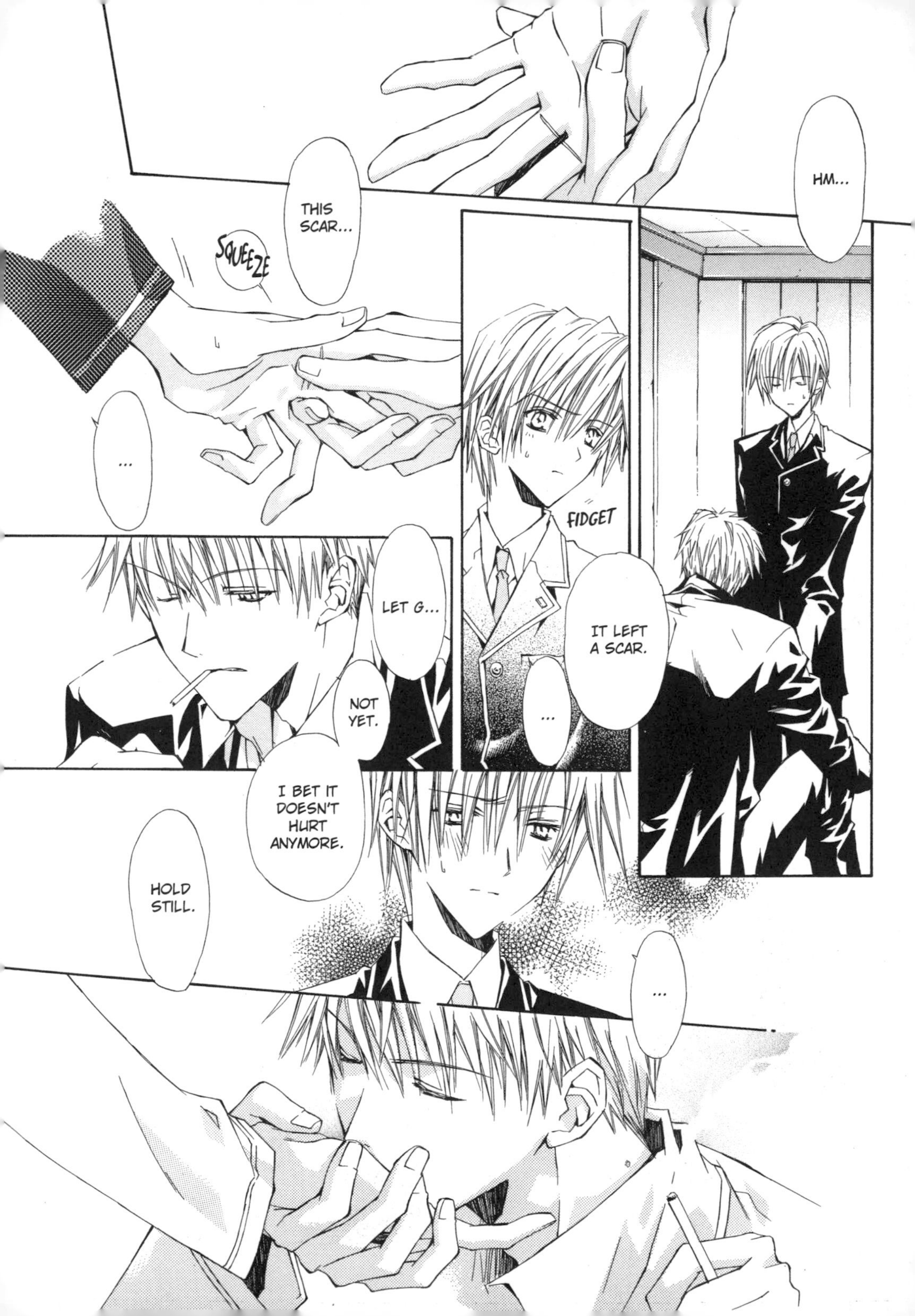
HM...
THIS SCAR...
IT LEFT A SCAR.
FIDGET
...
SQUEEZE
...
LET G...
NOT YET.
I BET IT DOESN'T HURT ANYMORE.
HOLD STILL.
...

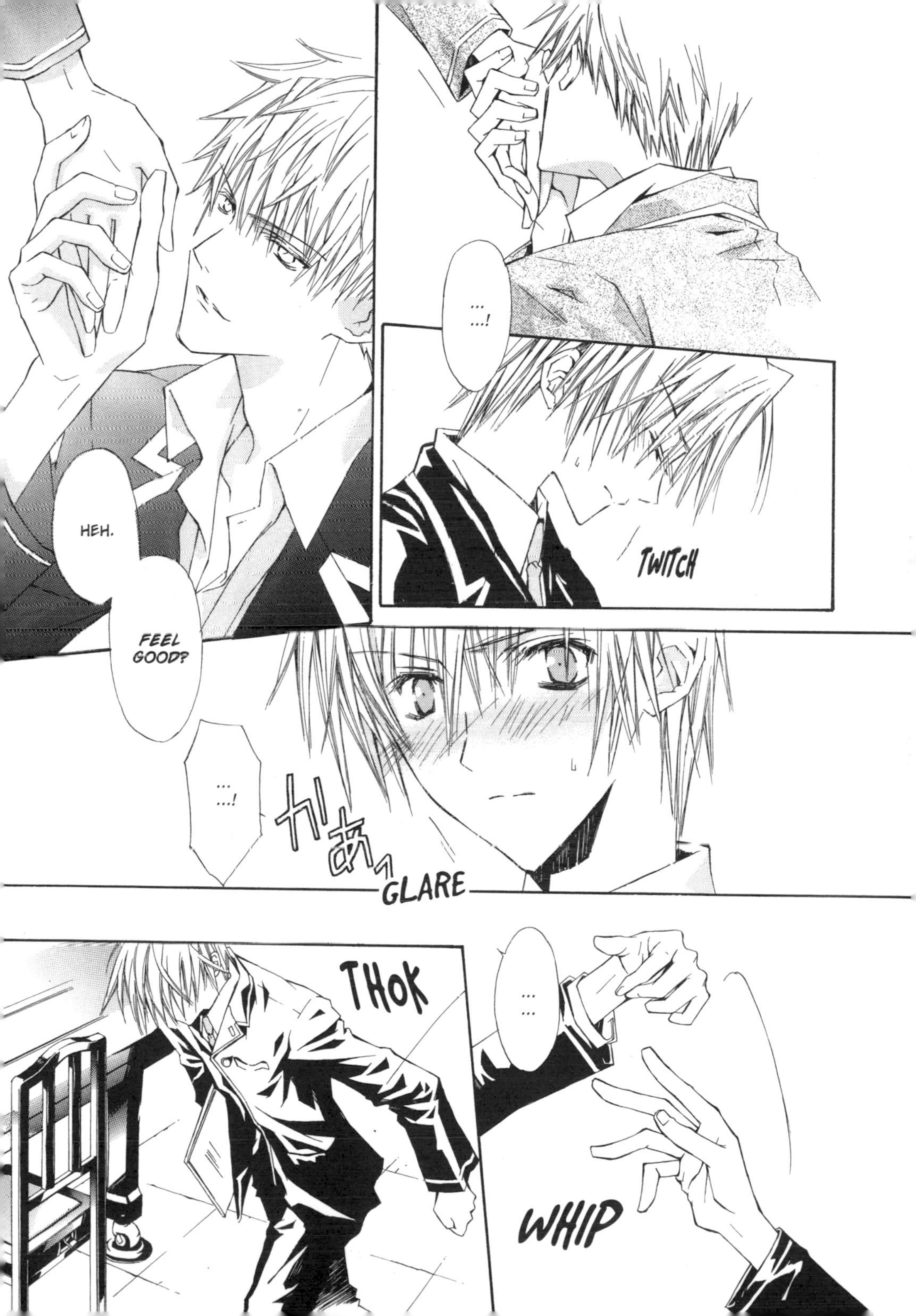
...
...!
TWITCH
HEH.
FEEL GOOD?
...
...!
かぁ
GLARE
...
...
WHIP
THOK

EPISODIO.1

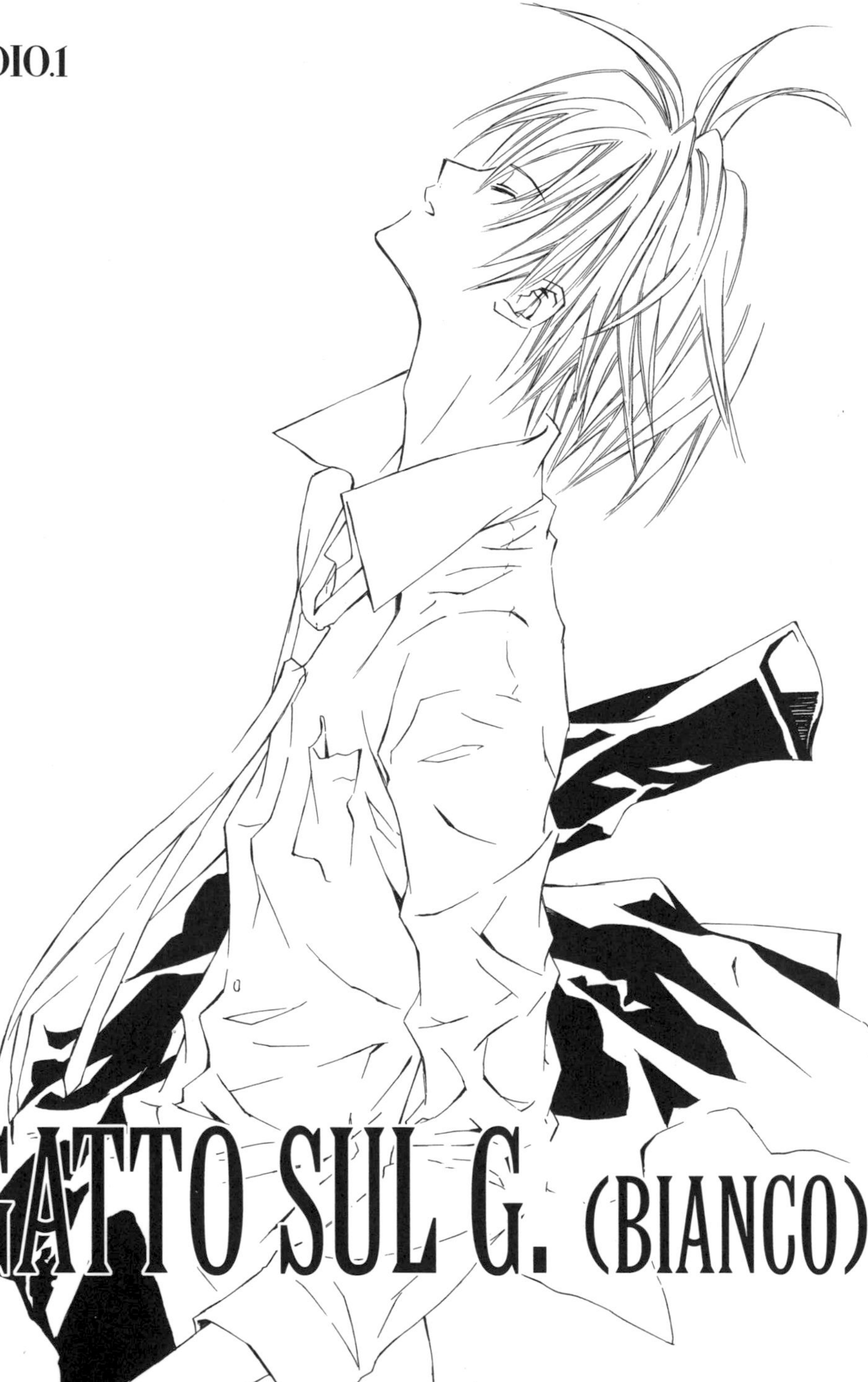

IL GATTO SUL G. (BIANCO)

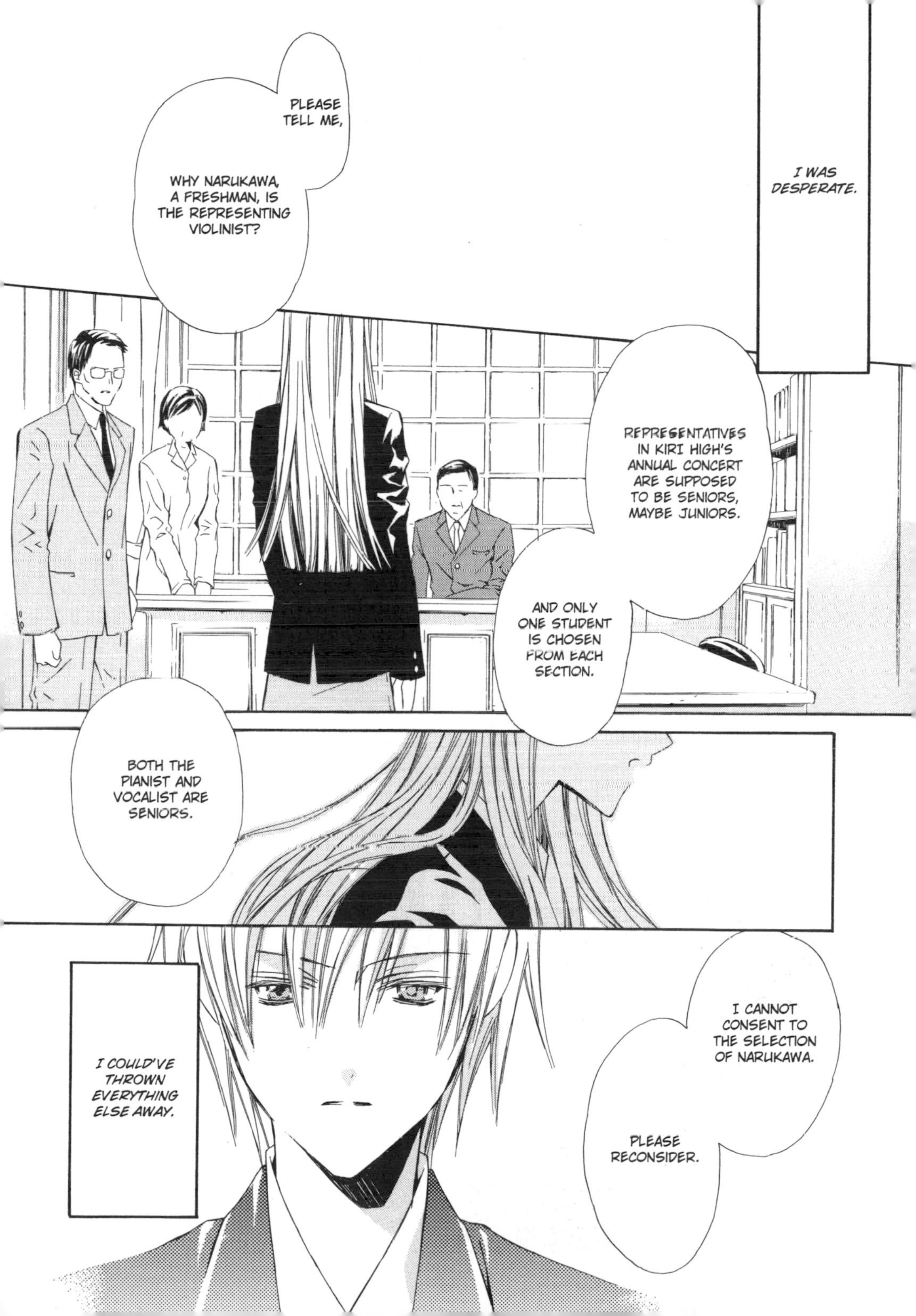
I WAS DESPERATE.
PLEASE TELL ME,
WHY NARUKAWA, A FRESHMAN, IS THE REPRESENTING VIOLINIST?
REPRESENTATIVES IN KIRI HIGH'S ANNUAL CONCERT ARE SUPPOSED TO BE SENIORS, MAYBE JUNIORS.
AND ONLY ONE STUDENT IS CHOSEN FROM EACH SECTION.
BOTH THE PIANIST AND VOCALIST ARE SENIORS.
I CANNOT CONSENT TO THE SELECTION OF NARUKAWA.
PLEASE RECONSIDER.
I COULD'VE THROWN EVERYTHING ELSE AWAY.

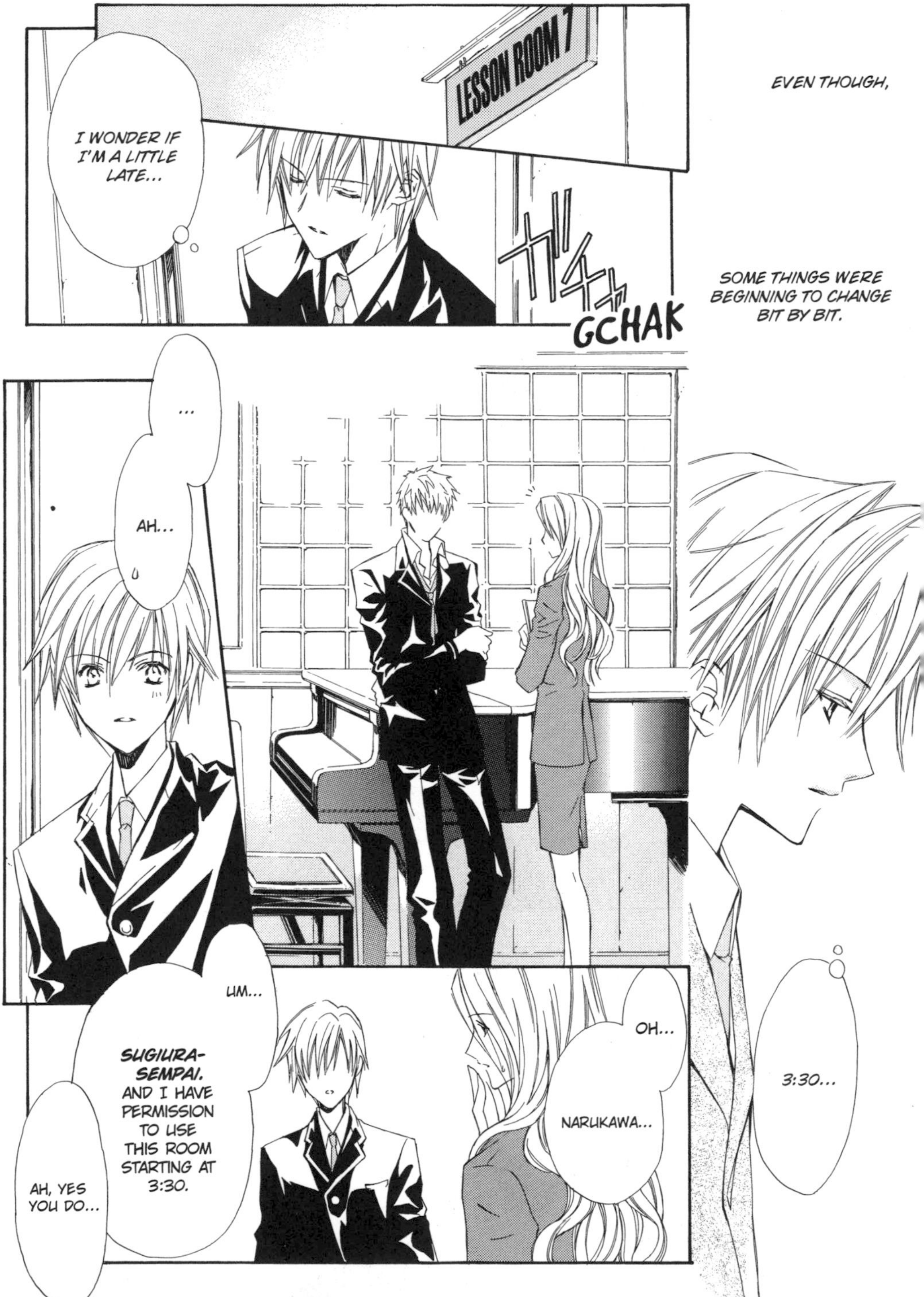
EVEN THOUGH,
LESSON ROOM 7
I WONDER IF I'M A LITTLE LATE...
GCHAK
SOME THINGS WERE BEGINNING TO CHANGE BIT BY BIT.
3:30...
...
AH...
OH...
NARUKAWA...
UM...
SUGIURA-SEMPAI. AND I HAVE PERMISSION TO USE THIS ROOM STARTING AT 3:30.
AH, YES YOU DO...

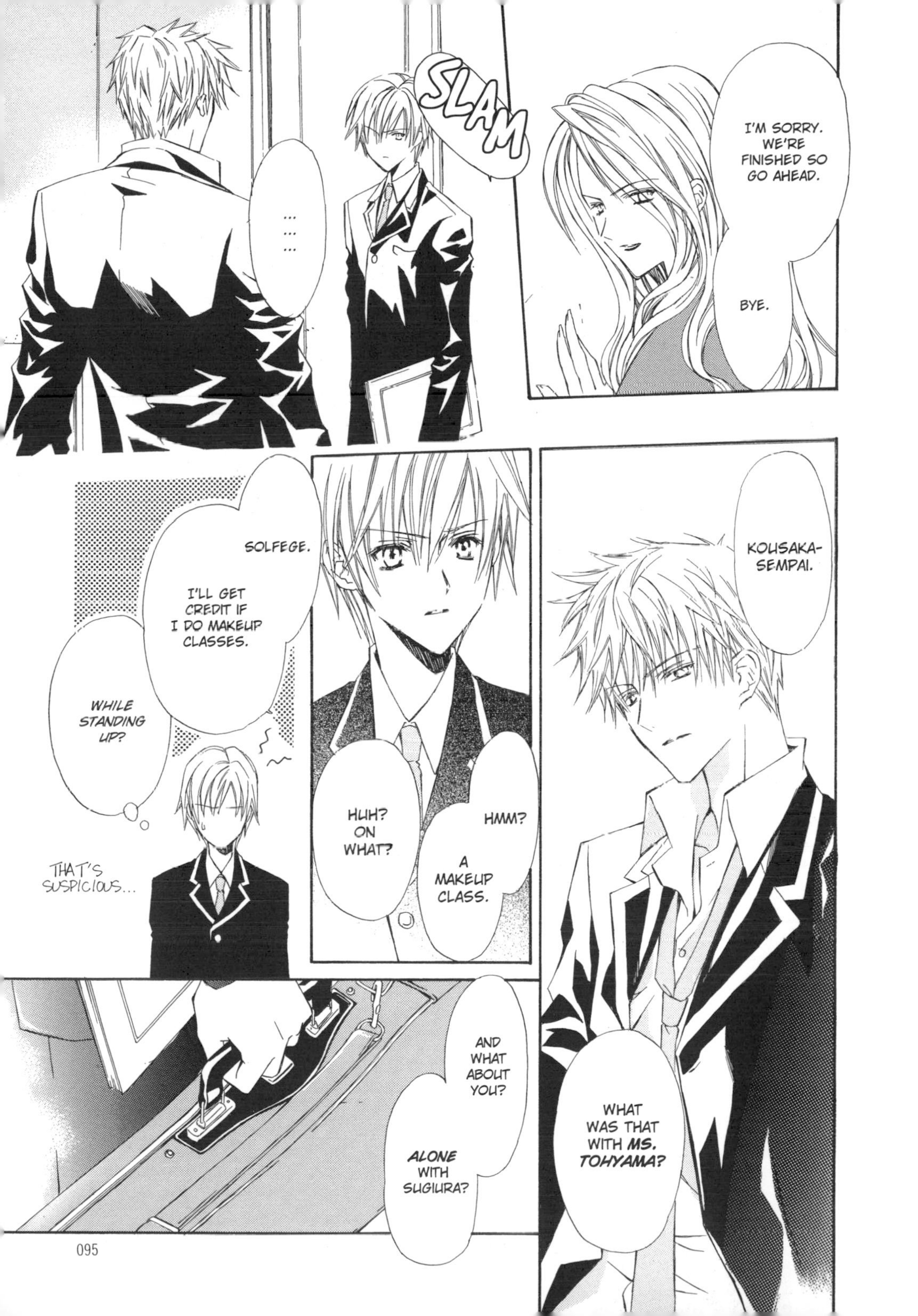
I'M SORRY. WE'RE FINISHED SO GO AHEAD.
BYE.
SLAM
... ...
KOUSAKA-SEMPAI.
HMM?
A MAKEUP CLASS.
HUH? ON WHAT?
SOLFEGE.
I'LL GET CREDIT IF I DO MAKEUP CLASSES.
WHILE STANDING UP?
THAT'S SUSPICIOUS...
WHAT WAS THAT WITH MS. TOHYAMA?
AND WHAT ABOUT YOU?
ALONE WITH SUGIURA?

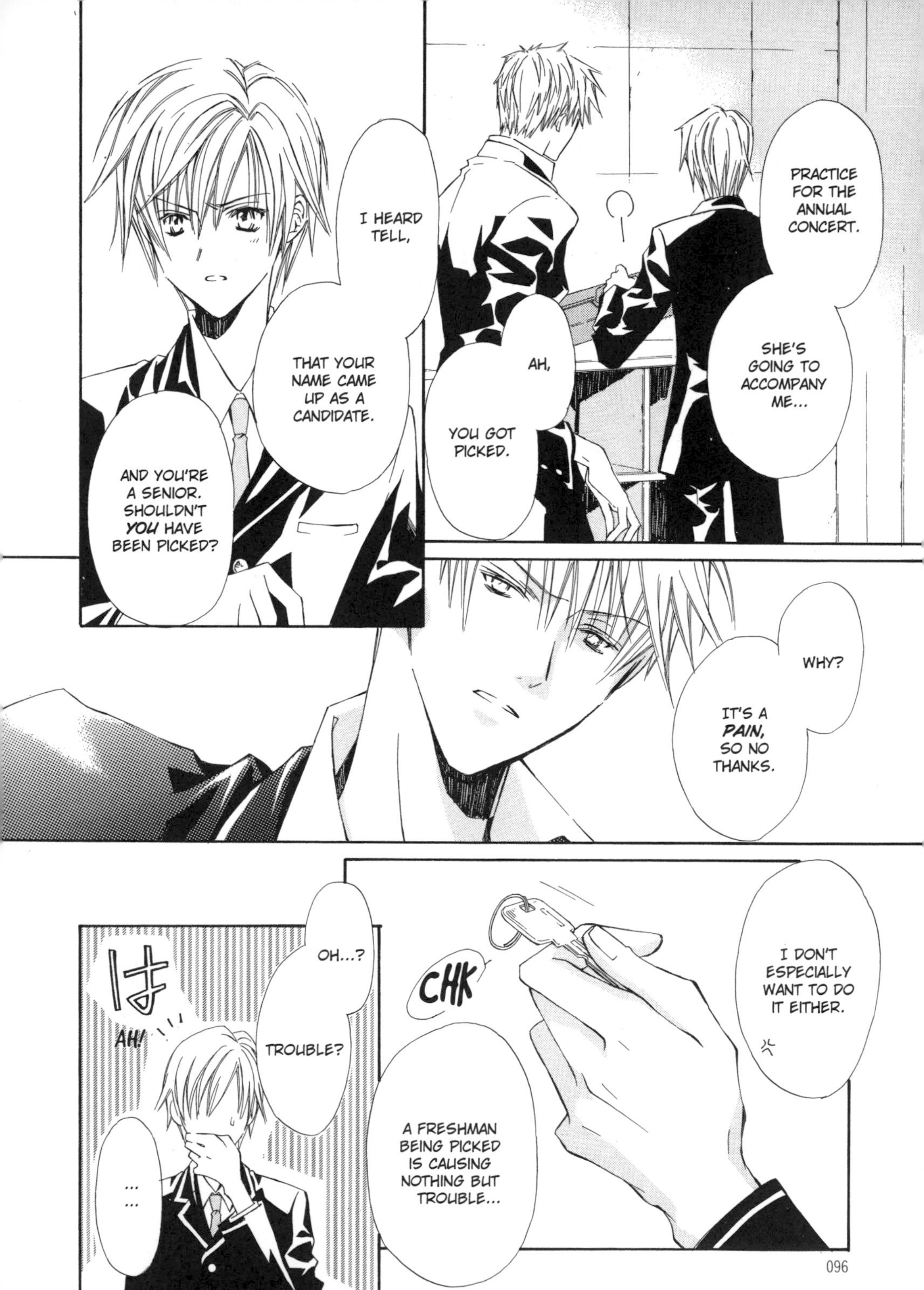
PRACTICE FOR THE ANNUAL CONCERT.
SHE'S GOING TO ACCOMPANY ME...
AH, YOU GOT PICKED.
I HEARD TELL,
THAT YOUR NAME CAME UP AS A CANDIDATE.
AND YOU'RE A SENIOR. SHOULDN'T *YOU* HAVE BEEN PICKED?
WHY?
IT'S A *PAIN,* SO NO THANKS.
I DON'T ESPECIALLY WANT TO DO IT EITHER.
CHK
A FRESHMAN BEING PICKED IS CAUSING NOTHING BUT TROUBLE...
OH...?
TROUBLE?
は
AH!
... ...

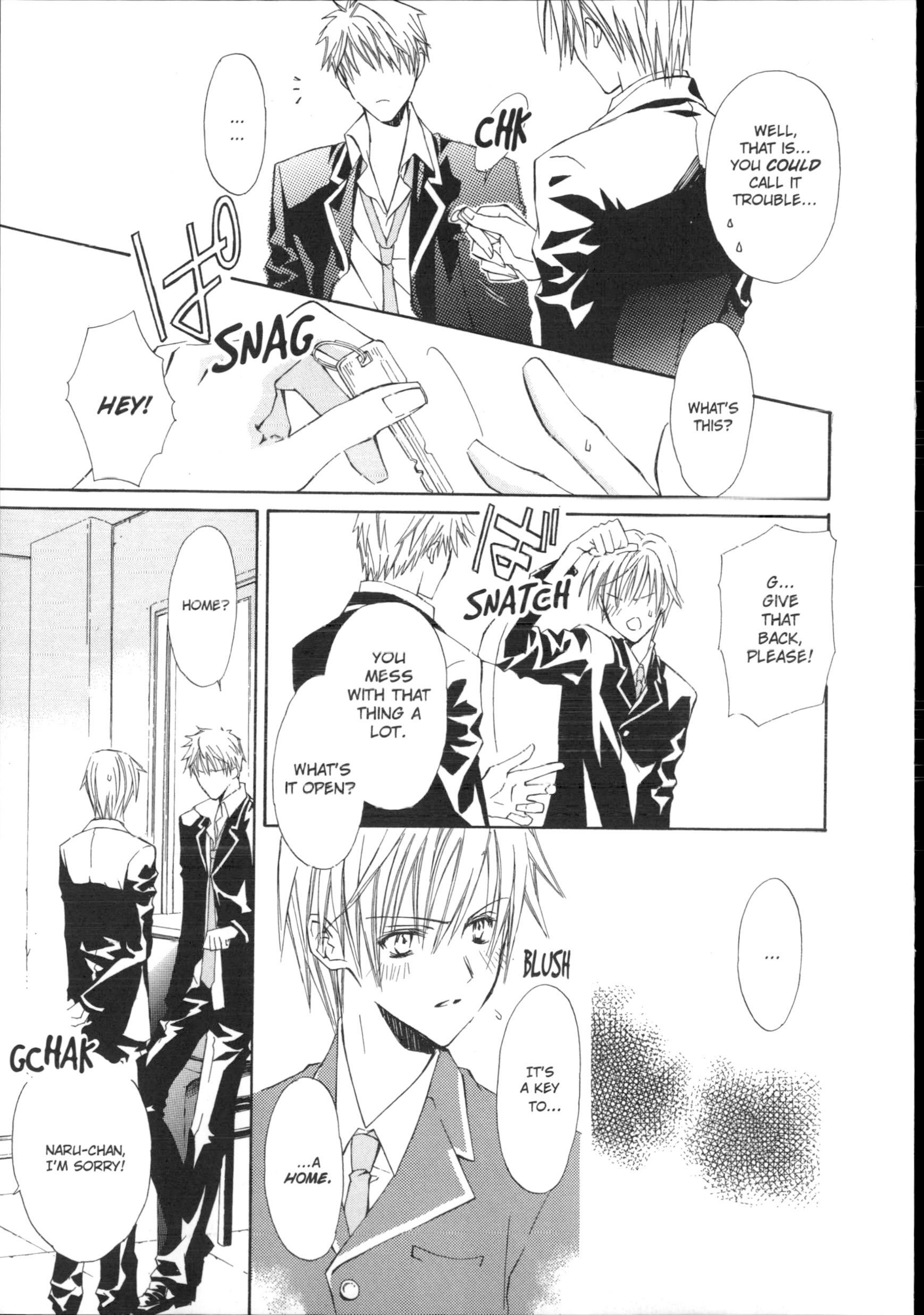
WELL, THAT IS... YOU COULD CALL IT TROUBLE...
CHK
......
WHAT'S THIS?
SNAG
HEY!
G... GIVE THAT BACK, PLEASE!
SNATCH
YOU MESS WITH THAT THING A LOT.
WHAT'S IT OPEN?
...
BLUSH
IT'S A KEY TO...
...A HOME.
HOME?
GCHAK
NARU-CHAN, I'M SORRY!

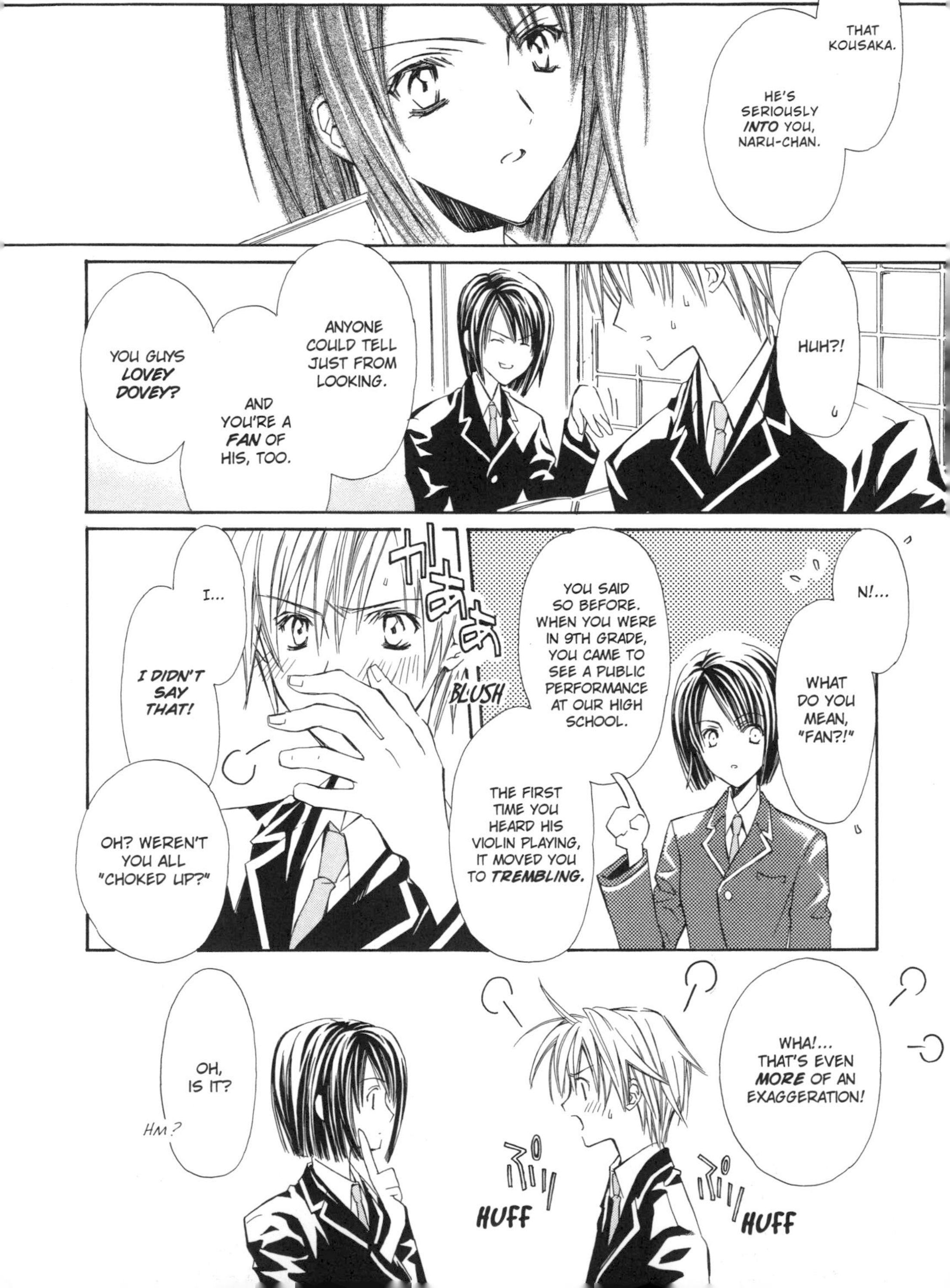

THAT KOUSAKA.
HE'S SERIOUSLY **INTO** YOU, NARU-CHAN.
HUH?!
ANYONE COULD TELL JUST FROM LOOKING.
AND YOU'RE A **FAN** OF HIS, TOO.
YOU GUYS **LOVEY DOVEY?**
N!...
WHAT DO YOU MEAN, "FAN?!"
YOU SAID SO BEFORE. WHEN YOU WERE IN 9TH GRADE, YOU CAME TO SEE A PUBLIC PERFORMANCE AT OUR HIGH SCHOOL.
THE FIRST TIME YOU HEARD HIS VIOLIN PLAYING, IT MOVED YOU TO **TREMBLING.**
BLUSH
I...
I DIDN'T SAY THAT!
OH? WEREN'T YOU ALL "CHOKED UP?"
WHA!... THAT'S EVEN **MORE** OF AN EXAGGERATION!
HUFF
HUFF
OH, IS IT?
HM?

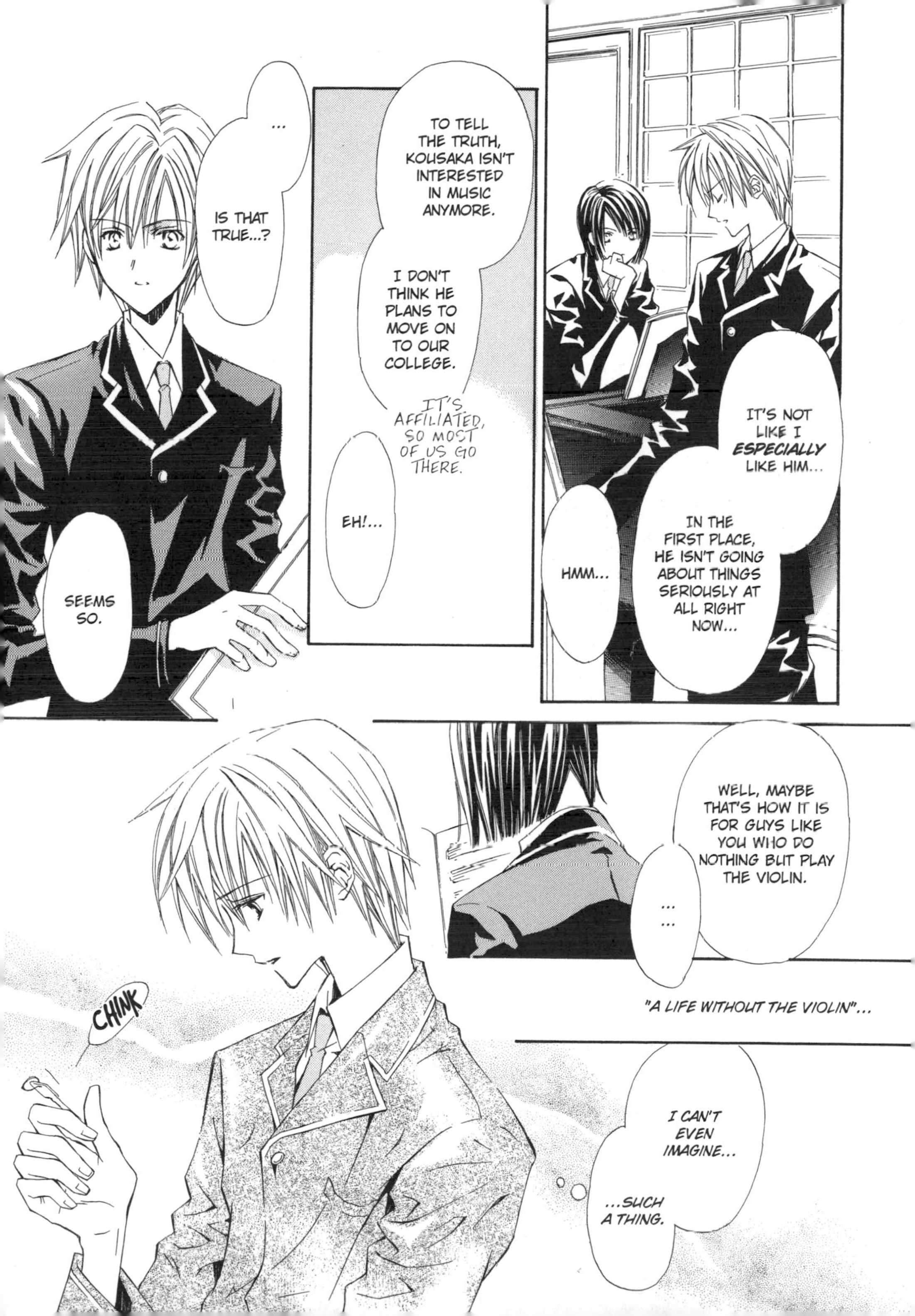
IT'S NOT LIKE I ESPECIALLY LIKE HIM...
IN THE FIRST PLACE, HE ISN'T GOING ABOUT THINGS SERIOUSLY AT ALL RIGHT NOW...
HMM...
TO TELL THE TRUTH, KOUSAKA ISN'T INTERESTED IN MUSIC ANYMORE.
I DON'T THINK HE PLANS TO MOVE ON TO OUR COLLEGE.
IT'S AFFILIATED, SO MOST OF US GO THERE.
EH!...
...
IS THAT TRUE...?
SEEMS SO.
WELL, MAYBE THAT'S HOW IT IS FOR GUYS LIKE YOU WHO DO NOTHING BUT PLAY THE VIOLIN.
... ...
"A LIFE WITHOUT THE VIOLIN"...
I CAN'T EVEN IMAGINE...
...SUCH A THING.
CHINK

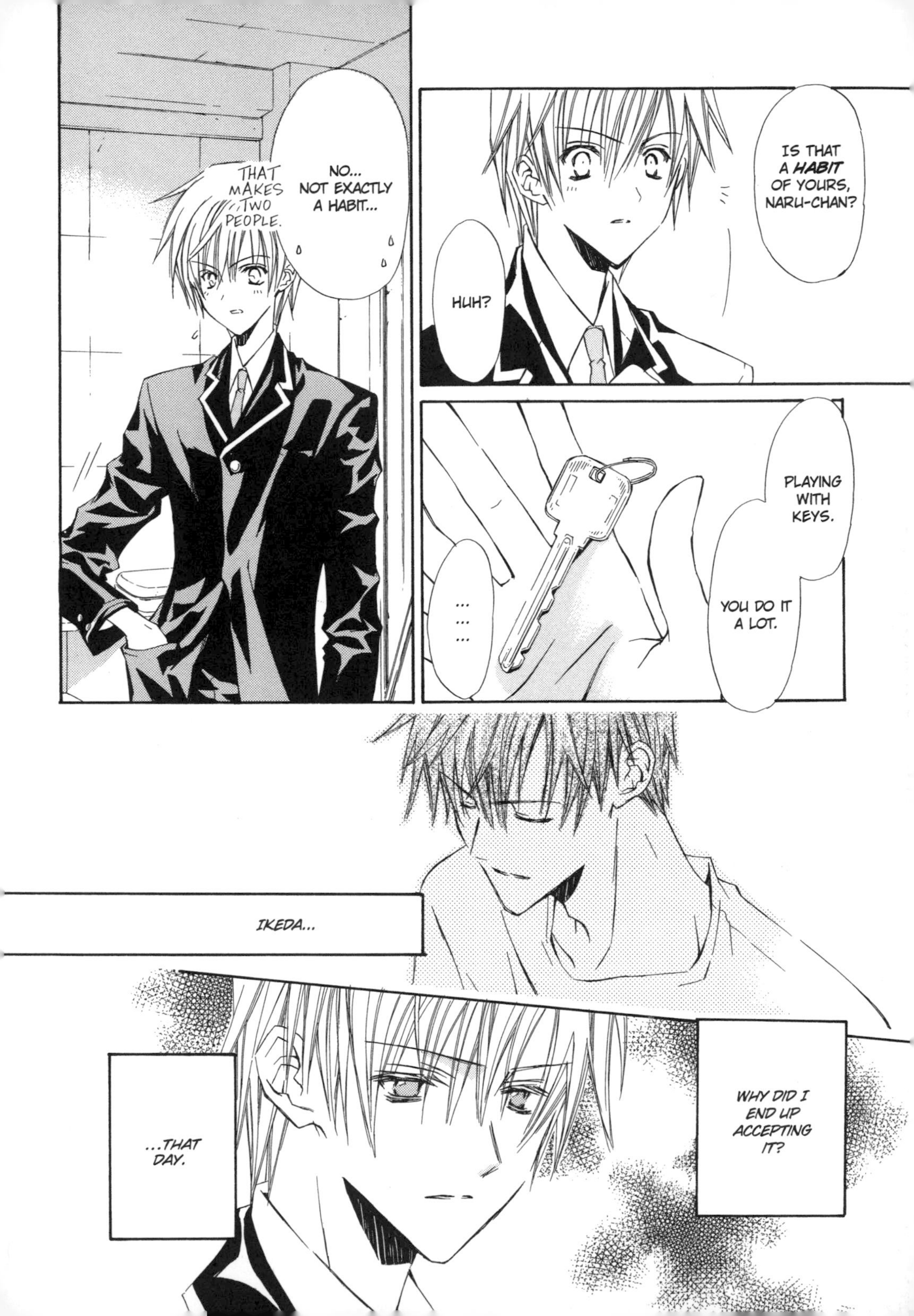
IS THAT A ***HABIT*** OF YOURS, NARU-CHAN?
HUH?
PLAYING WITH KEYS.
YOU DO IT A LOT.
... ...
NO... NOT EXACTLY A HABIT...
THAT MAKES TWO PEOPLE.
IKEDA...
WHY DID I END UP ACCEPTING IT?
...THAT DAY.

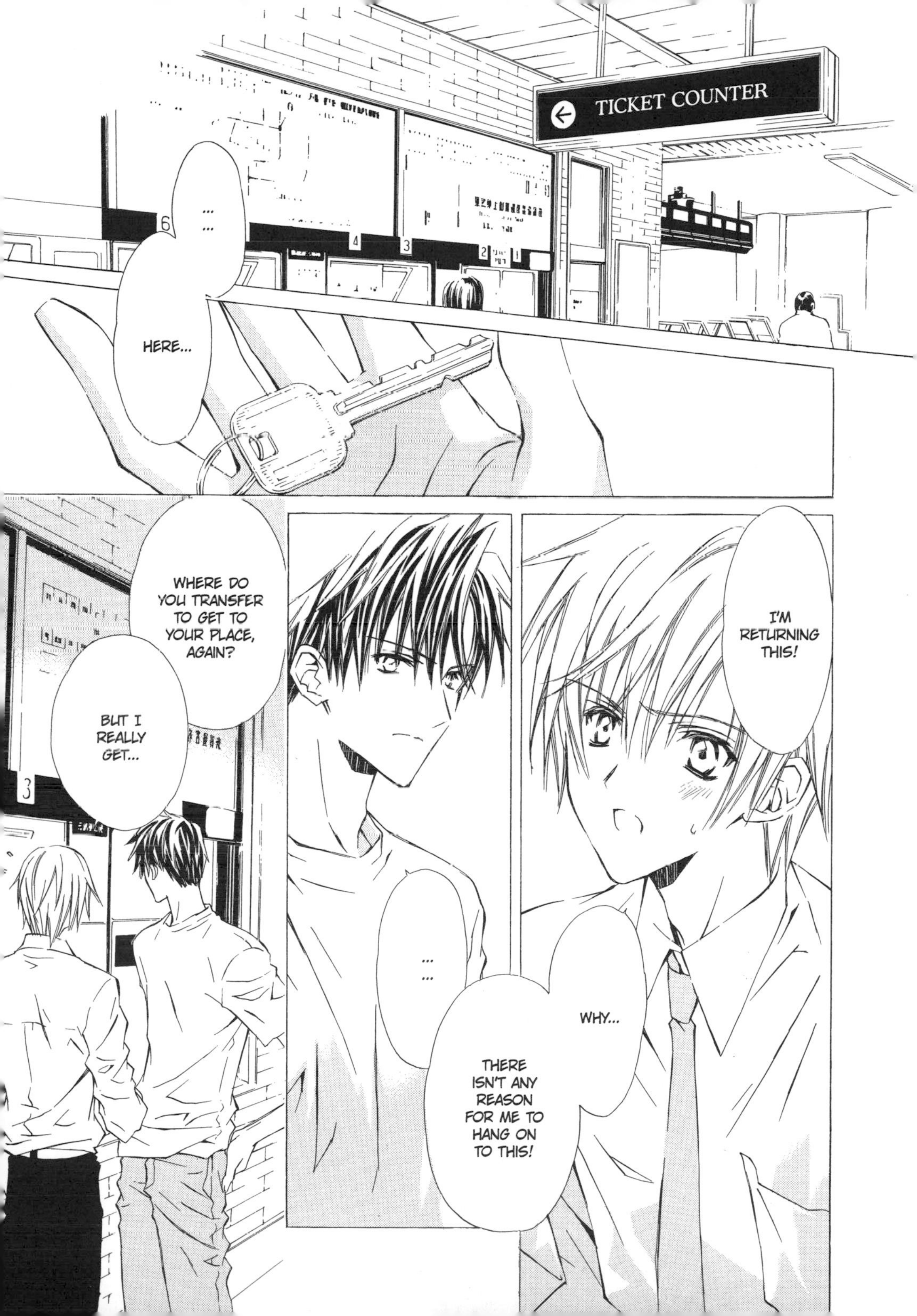
TICKET COUNTER
……
HERE...
I'M RETURNING THIS!
WHY...
THERE ISN'T ANY REASON FOR ME TO HANG ON TO THIS!
……
WHERE DO YOU TRANSFER TO GET TO YOUR PLACE, AGAIN?
BUT I REALLY GET...

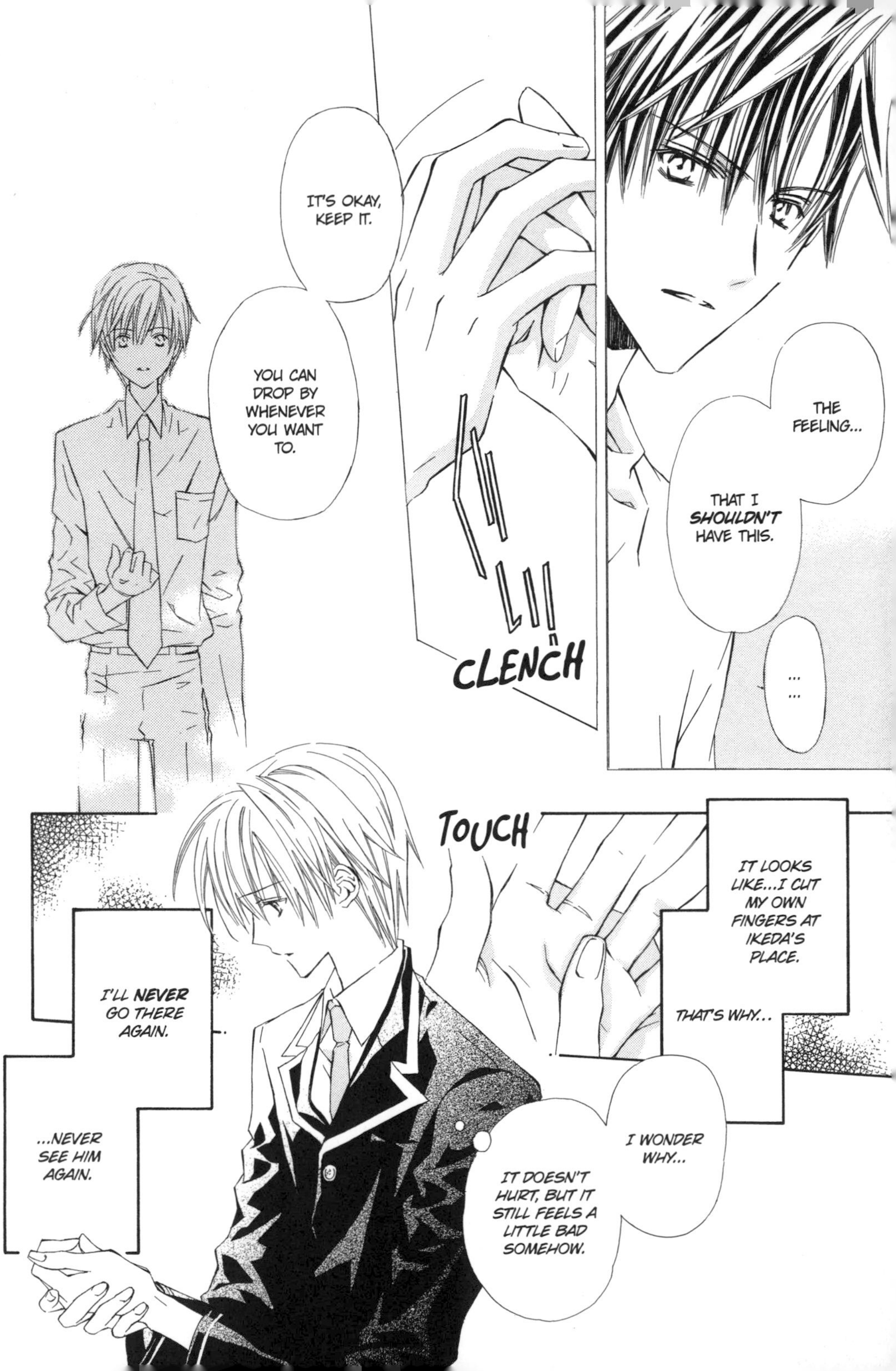

THE FEELING...
THAT I SHOULDN'T HAVE THIS.
... ...
CLENCH
IT'S OKAY, KEEP IT.
YOU CAN DROP BY WHENEVER YOU WANT TO.
TOUCH
IT LOOKS LIKE...I CUT MY OWN FINGERS AT IKEDA'S PLACE.
THAT'S WHY...
I WONDER WHY...
IT DOESN'T HURT, BUT IT STILL FEELS A LITTLE BAD SOMEHOW.
I'LL NEVER GO THERE AGAIN.
...NEVER SEE HIM AGAIN.

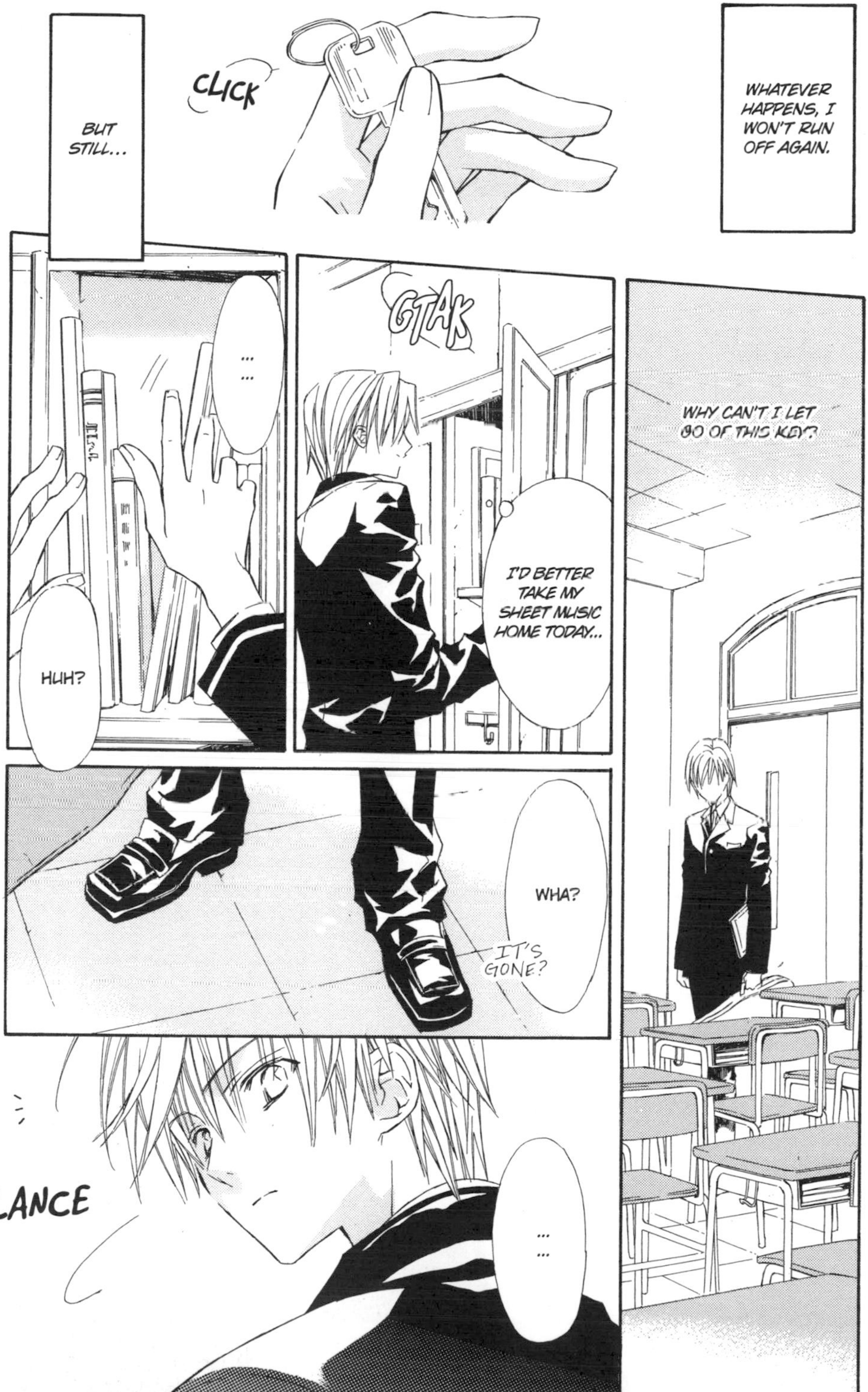
WHATEVER HAPPENS, I WON'T RUN OFF AGAIN.
CLICK
BUT STILL...
WHY CAN'T I LET GO OF THIS KEY?
GTAK
I'D BETTER TAKE MY SHEET MUSIC HOME TODAY...
... ...
HUH?
WHA?
IT'S GONE?
GLANCE
... ...

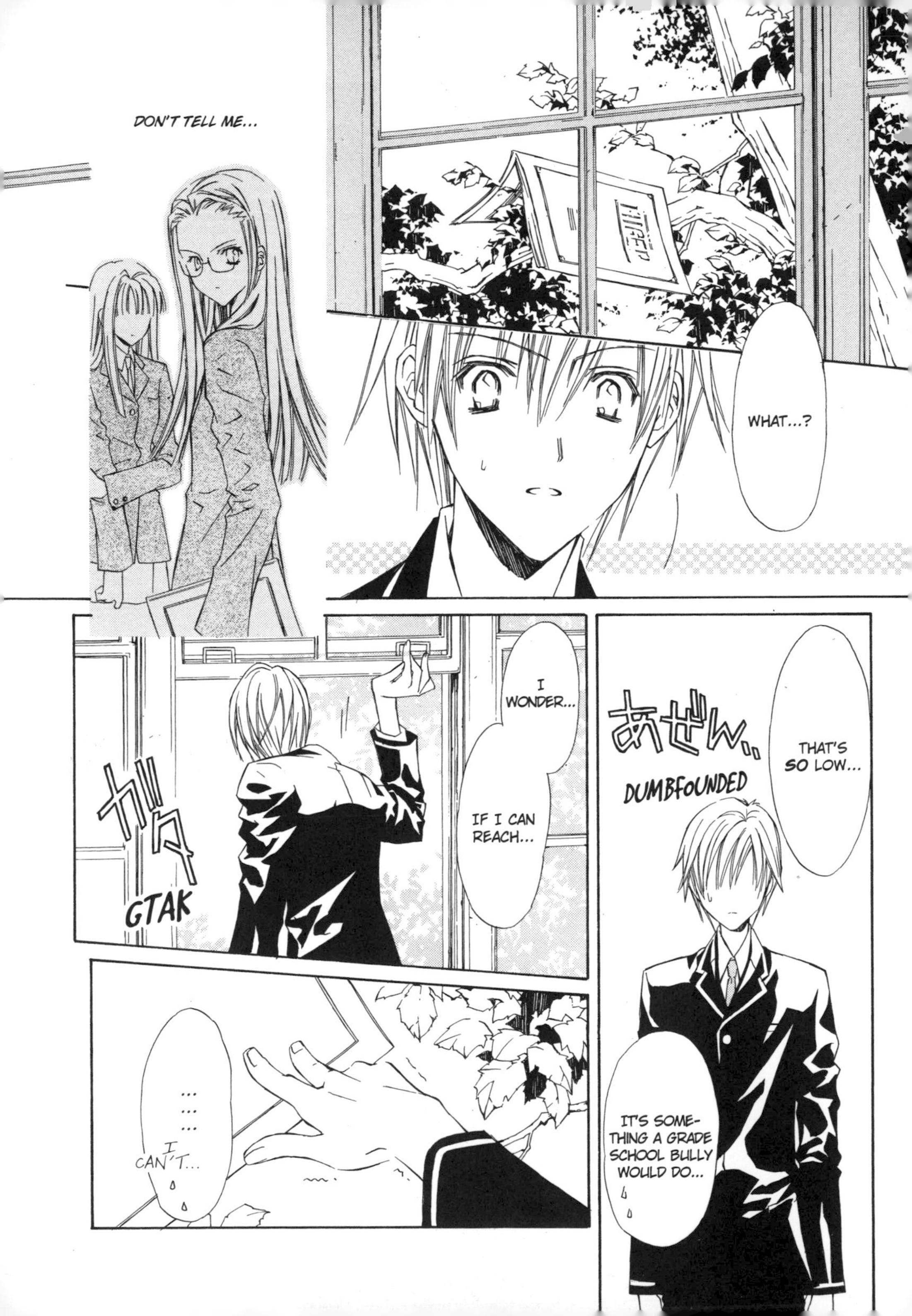
WHAT...?
DON'T TELL ME...
あぜん
DUMBFOUNDED
THAT'S SO LOW...
IT'S SOMETHING A GRADE SCHOOL BULLY WOULD DO...
ガタ
GTAK
I WONDER...
IF I CAN REACH...
...
...
...
I CAN'T...

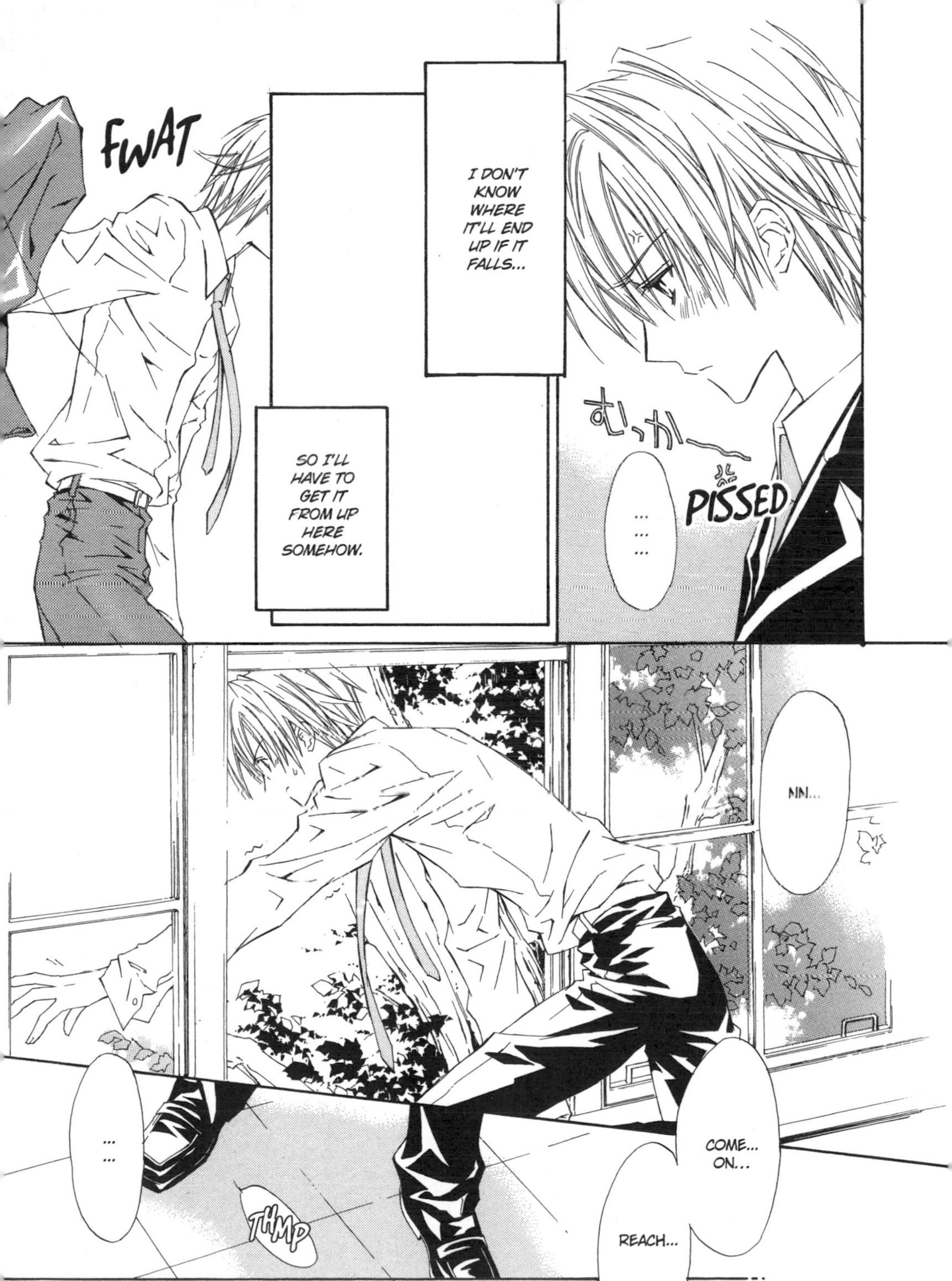
むっかー
PISSED
... ...
I DON'T KNOW WHERE IT'LL END UP IF IT FALLS...
SO I'LL HAVE TO GET IT FROM UP HERE SOMEHOW.
FWAT
NN...
COME... ON...
REACH...
THMP
... ...

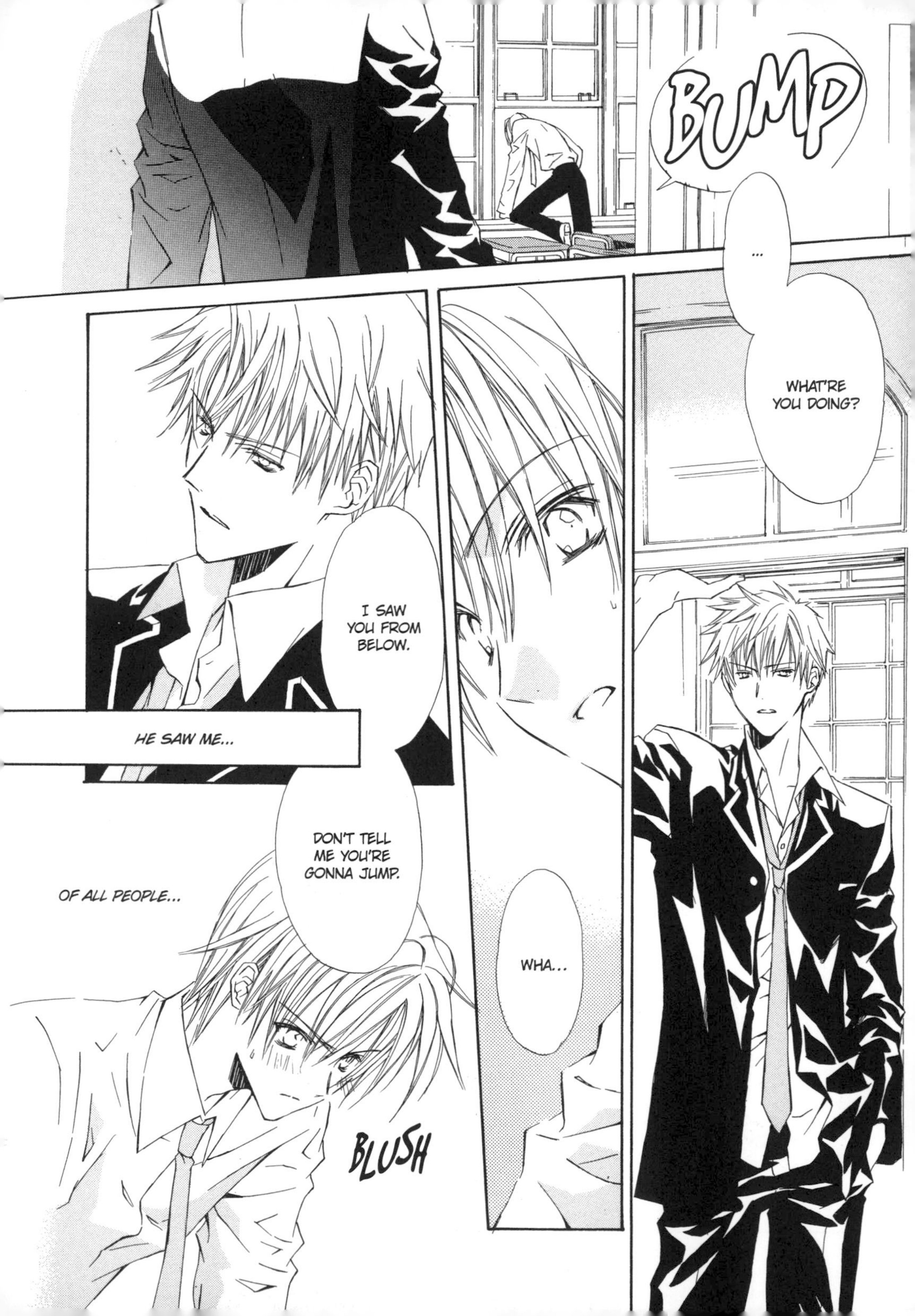
BUMP
...
WHAT'RE YOU DOING?
I SAW YOU FROM BELOW.
HE SAW ME...
DON'T TELL ME YOU'RE GONNA JUMP.
WHA...
OF ALL PEOPLE...
BLUSH

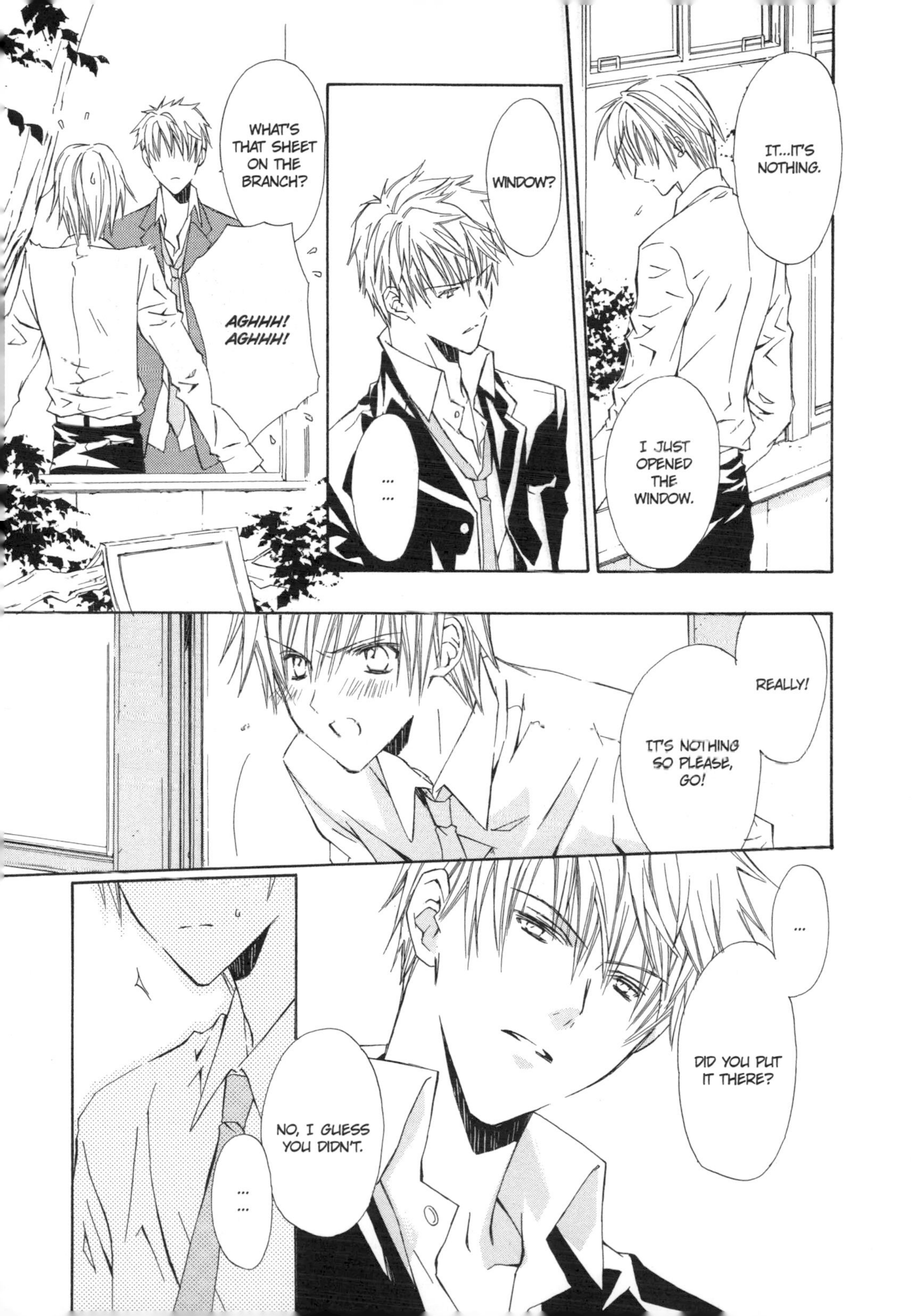
IT...IT'S NOTHING.
I JUST OPENED THE WINDOW.
WINDOW?
... ...
WHAT'S THAT SHEET ON THE BRANCH?
AGHHH! AGHHH!
REALLY!
IT'S NOTHING SO PLEASE, GO!
...
DID YOU PUT IT THERE?
NO, I GUESS YOU DIDN'T.
... ...

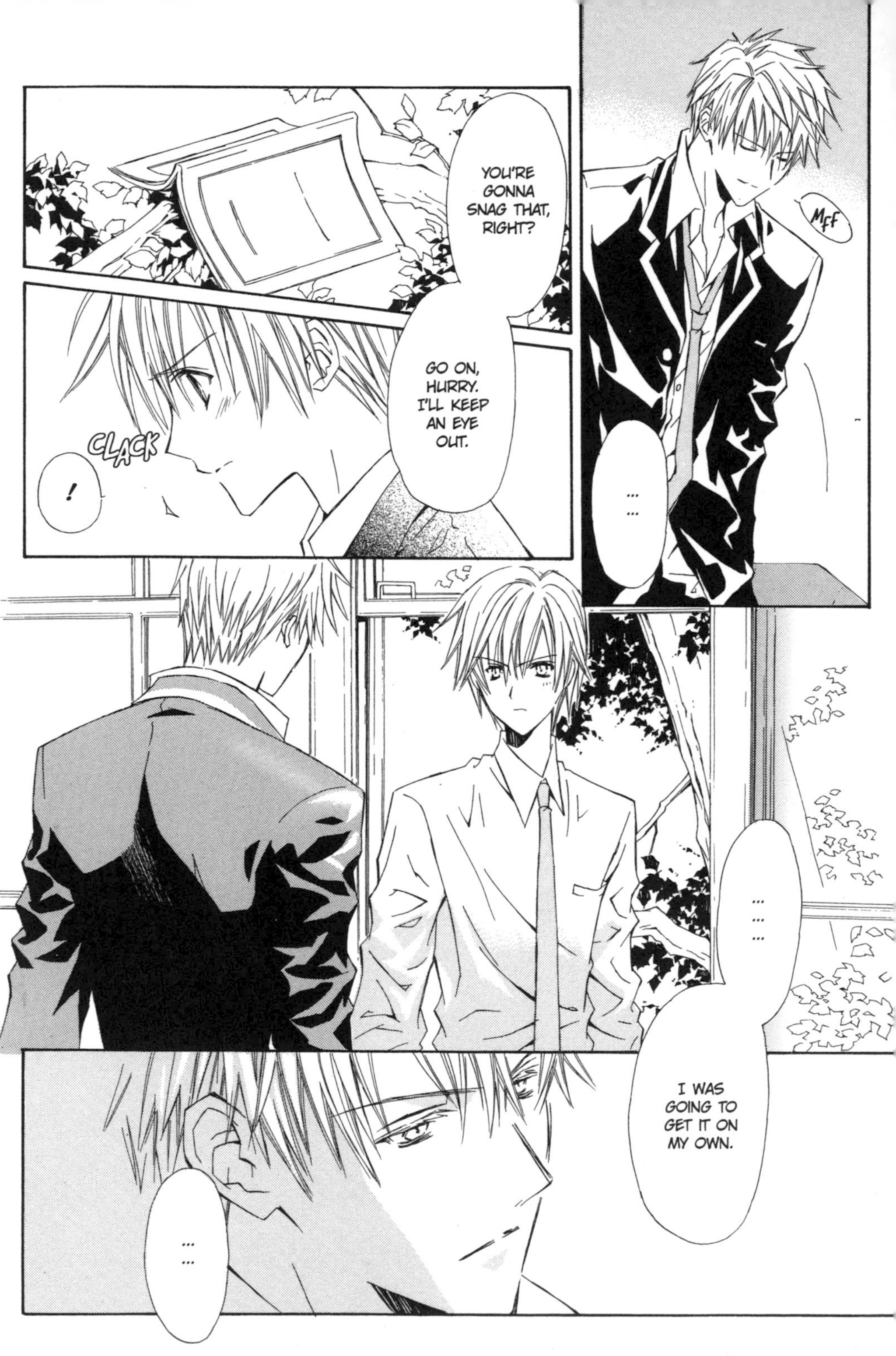
MFF
... ...
YOU'RE GONNA SNAG THAT, RIGHT?
GO ON, HURRY. I'LL KEEP AN EYE OUT.
CLACK
!
... ...
I WAS GOING TO GET IT ON MY OWN.
... ...

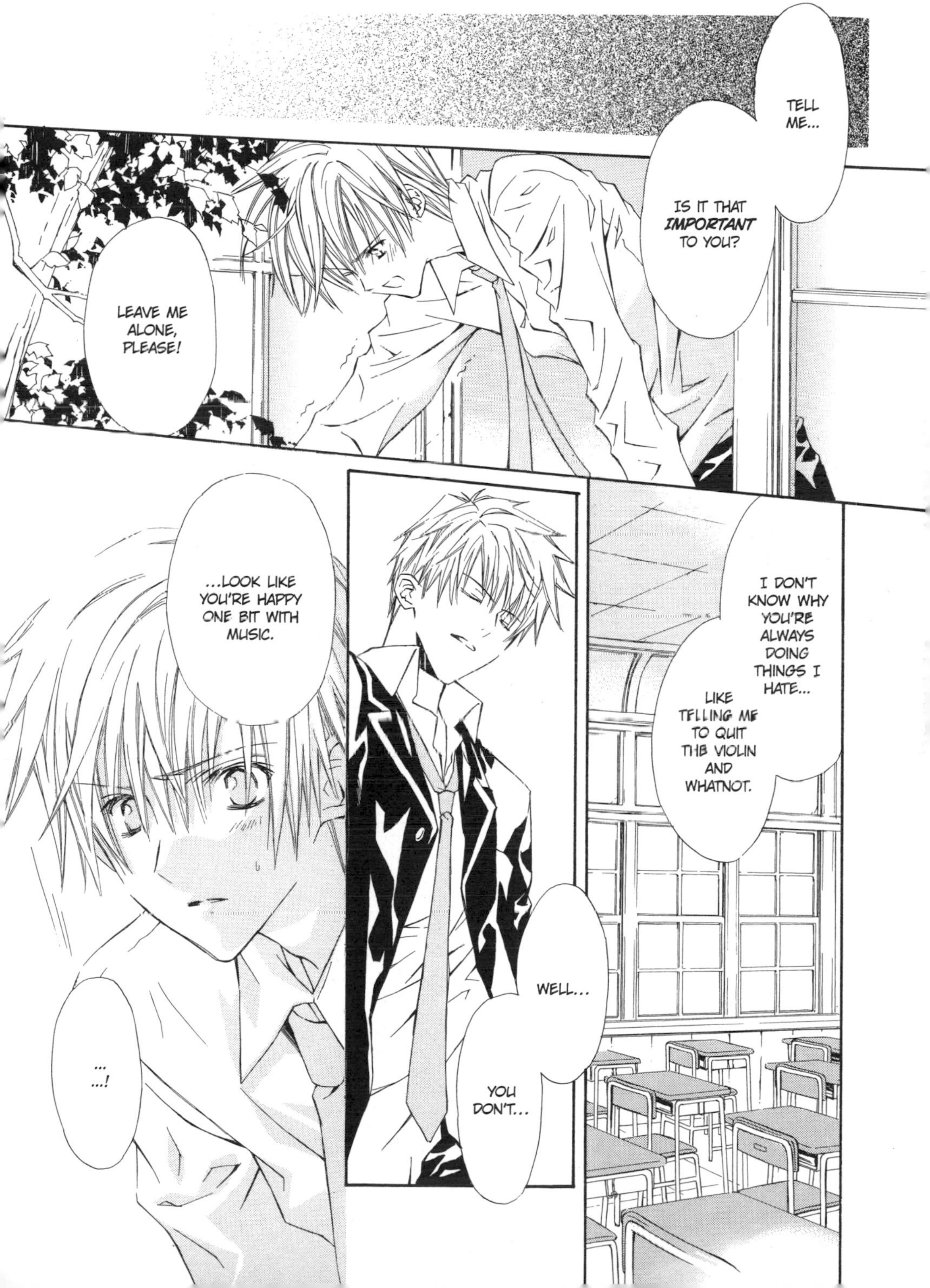
TELL ME...
IS IT THAT **IMPORTANT** TO YOU?
LEAVE ME ALONE, PLEASE!
I DON'T KNOW WHY YOU'RE ALWAYS DOING THINGS I HATE...
LIKE TELLING ME TO QUIT THE VIOLIN AND WHATNOT.
WELL...
YOU DON'T...
...LOOK LIKE YOU'RE HAPPY ONE BIT WITH MUSIC.
...
...!

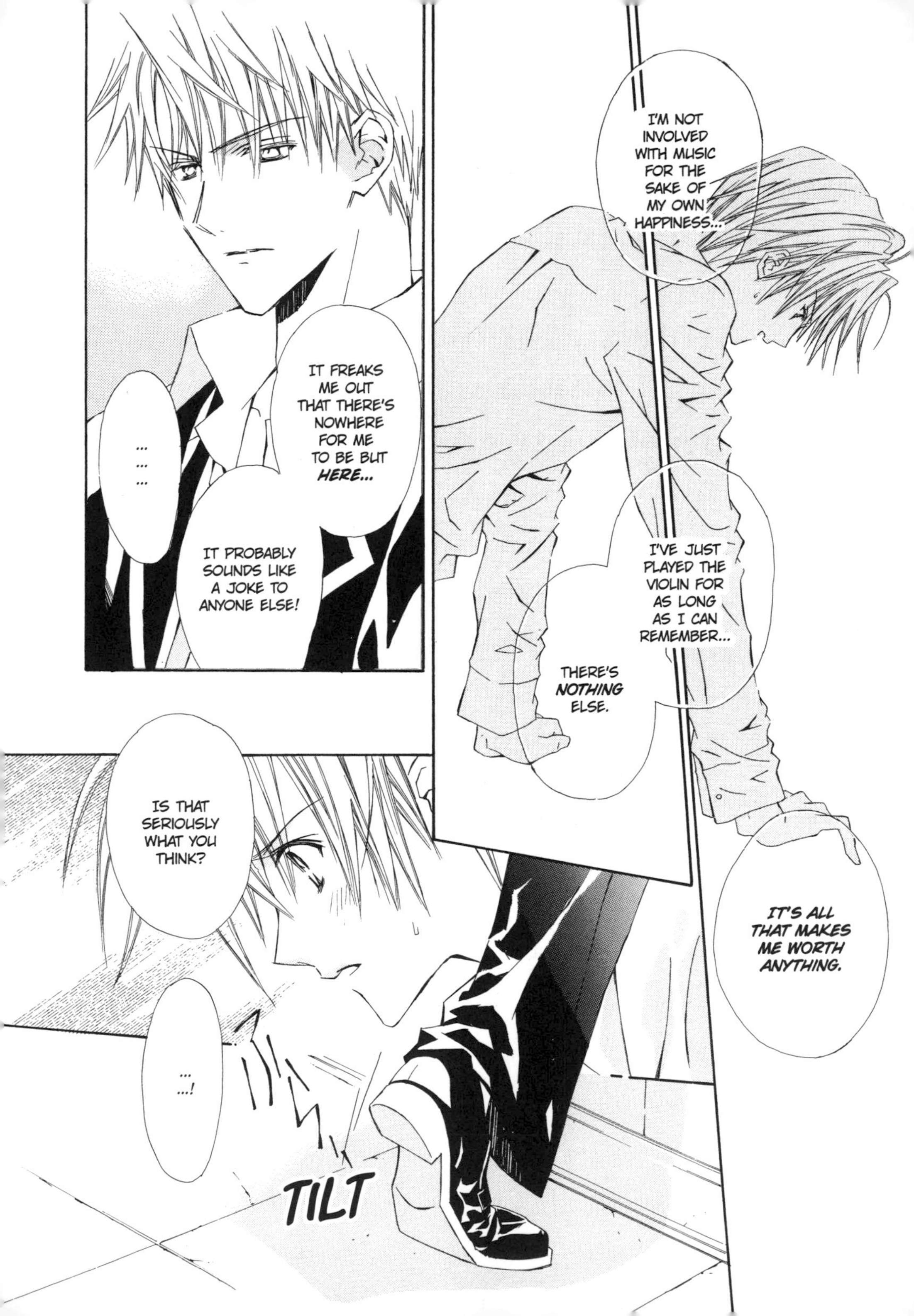
I'M NOT INVOLVED WITH MUSIC FOR THE SAKE OF MY OWN HAPPINESS...
I'VE JUST PLAYED THE VIOLIN FOR AS LONG AS I CAN REMEMBER...
THERE'S *NOTHING* ELSE.
IT'S ALL THAT MAKES ME WORTH ANYTHING.
IT FREAKS ME OUT THAT THERE'S NOWHERE FOR ME TO BE BUT *HERE*...
IT PROBABLY SOUNDS LIKE A JOKE TO ANYONE ELSE!
... ...
IS THAT SERIOUSLY WHAT YOU THINK?
... ...!
TILT

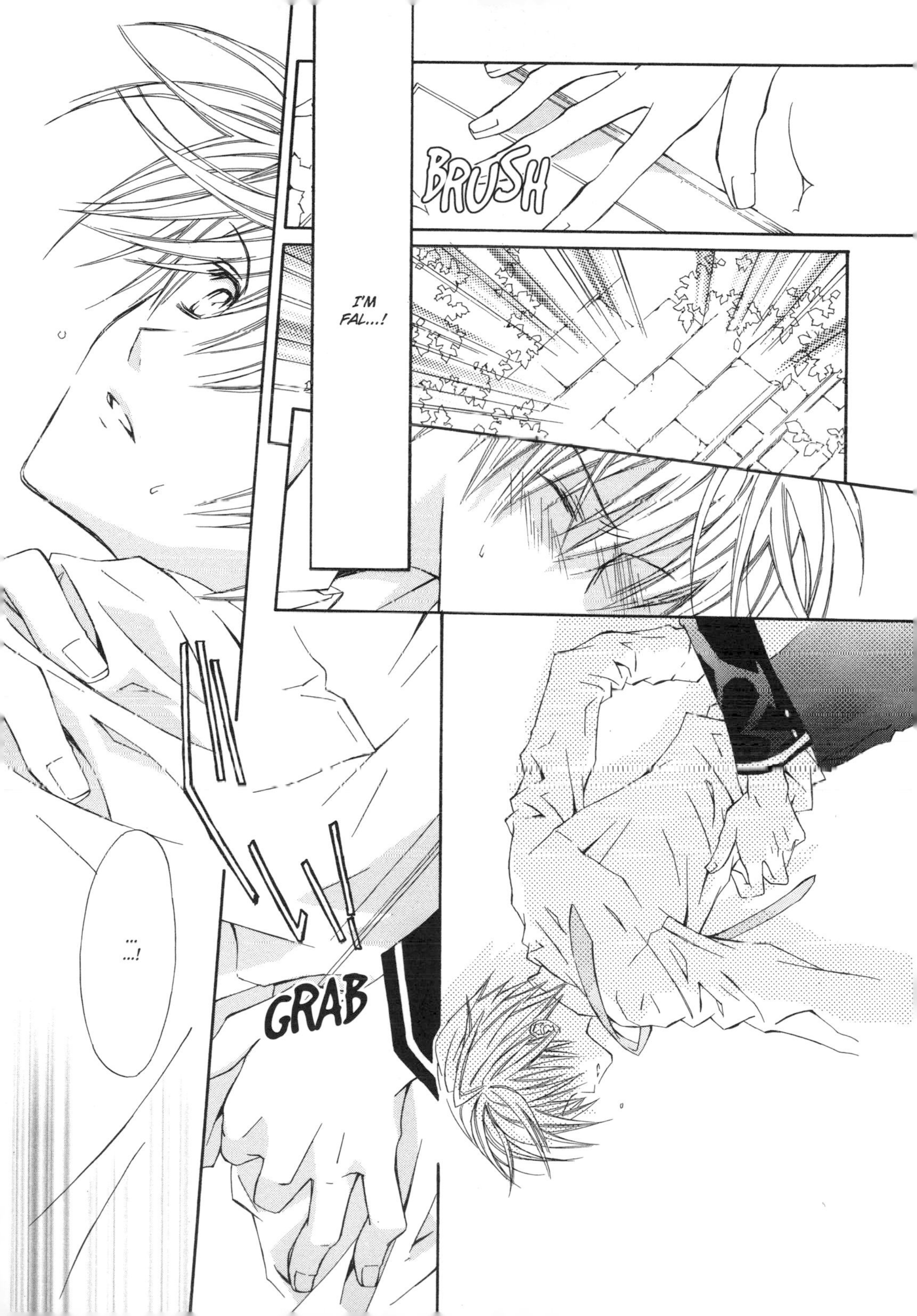
BRUSH
I'M FAL...!
GRAB
... ...!

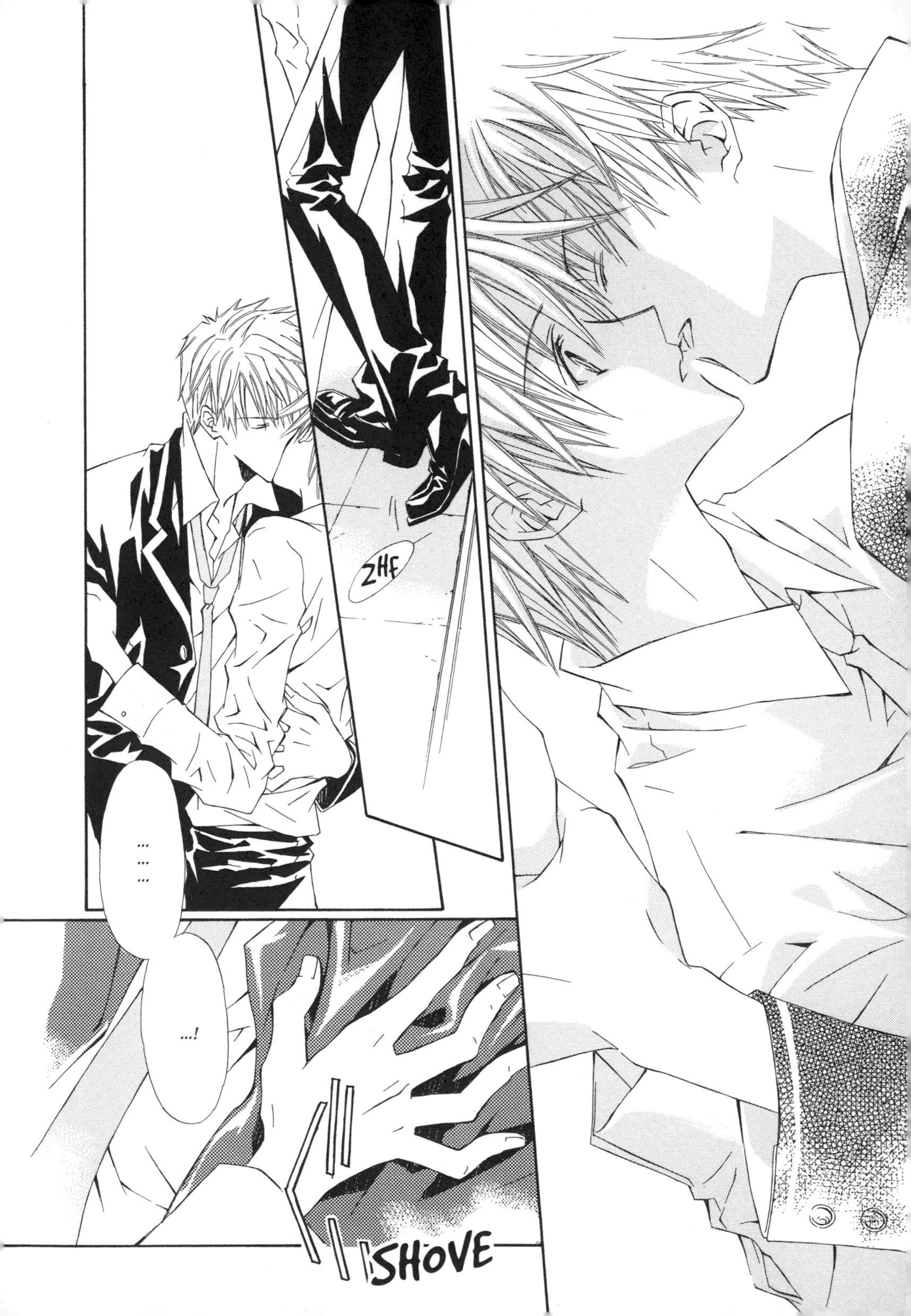
ZHF
...
...
...
...!
SHOVE

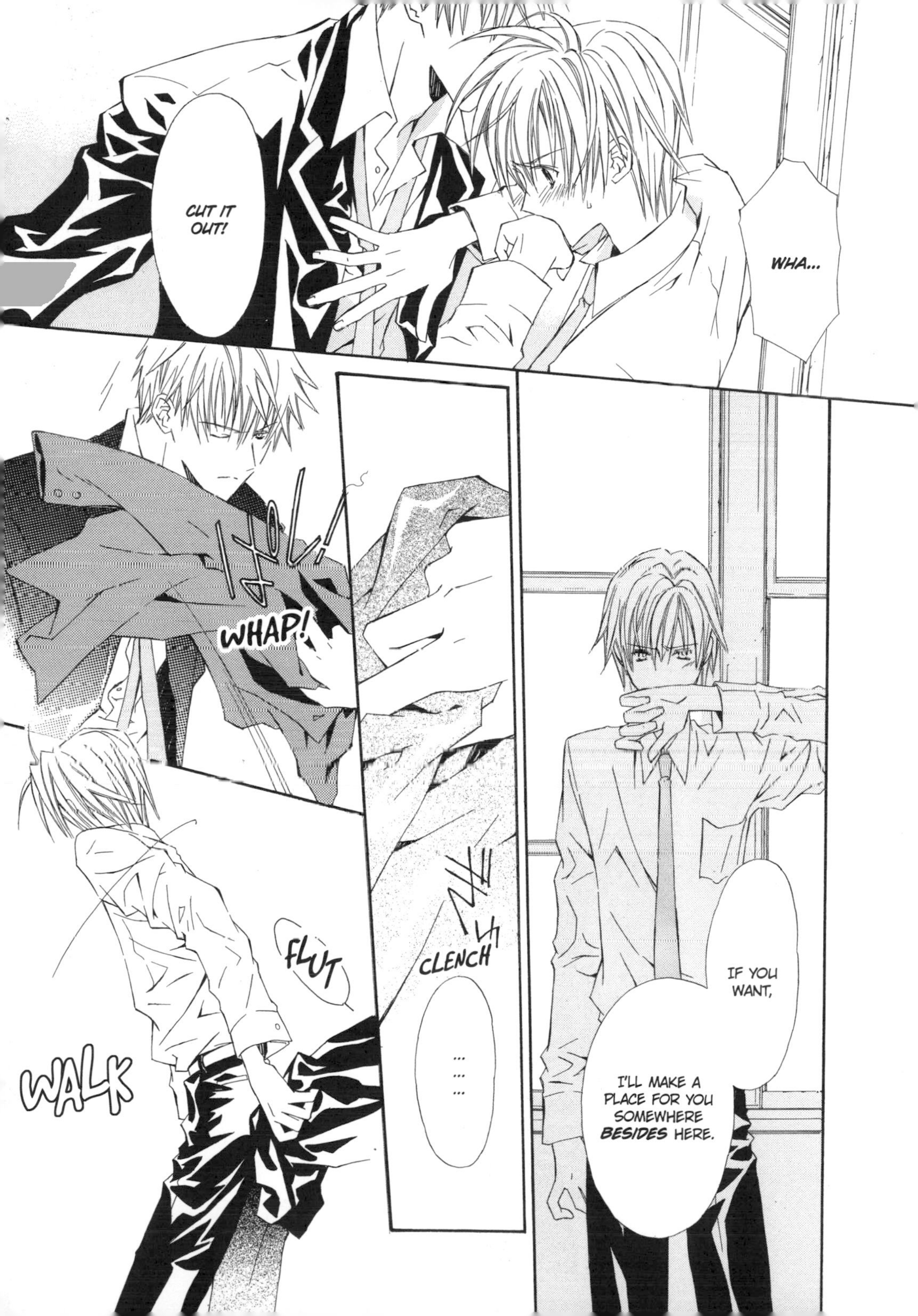
WHA...
CUT IT OUT!
IF YOU WANT,
I'LL MAKE A PLACE FOR YOU SOMEWHERE BESIDES HERE.
CLENCH
...
...
...
WHAP!
FLUT
WALK

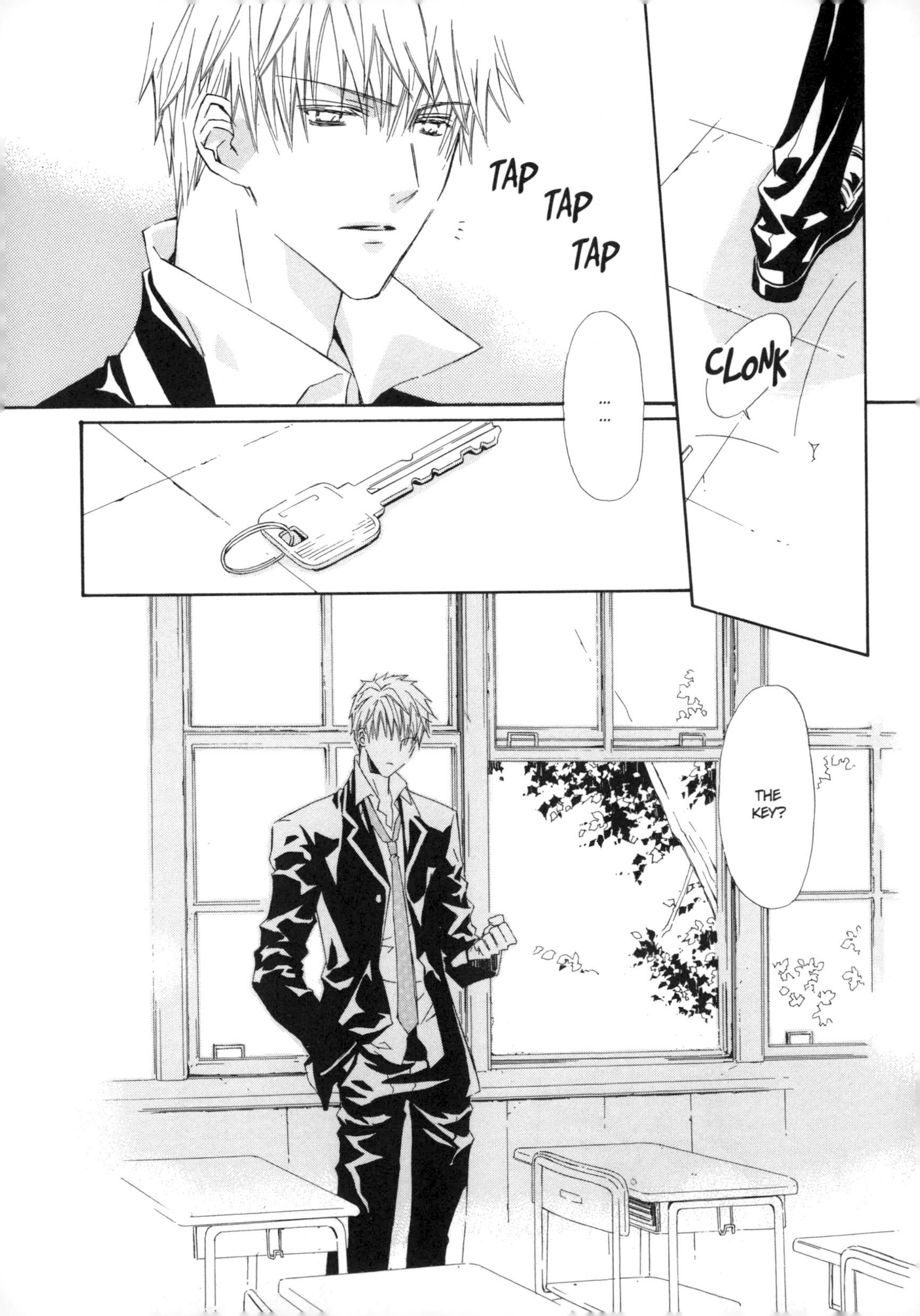
CLONK
TAP TAP TAP
……
THE KEY?

Episodio.2

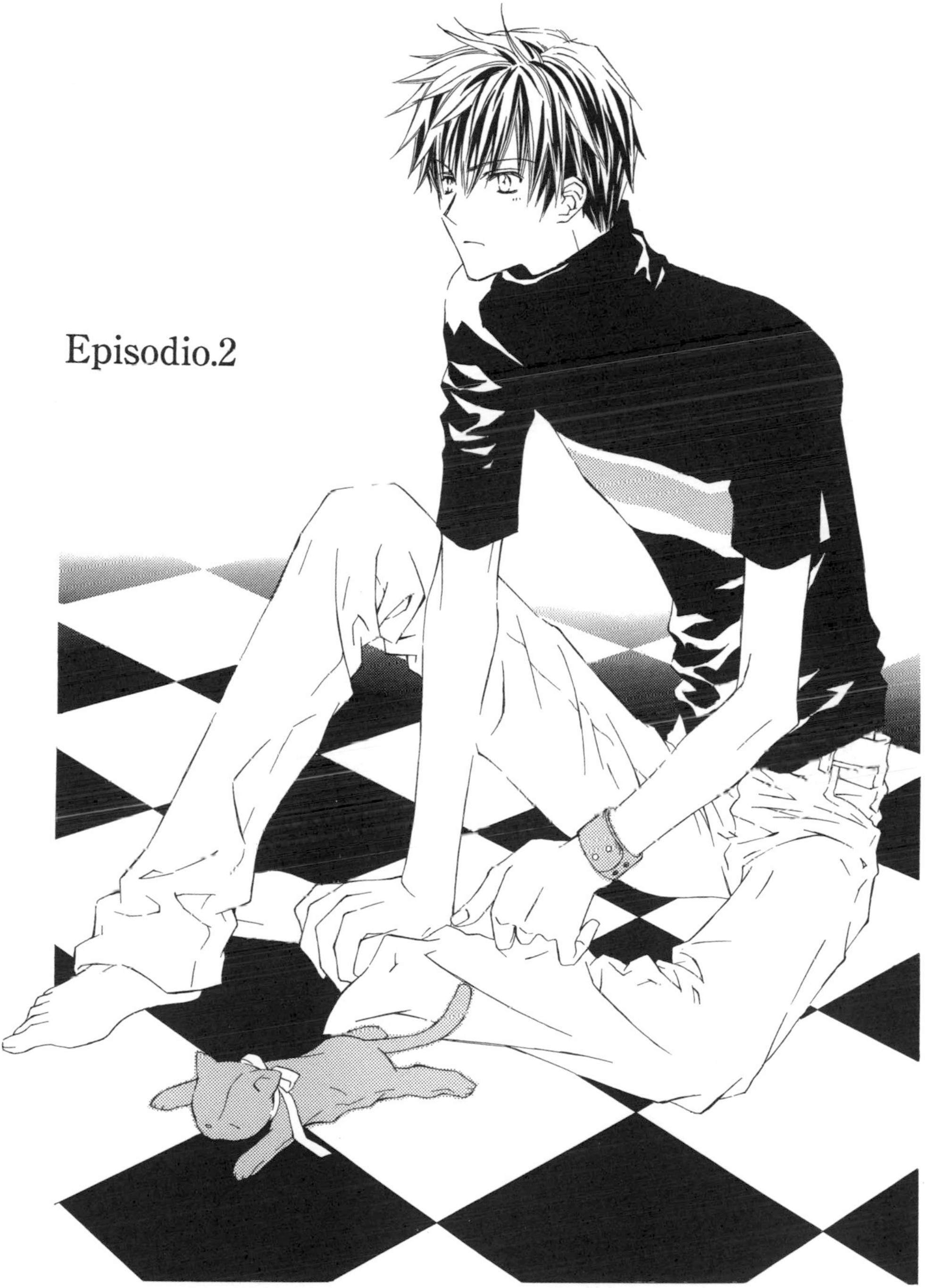

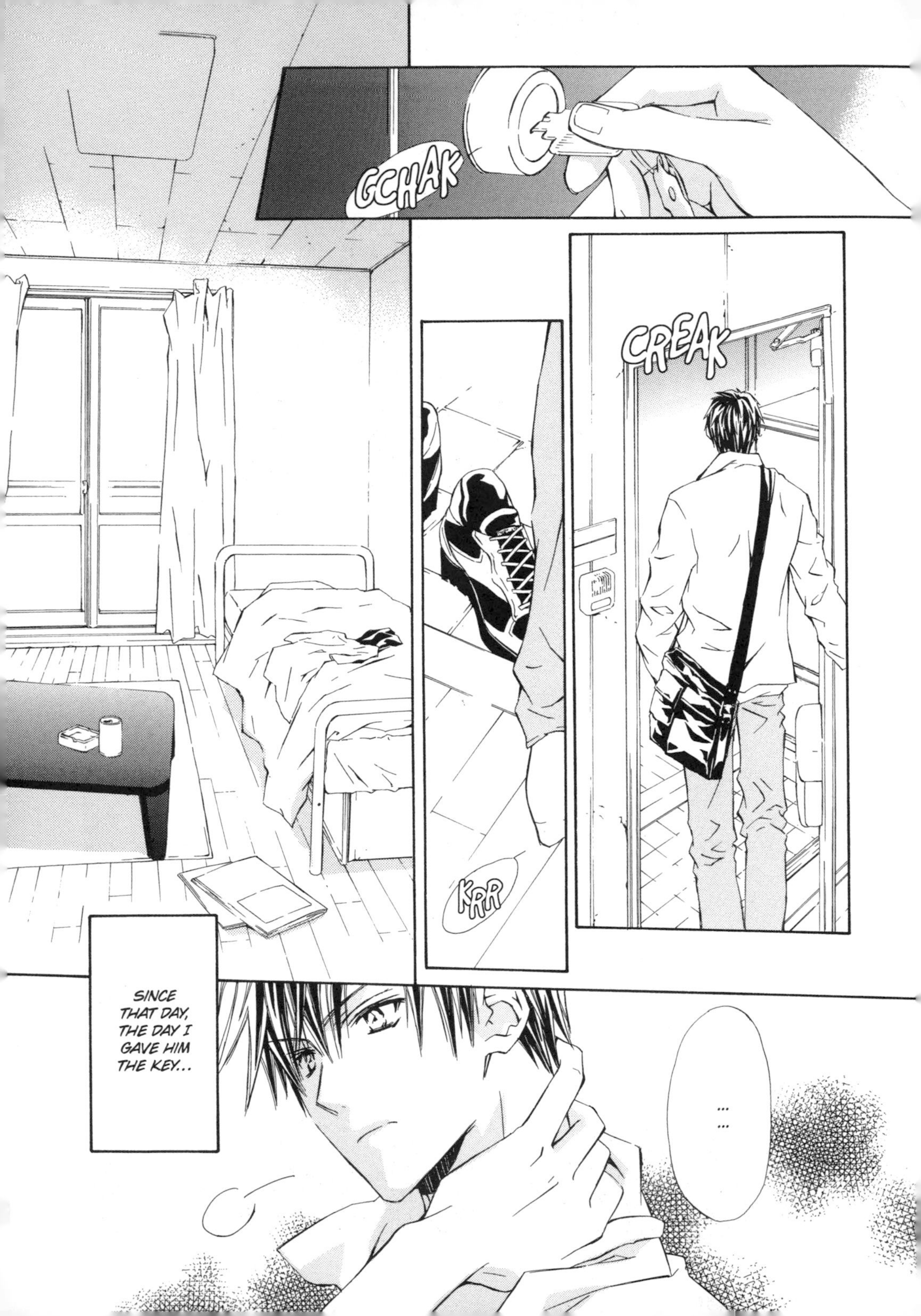
GCHAK
CREAK
KRR
SINCE THAT DAY, THE DAY I GAVE HIM THE KEY...
......

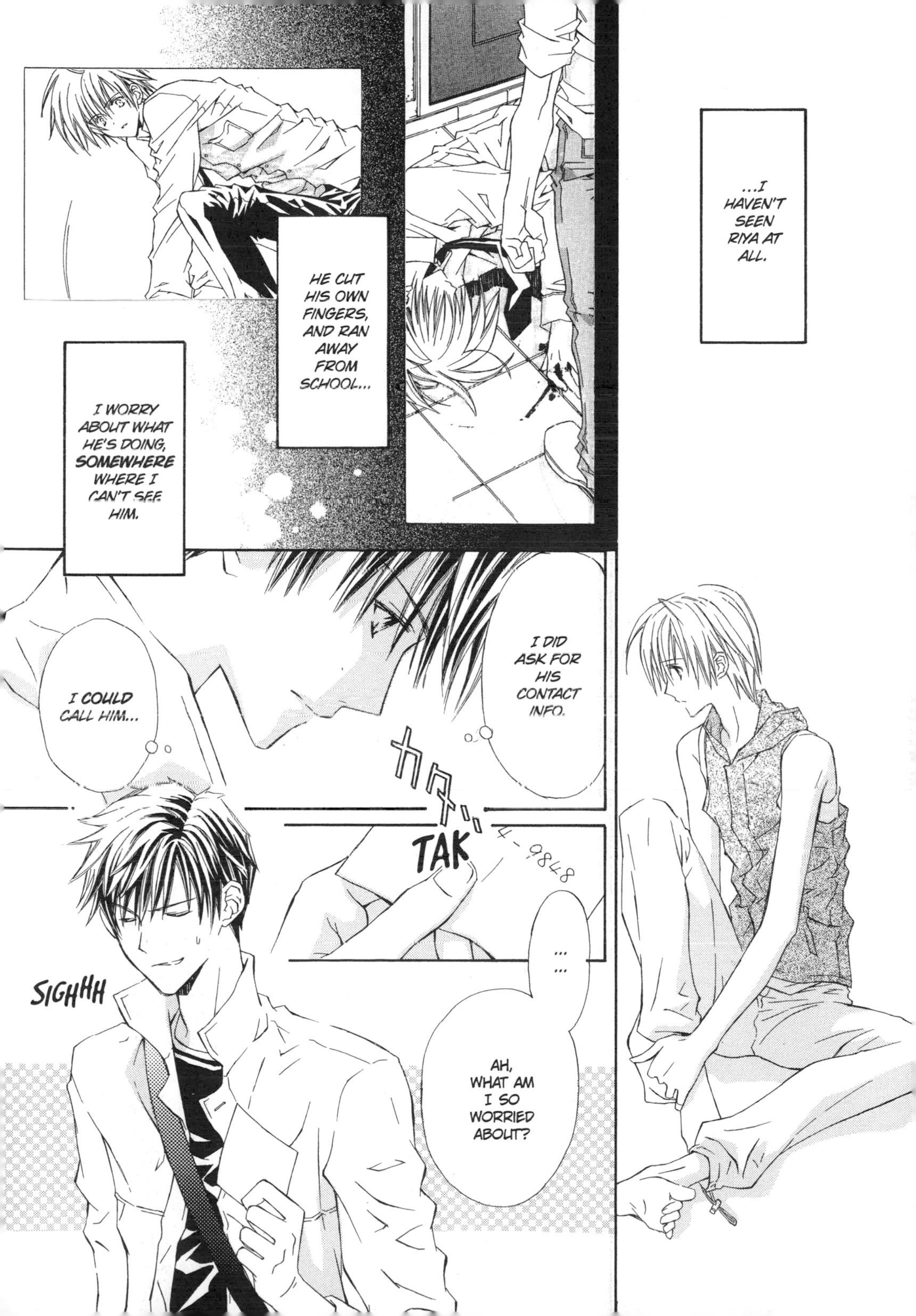
...I HAVEN'T SEEN RIYA AT ALL.
HE CUT HIS OWN FINGERS, AND RAN AWAY FROM SCHOOL...
I WORRY ABOUT WHAT HE'S DOING, SOMEWHERE WHERE I CAN'T SEE HIM.
I DID ASK FOR HIS CONTACT INFO.
I COULD CALL HIM...
TAK
......
SIGHHH
AH, WHAT AM I SO WORRIED ABOUT?

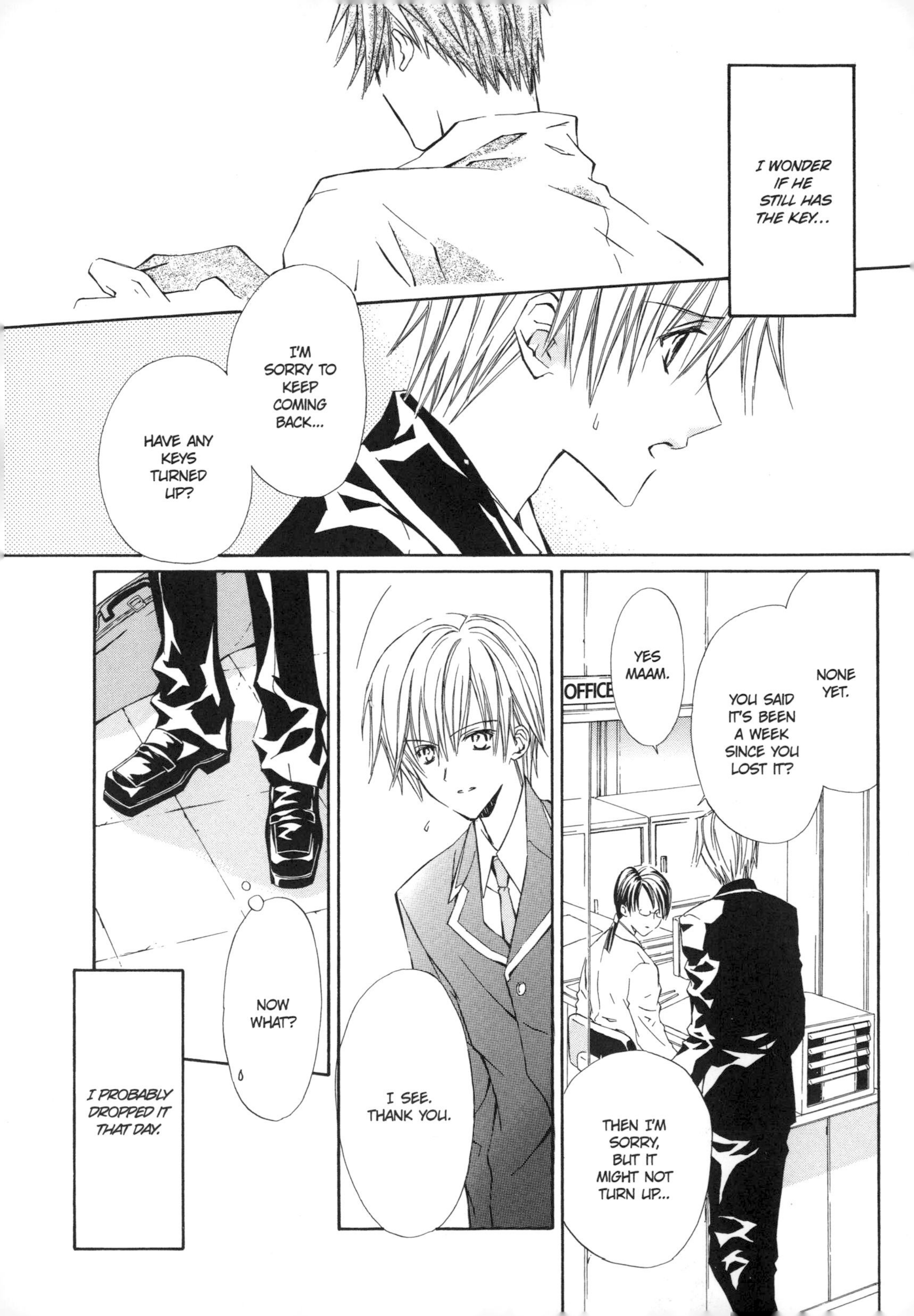
I WONDER IF HE STILL HAS THE KEY...
I'M SORRY TO KEEP COMING BACK...
HAVE ANY KEYS TURNED UP?
NONE YET.
YOU SAID IT'S BEEN A WEEK SINCE YOU LOST IT?
YES MAAM.
OFFICE
THEN I'M SORRY, BUT IT MIGHT NOT TURN UP...
I SEE. THANK YOU.
NOW WHAT?
I PROBABLY DROPPED IT THAT DAY.

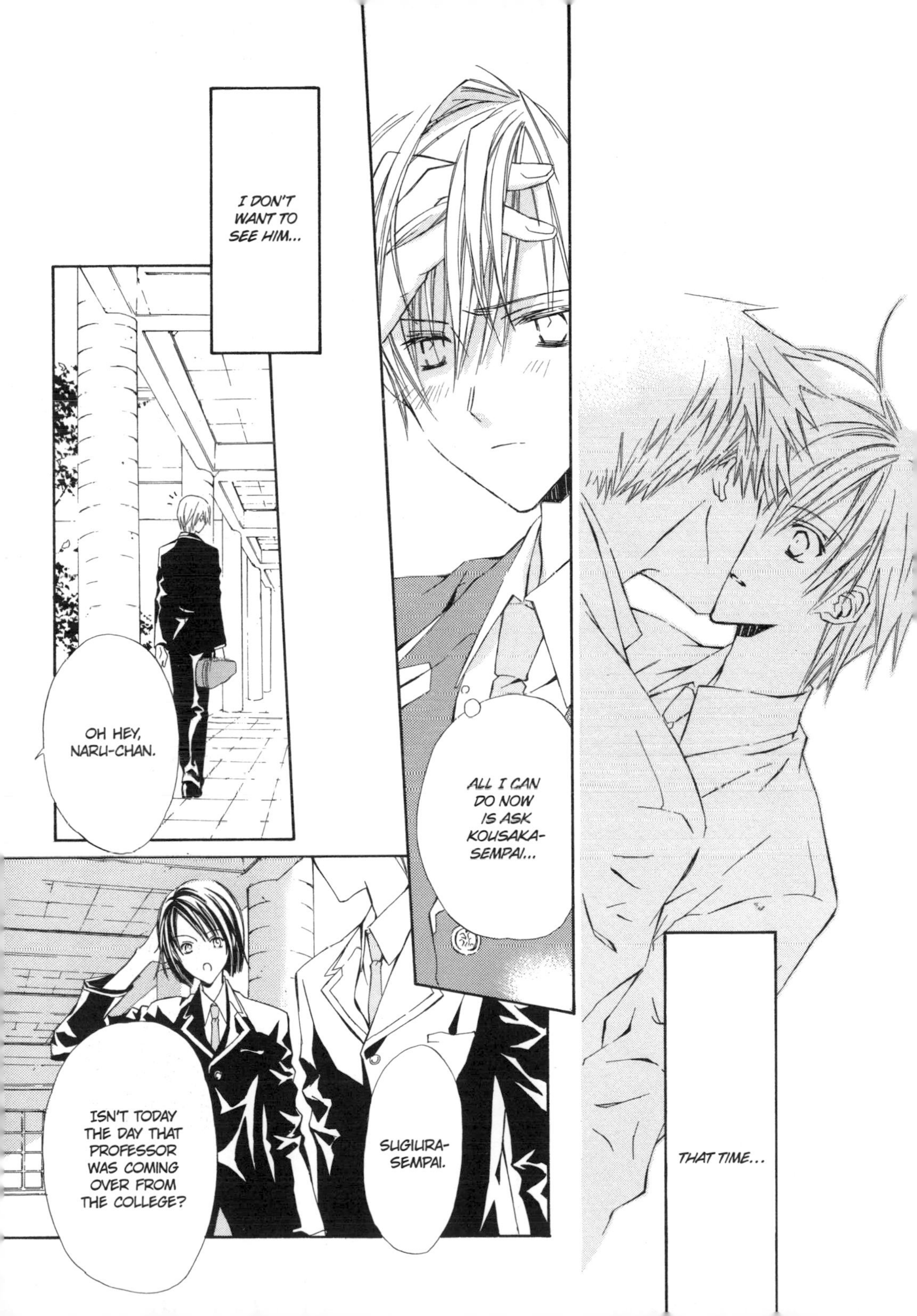
THAT TIME…
I DON'T WANT TO SEE HIM…
ALL I CAN DO NOW IS ASK KOUSAKA-SEMPAI…
OH HEY, NARU-CHAN.
SUGIURA-SEMPAI.
ISN'T TODAY THE DAY THAT PROFESSOR WAS COMING OVER FROM THE COLLEGE?

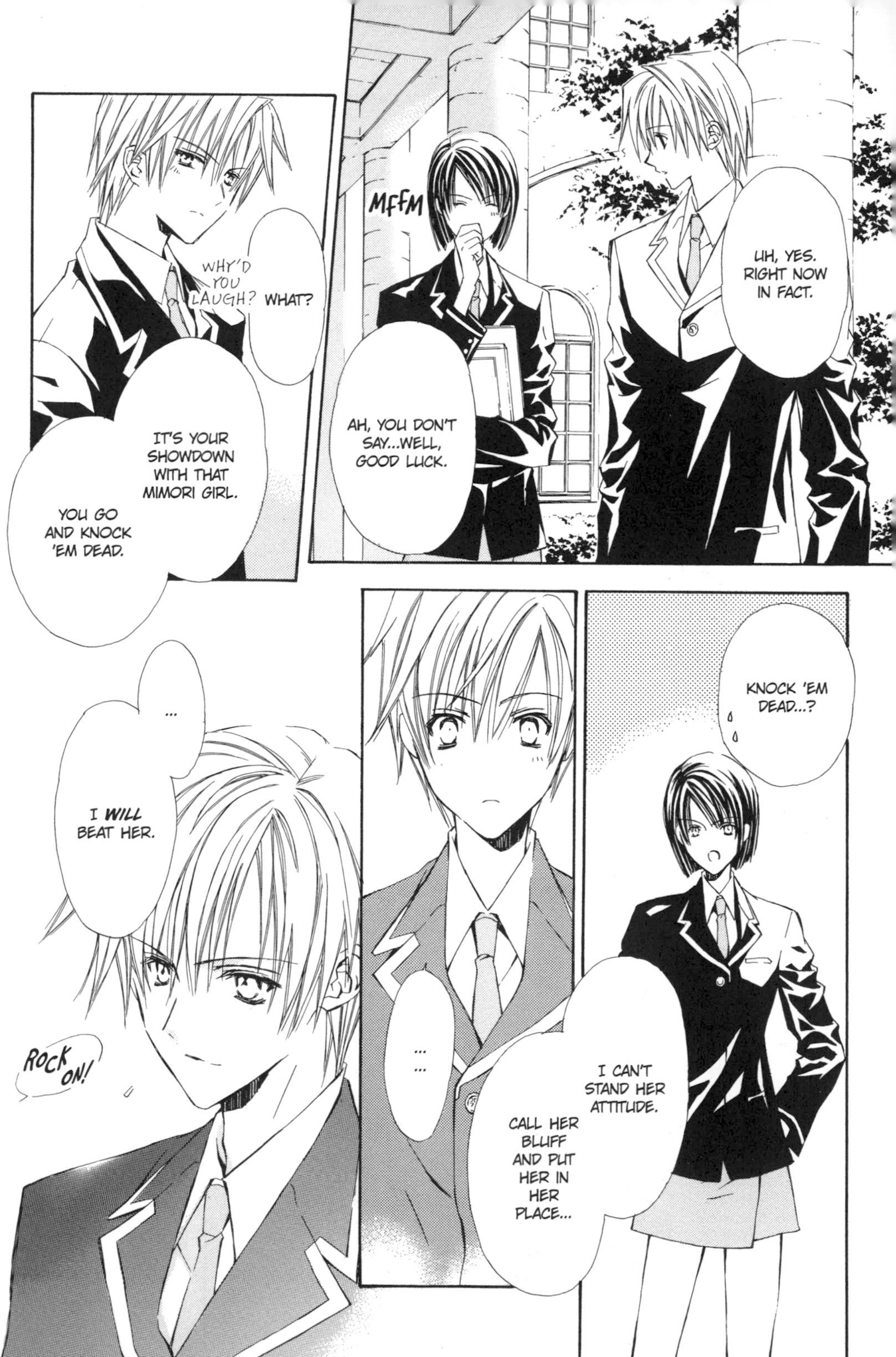
UH, YES. RIGHT NOW IN FACT.
MFFM
AH, YOU DON'T SAY...WELL, GOOD LUCK.
WHAT?
WHY'D YOU LAUGH?
IT'S YOUR SHOWDOWN WITH THAT MIMORI GIRL.
YOU GO AND KNOCK 'EM DEAD.
KNOCK 'EM DEAD...?
I CAN'T STAND HER ATTITUDE.
CALL HER BLUFF AND PUT HER IN HER PLACE...
... ...
...
I *WILL* BEAT HER.
ROCK ON!

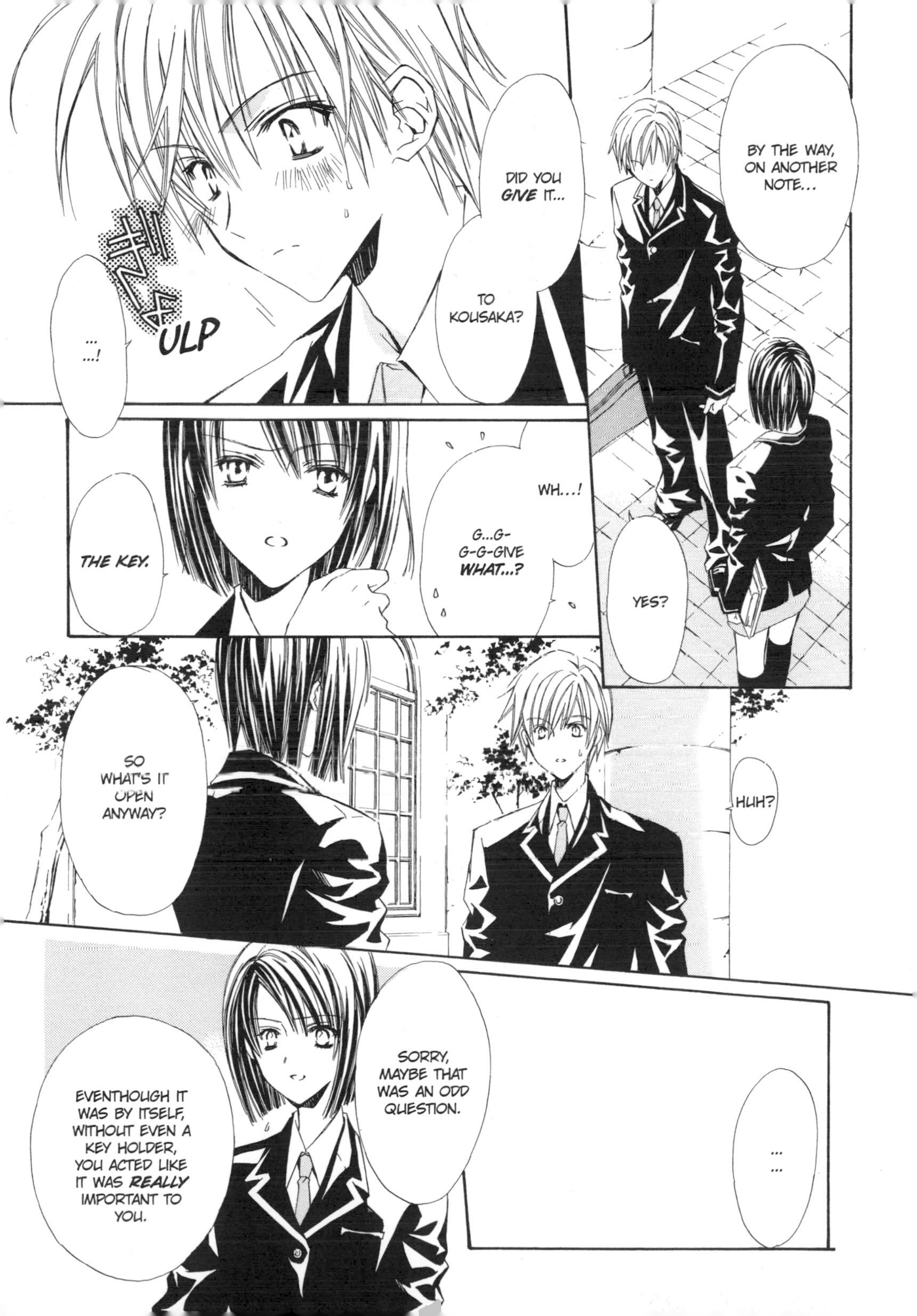

BY THE WAY, ON ANOTHER NOTE...
YES?
DID YOU GIVE IT...
TO KOUSAKA?
ULP
... ...!
WH...!
G...G-G-G-GIVE WHAT...?
THE KEY.
HUH?
SO WHAT'S IT OPEN ANYWAY?
... ...
SORRY, MAYBE THAT WAS AN ODD QUESTION.
EVENTHOUGH IT WAS BY ITSELF, WITHOUT EVEN A KEY HOLDER, YOU ACTED LIKE IT WAS REALLY IMPORTANT TO YOU.

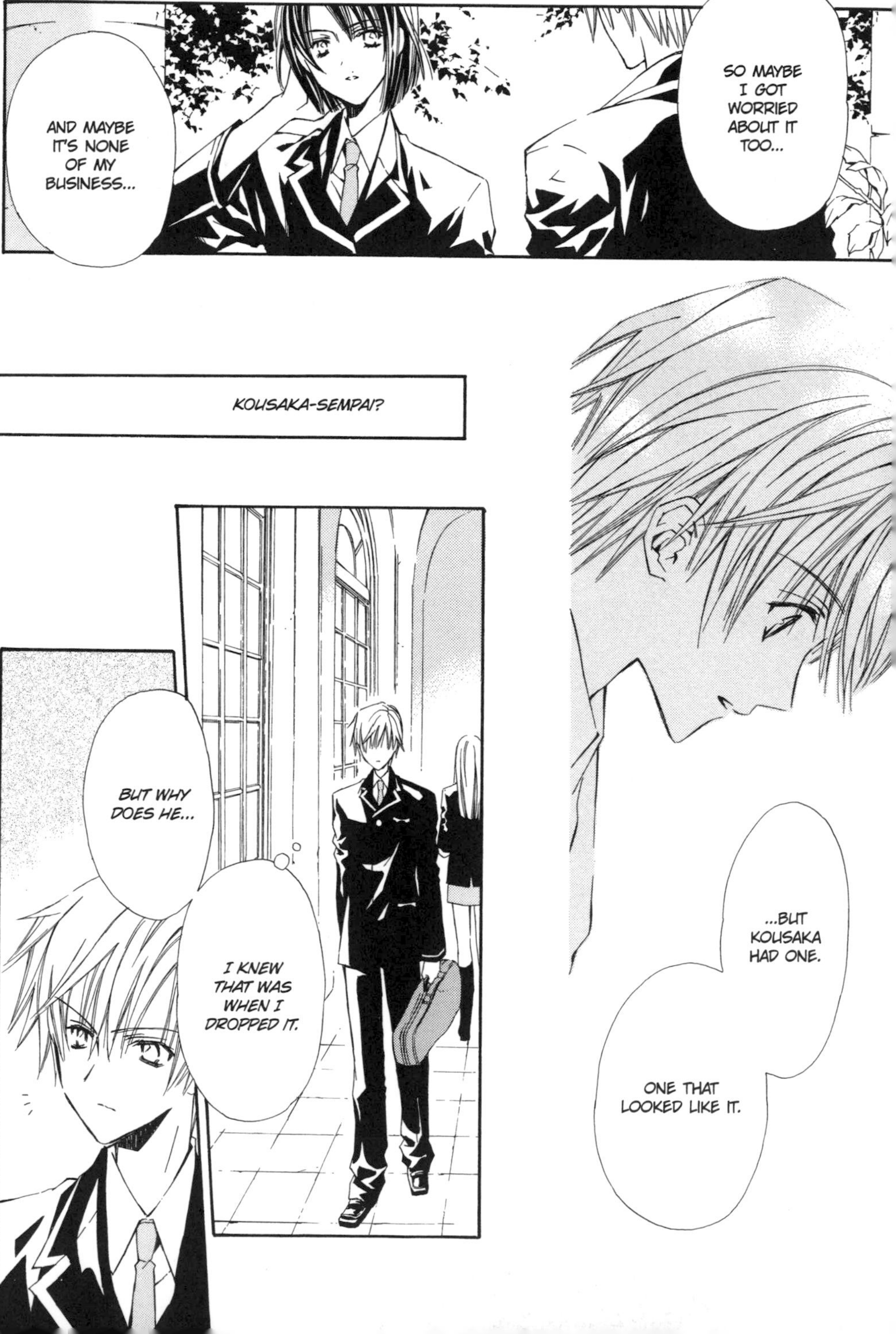
SO MAYBE I GOT WORRIED ABOUT IT TOO...
AND MAYBE IT'S NONE OF MY BUSINESS...
...BUT KOUSAKA HAD ONE.
ONE THAT LOOKED LIKE IT.
KOUSAKA-SEMPAI?
I KNEW THAT WAS WHEN I DROPPED IT.
BUT WHY DOES HE...

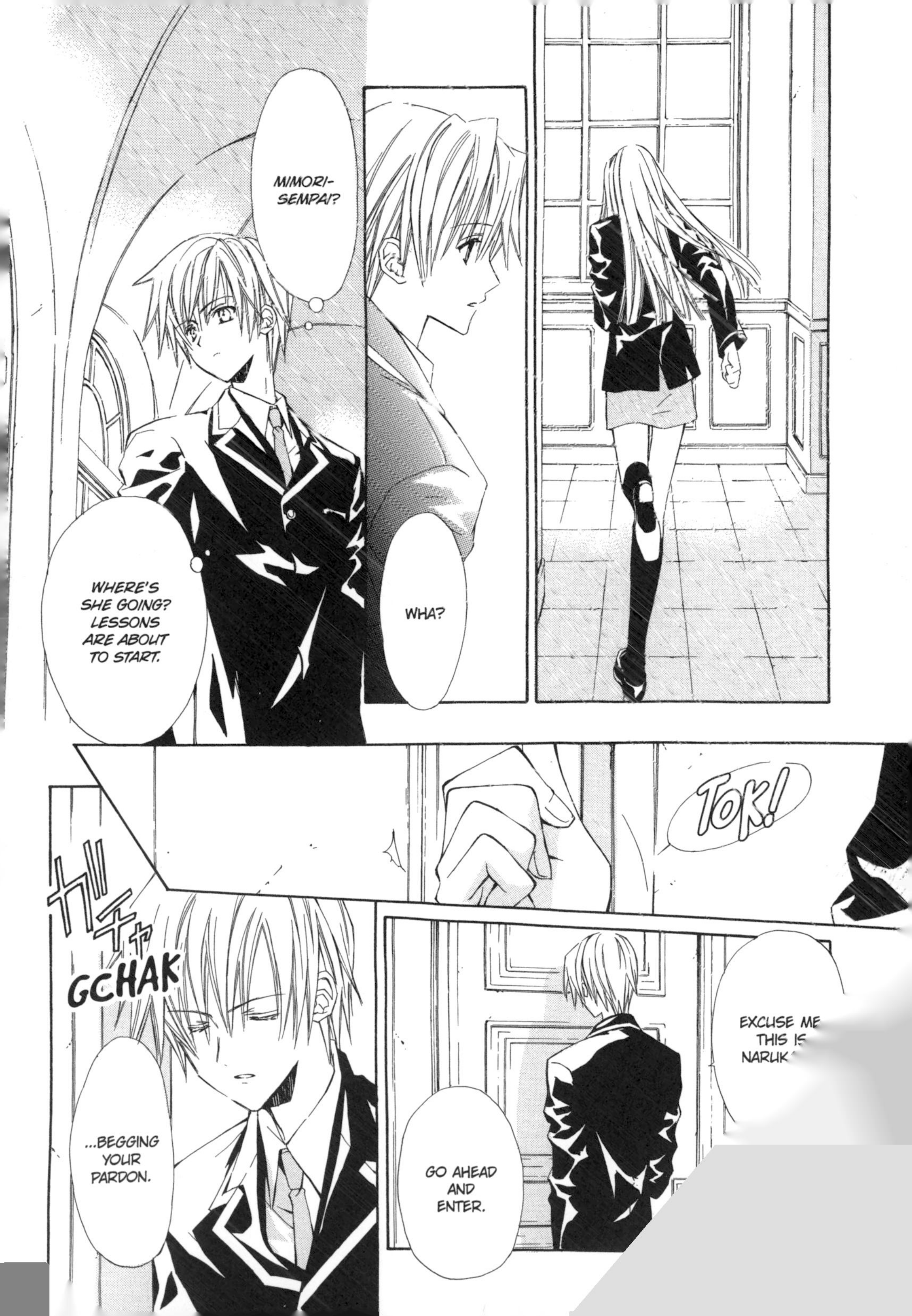
WHA?
MIMORI-SEMPAI?
WHERE'S SHE GOING? LESSONS ARE ABOUT TO START.
TOK!
EXCUSE ME THIS IS
GO AHEAD AND ENTER.
カチャ
GCHAK
...BEGGING YOUR PARDON.

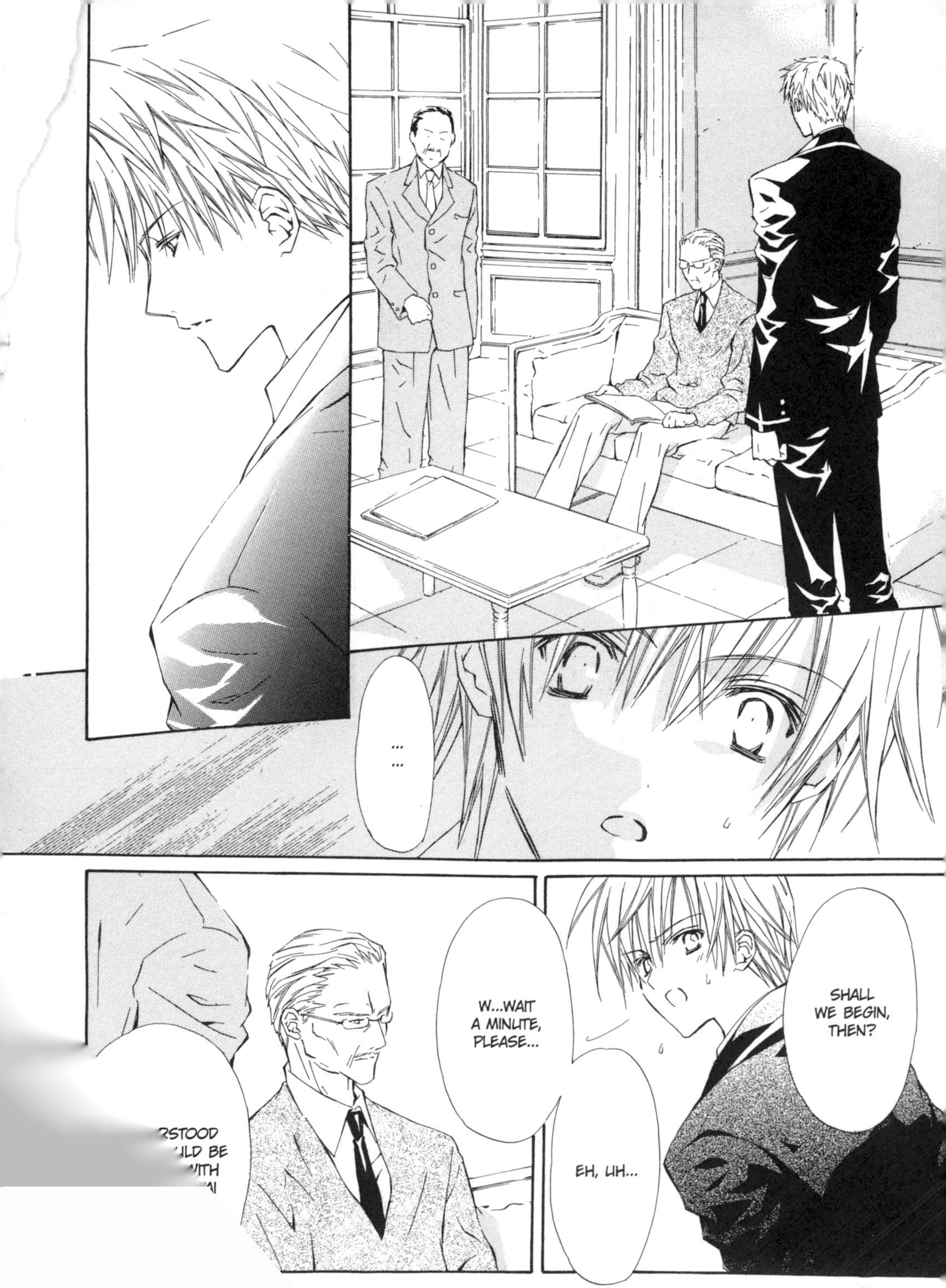
……
SHALL WE BEGIN, THEN?
EH, UH...
W...WAIT A MINUTE, PLEASE...
RSTOOD ULD BE WITH AI

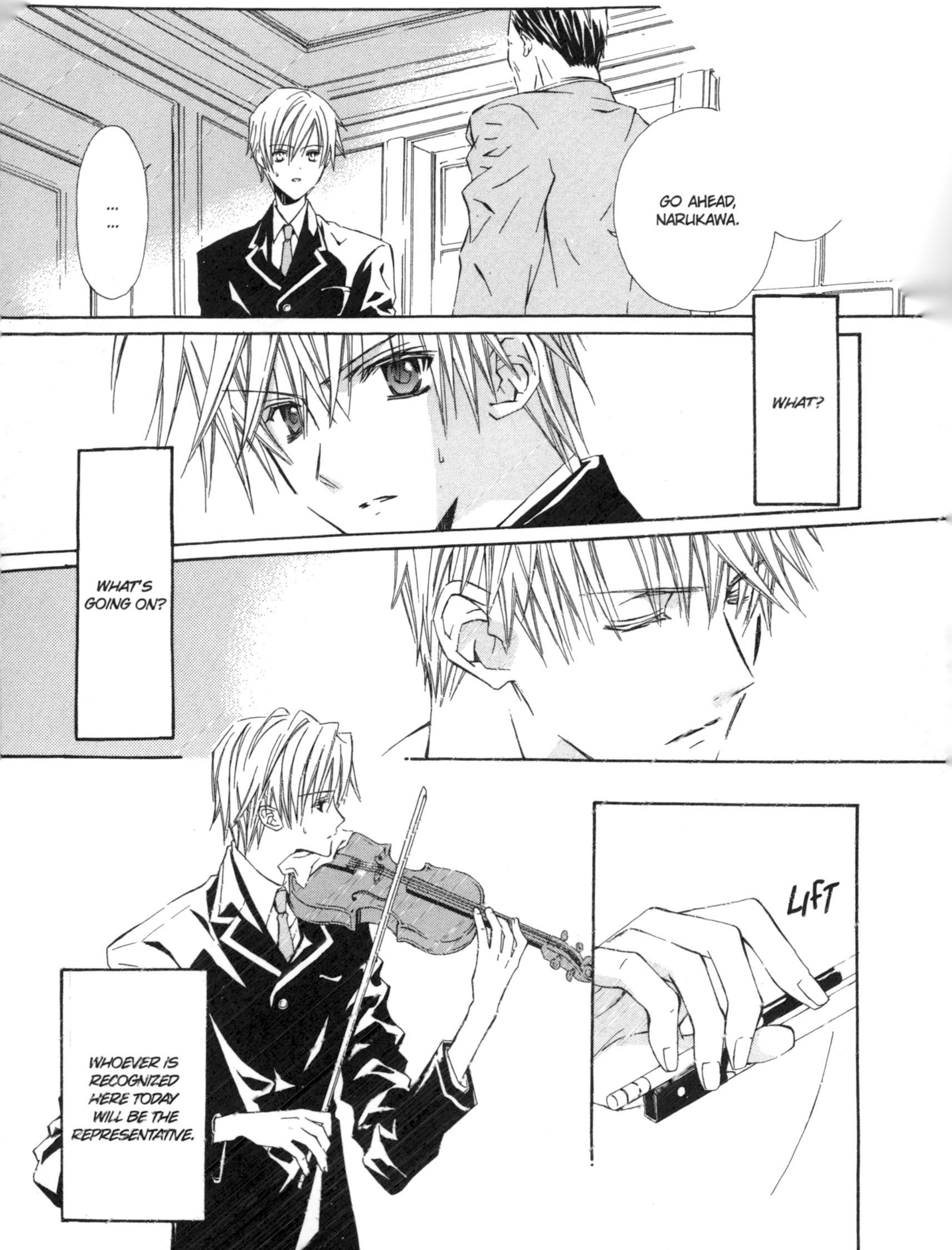
GO AHEAD, NARUKAWA.
... ...
WHAT?
WHAT'S GOING ON?
LIFT
WHOEVER IS RECOGNIZED HERE TODAY WILL BE THE REPRESENTATIVE.

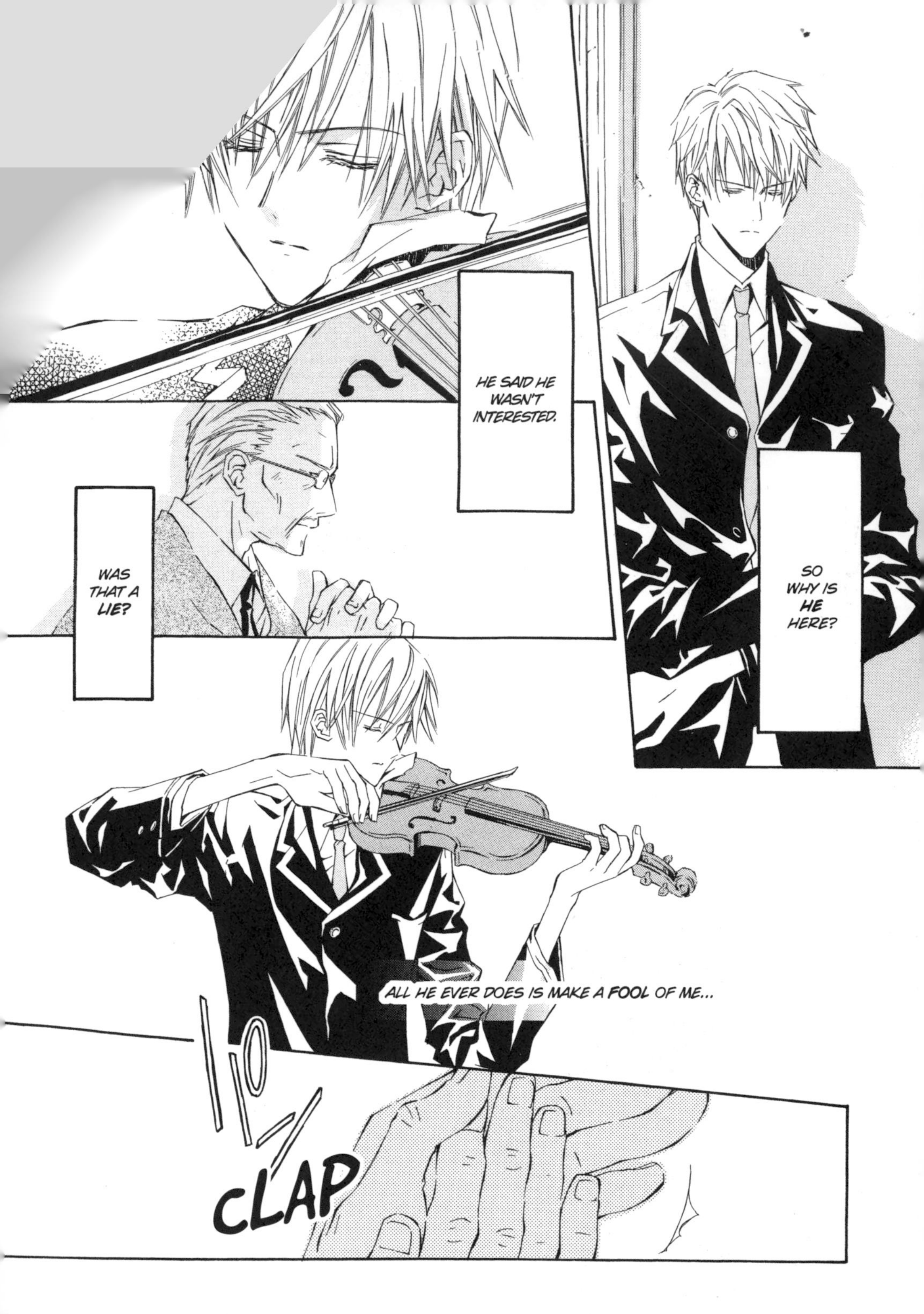
HE SAID HE WASN'T INTERESTED.
SO WHY IS HE HERE?
WAS THAT A LIE?
ALL HE EVER DOES IS MAKE A FOOL OF ME...
CLAP

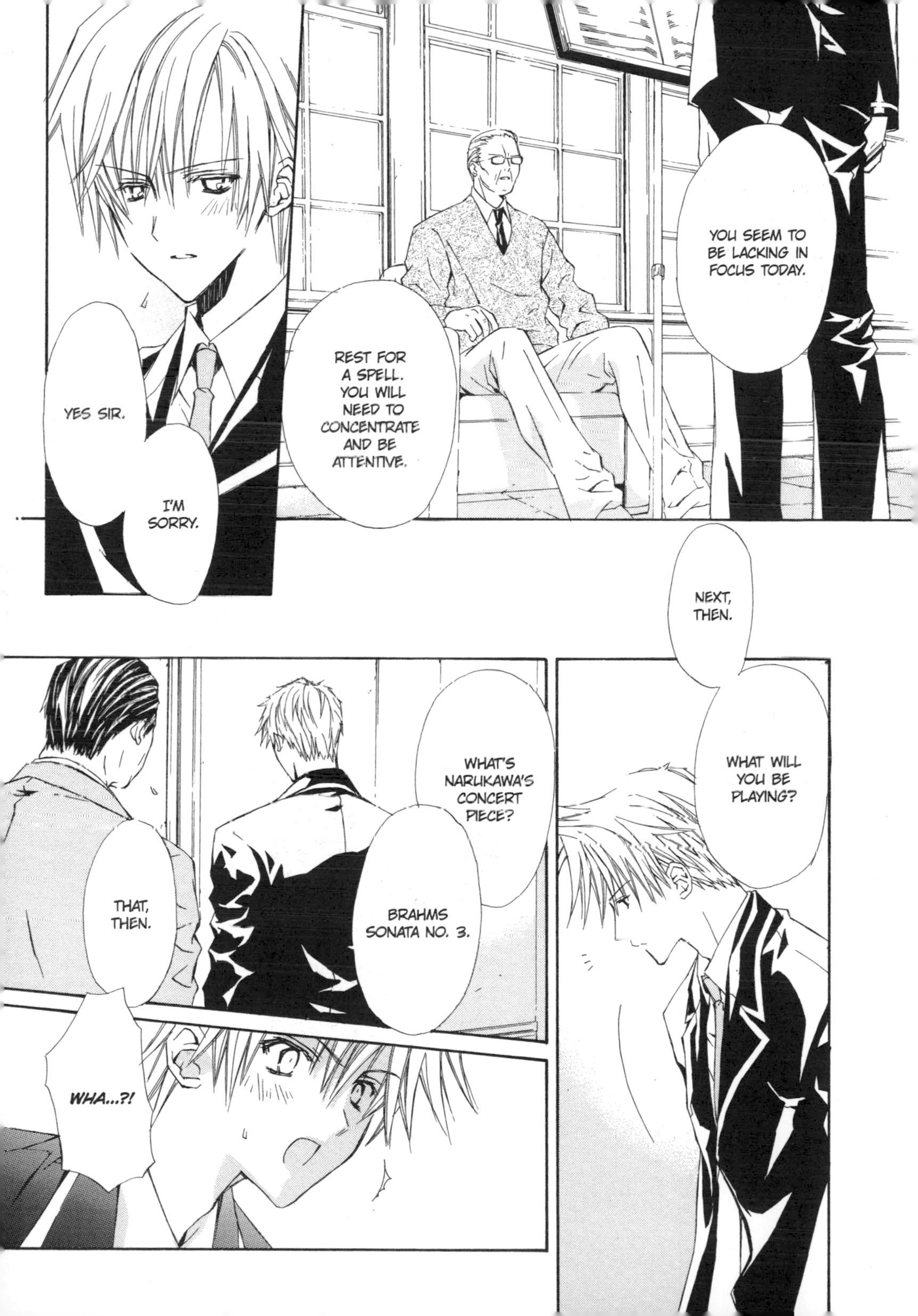
YOU SEEM TO BE LACKING IN FOCUS TODAY.
REST FOR A SPELL. YOU WILL NEED TO CONCENTRATE AND BE ATTENTIVE.
YES SIR.
I'M SORRY.
NEXT, THEN.
WHAT WILL YOU BE PLAYING?
WHAT'S NARUKAWA'S CONCERT PIECE?
BRAHMS SONATA NO. 3.
THAT, THEN.
WHA...?!

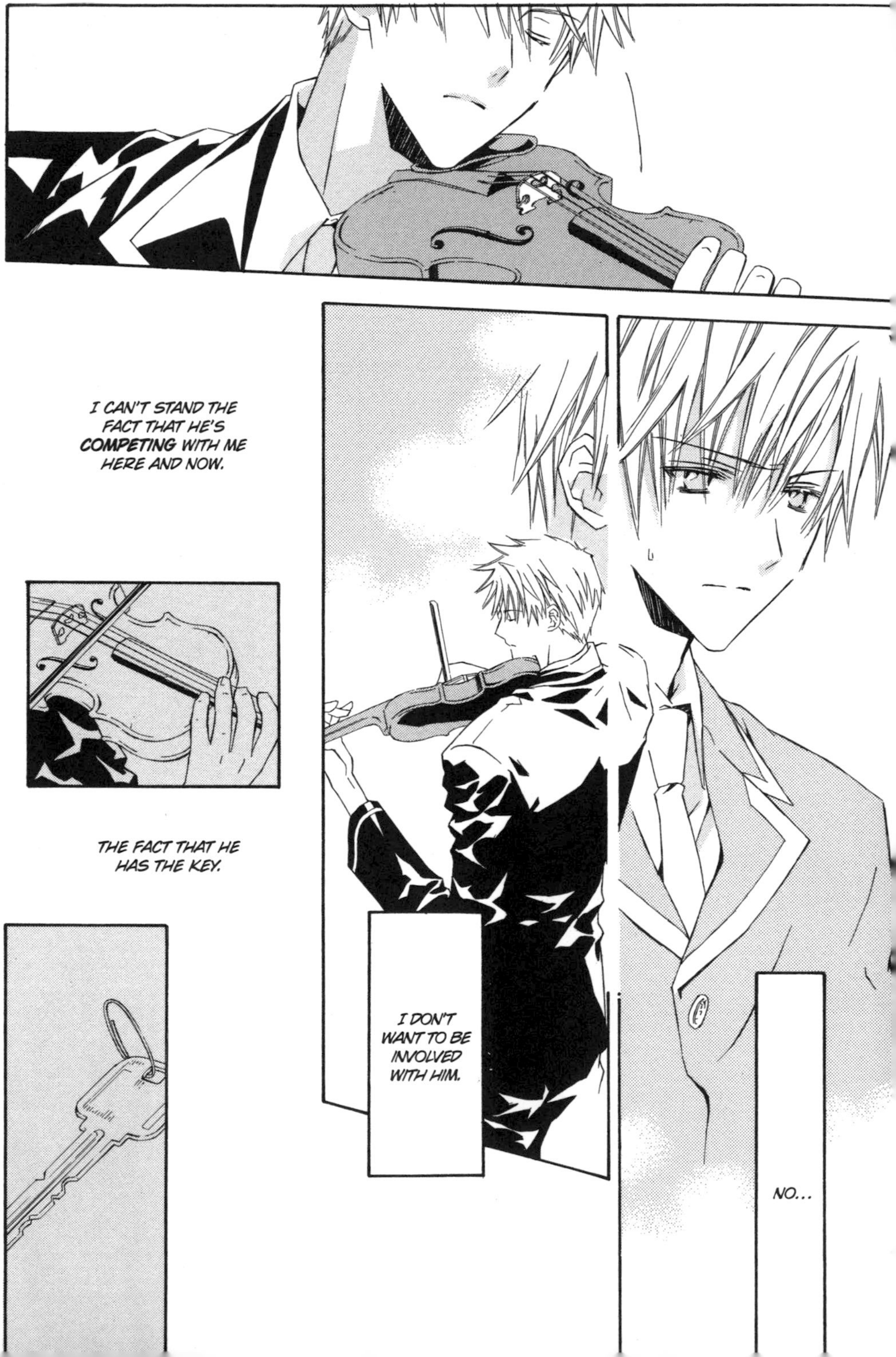
I DON'T WANT TO BE INVOLVED WITH HIM.
NO...
I CAN'T STAND THE FACT THAT HE'S **COMPETING** WITH ME HERE AND NOW.
THE FACT THAT HE HAS THE KEY.

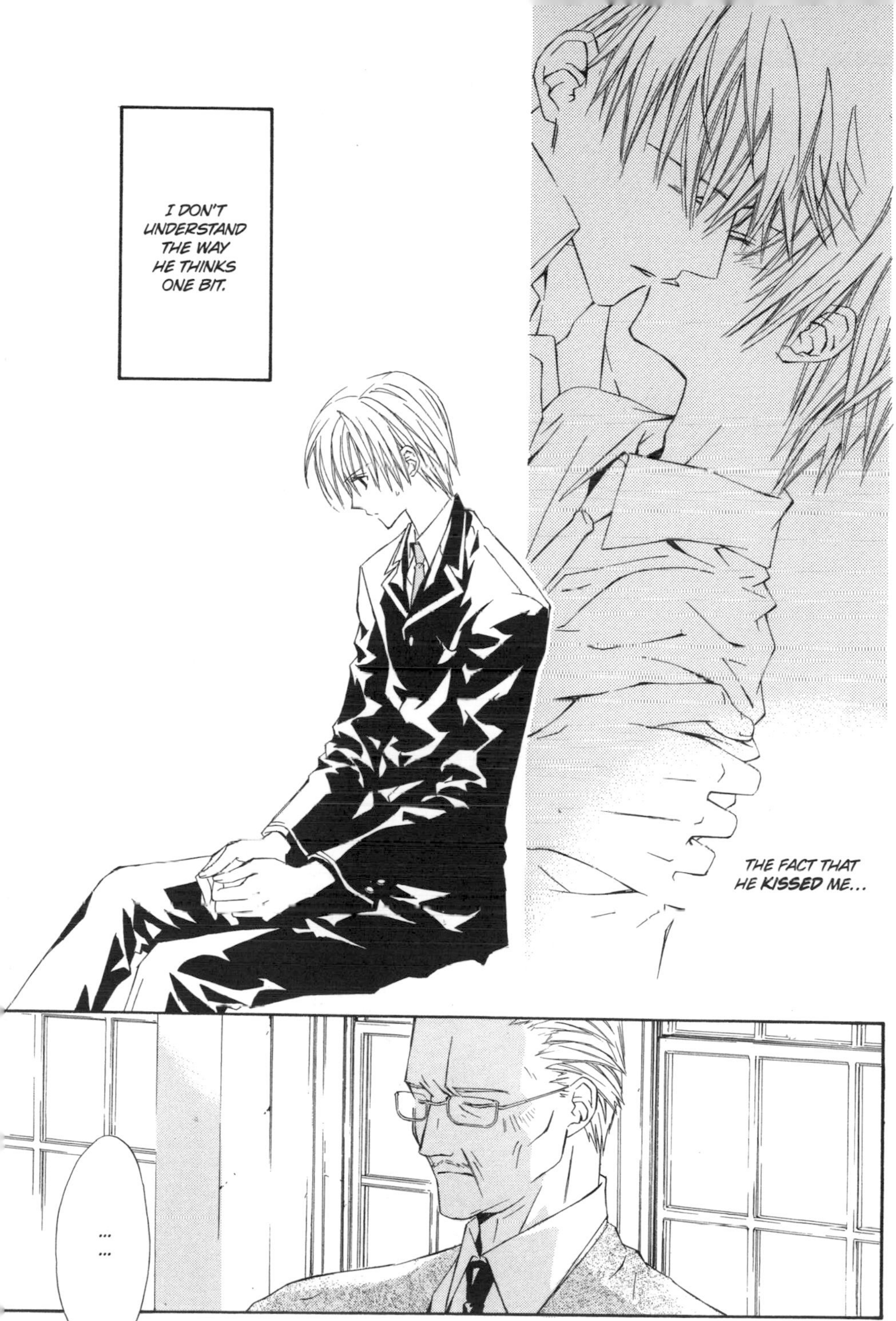
I DON'T UNDERSTAND THE WAY HE THINKS ONE BIT.
THE FACT THAT HE KISSED ME...
...
...

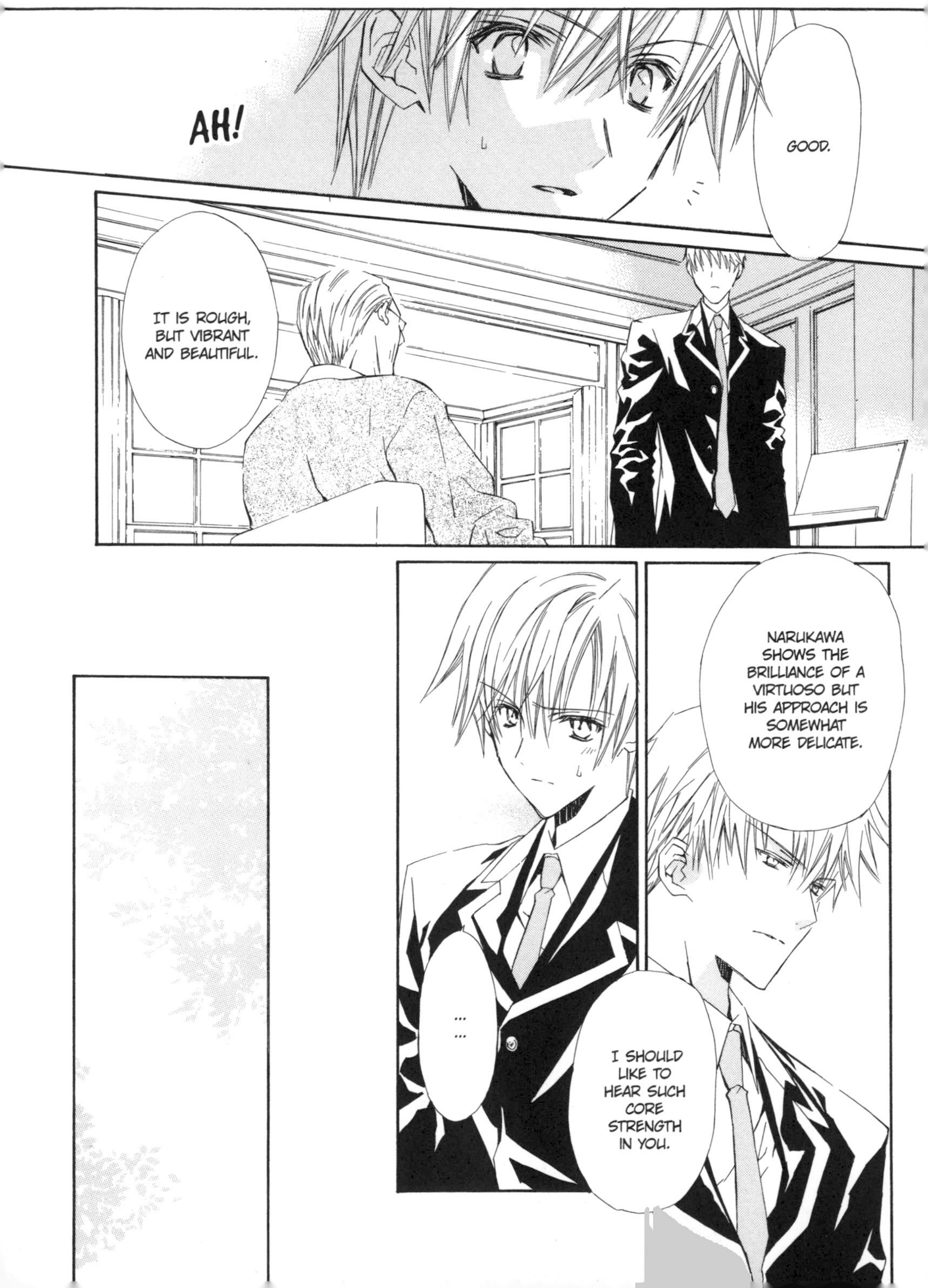
GOOD.
AH!
IT IS ROUGH, BUT VIBRANT AND BEAUTIFUL.
NARUKAWA SHOWS THE BRILLIANCE OF A VIRTUOSO BUT HIS APPROACH IS SOMEWHAT MORE DELICATE.
I SHOULD LIKE TO HEAR SUCH CORE STRENGTH IN YOU.
... ...

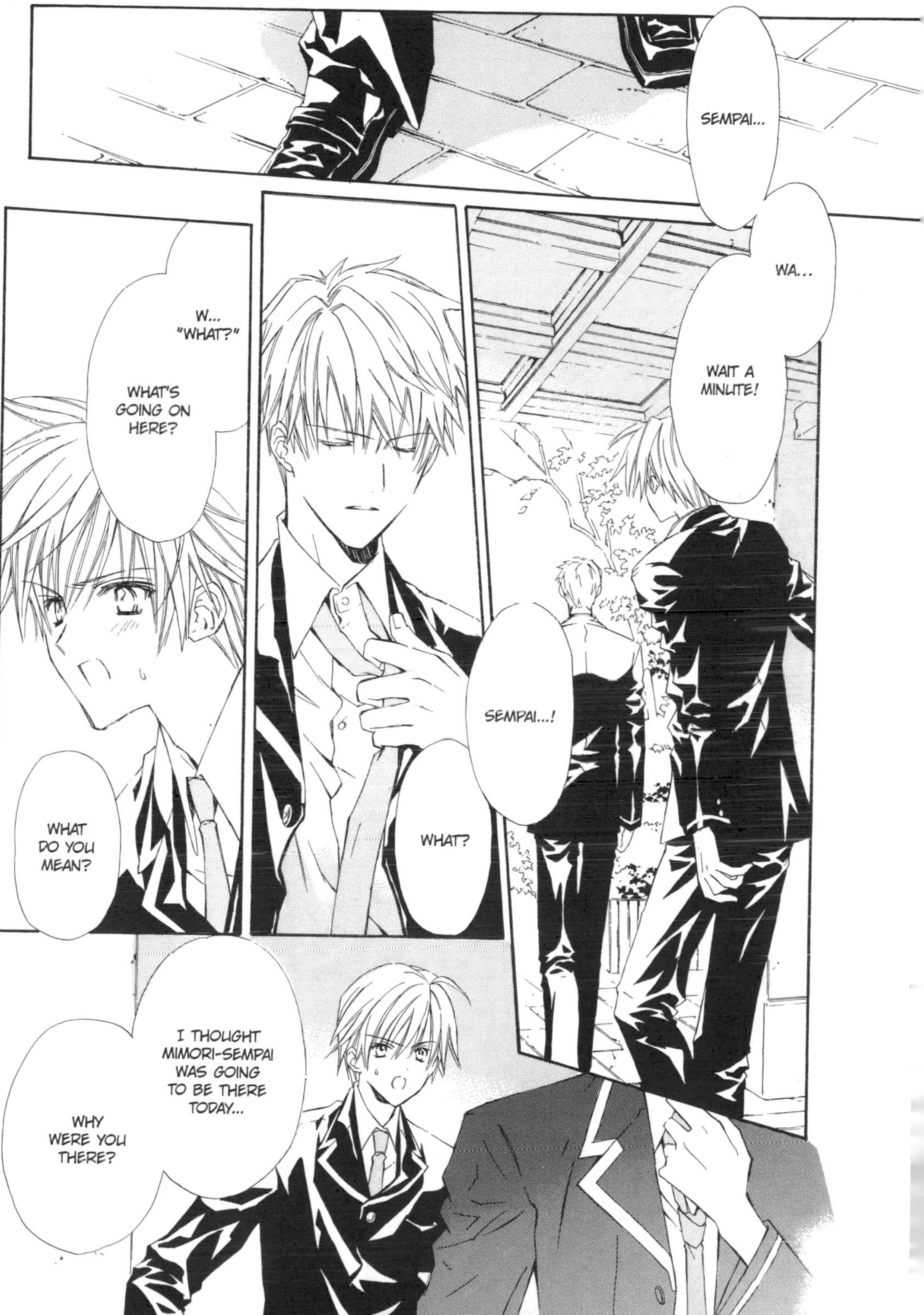
SEMPAI...
WA...
WAIT A MINUTE!
SEMPAI...!
WHAT?
W... "WHAT?"
WHAT'S GOING ON HERE?
WHAT DO YOU MEAN?
I THOUGHT MIMORI-SEMPAI WAS GOING TO BE THERE TODAY...
WHY WERE YOU THERE?

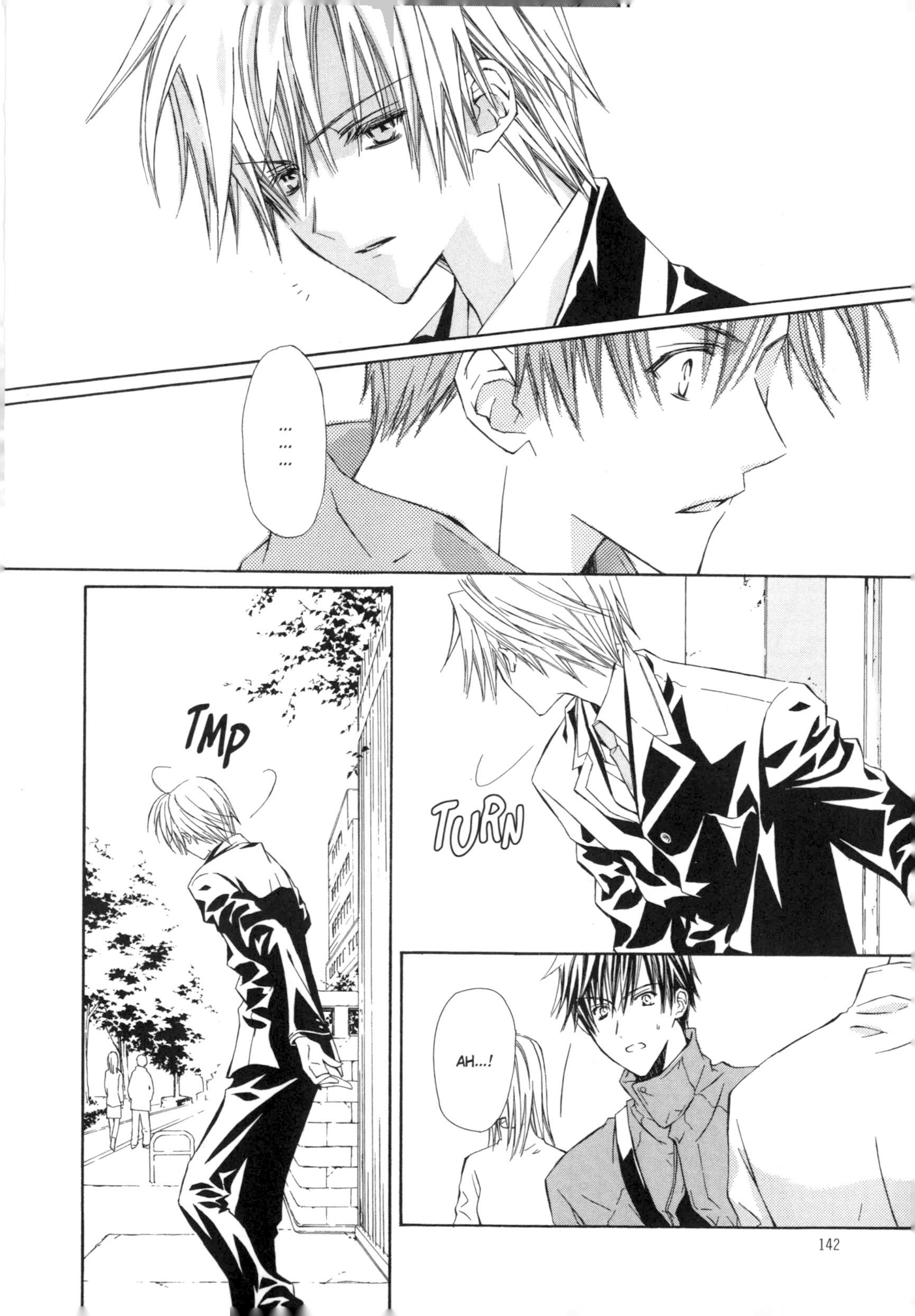
......
......
......
TURN
TMP
AH...!

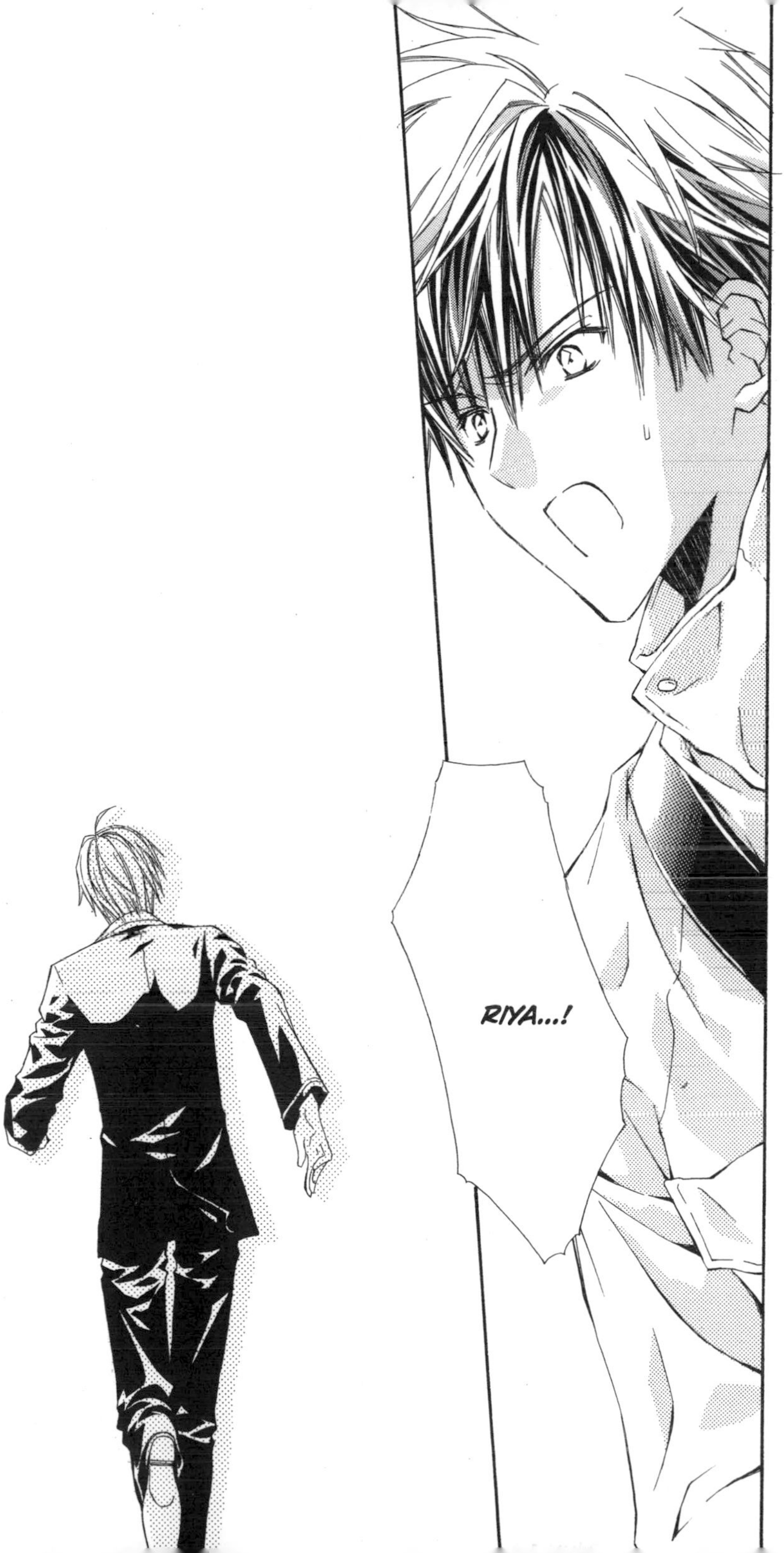
RIYA...!

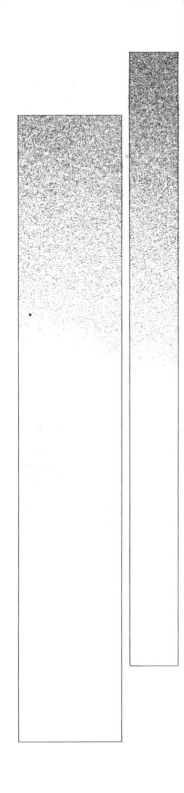

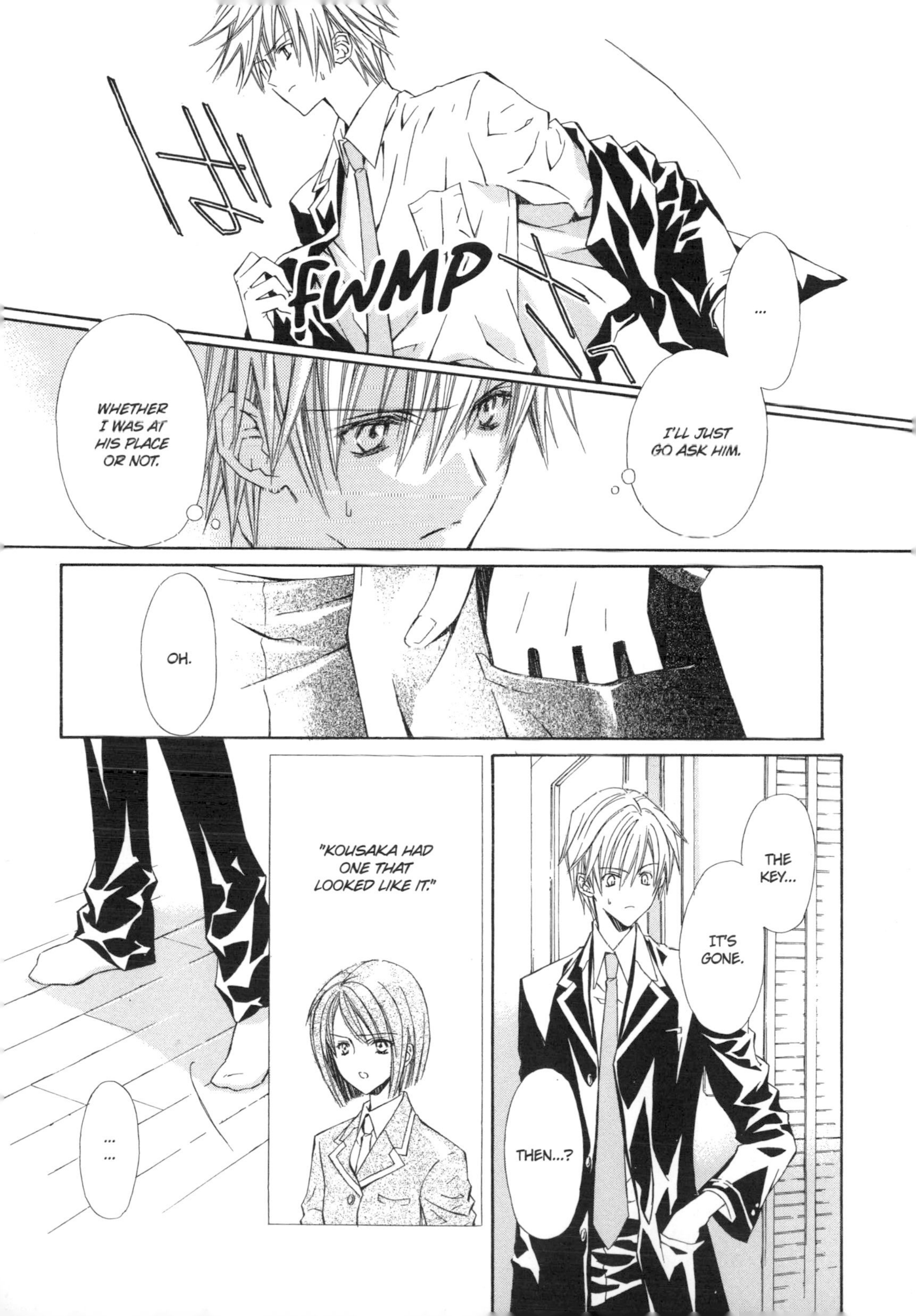
FWMP
...
I'LL JUST GO ASK HIM.
WHETHER I WAS AT HIS PLACE OR NOT.
OH.
THE KEY...
IT'S GONE.
THEN...?
"KOUSAKA HAD ONE THAT LOOKED LIKE IT."
... ...

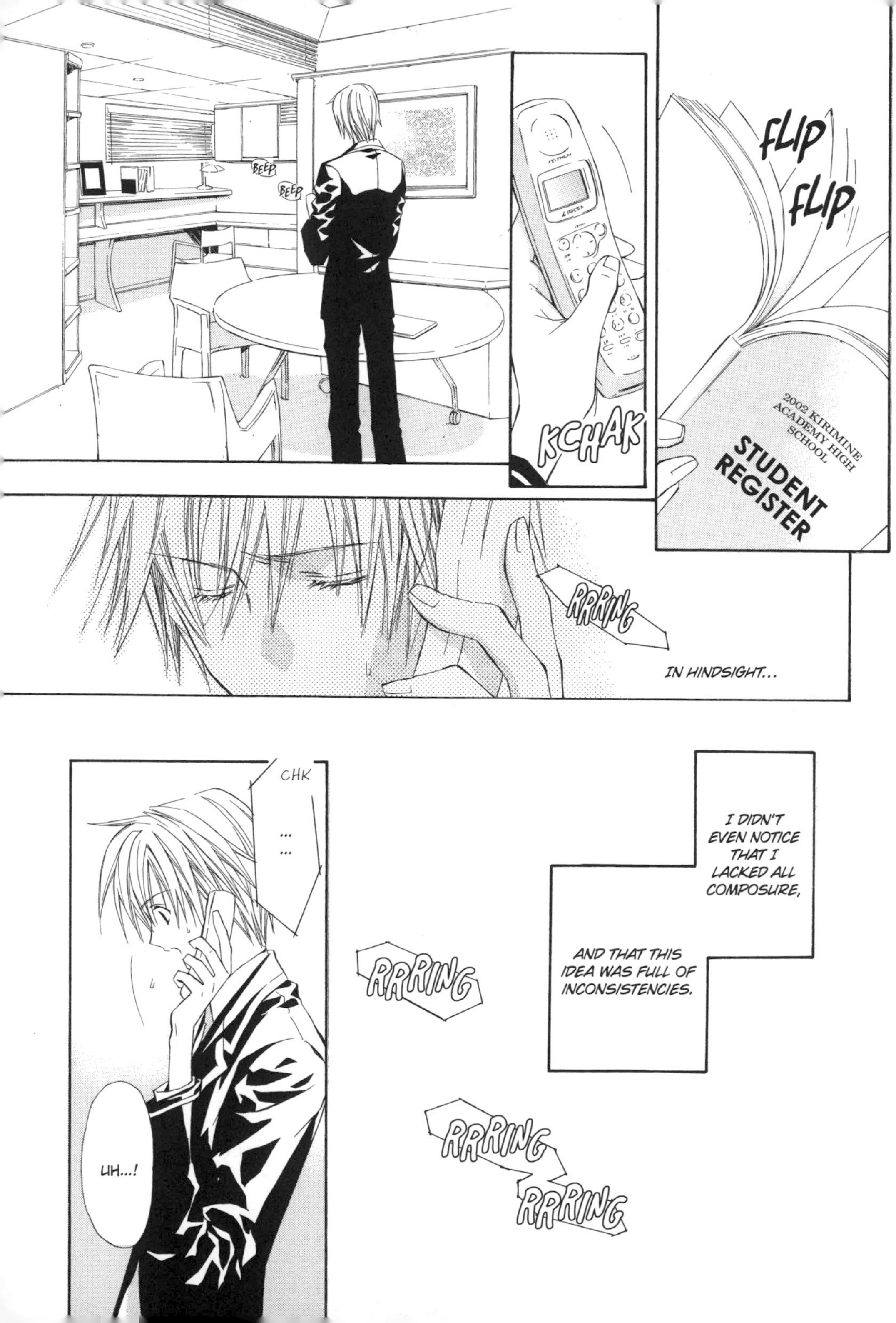
FLIP
FLIP
2002 KIRIMINE ACADEMY HIGH SCHOOL
STUDENT REGISTER
KCHAK
BEEP
BEEP
RRRING
IN HINDSIGHT...
I DIDN'T EVEN NOTICE THAT I LACKED ALL COMPOSURE,
AND THAT THIS IDEA WAS FULL OF INCONSISTENCIES.
RRRING
RRRING
RRRING
CHK
... ...
UH...!

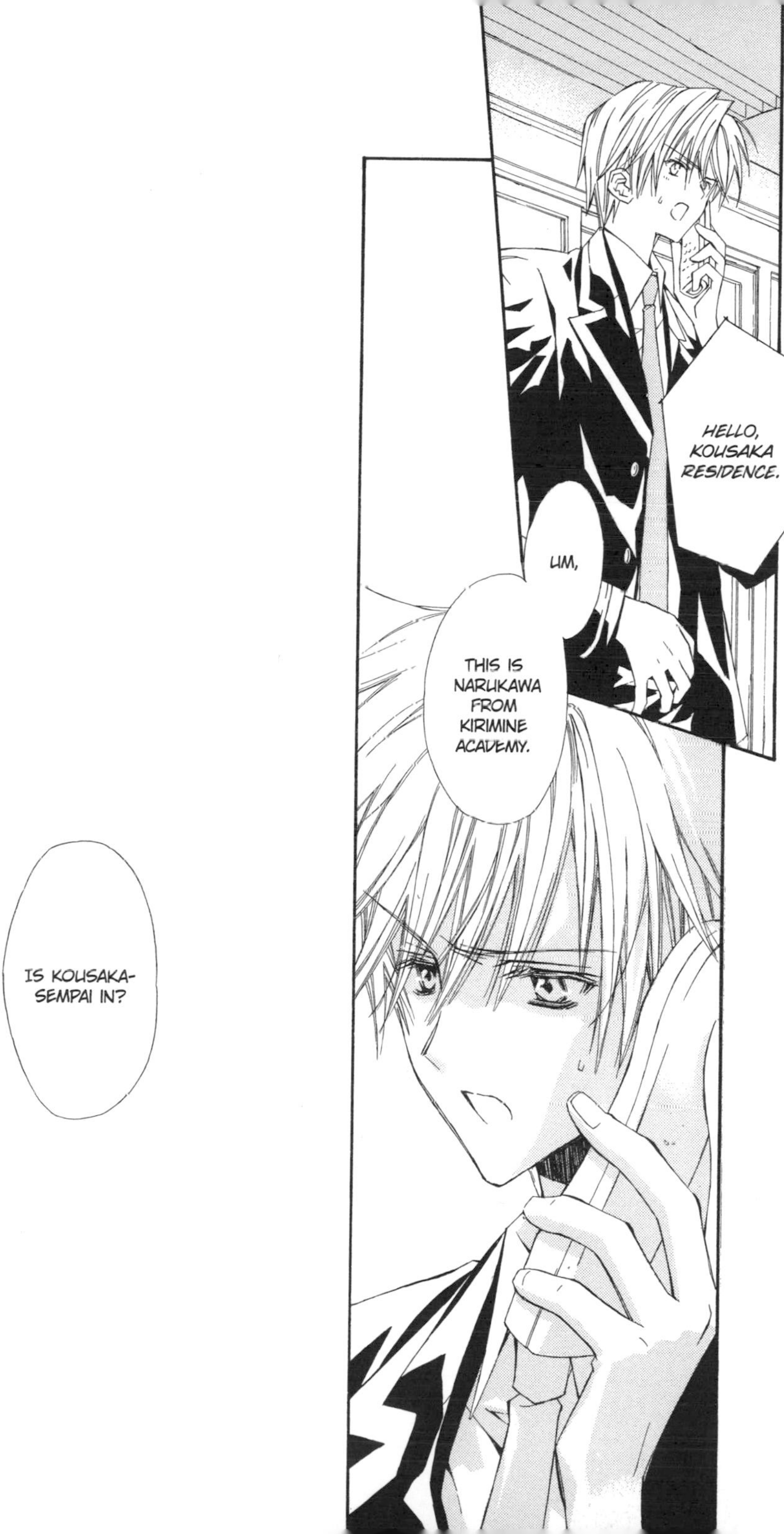
HELLO, KOUSAKA RESIDENCE.
UM,
THIS IS NARUKAWA FROM KIRIMINE ACADEMY.
IS KOUSAKA-SEMPAI IN?

Il gatto sul G.

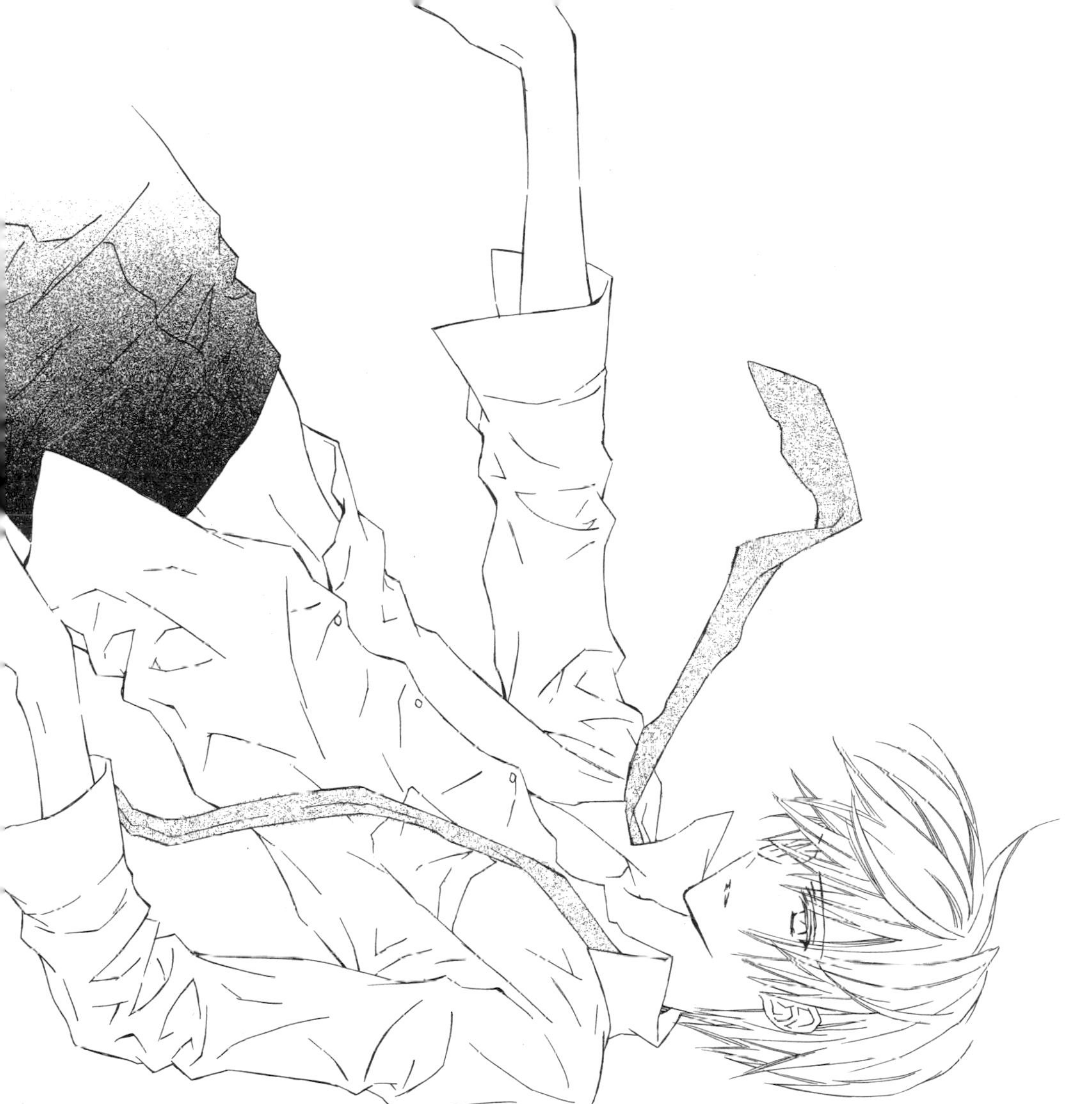

Episodio.3

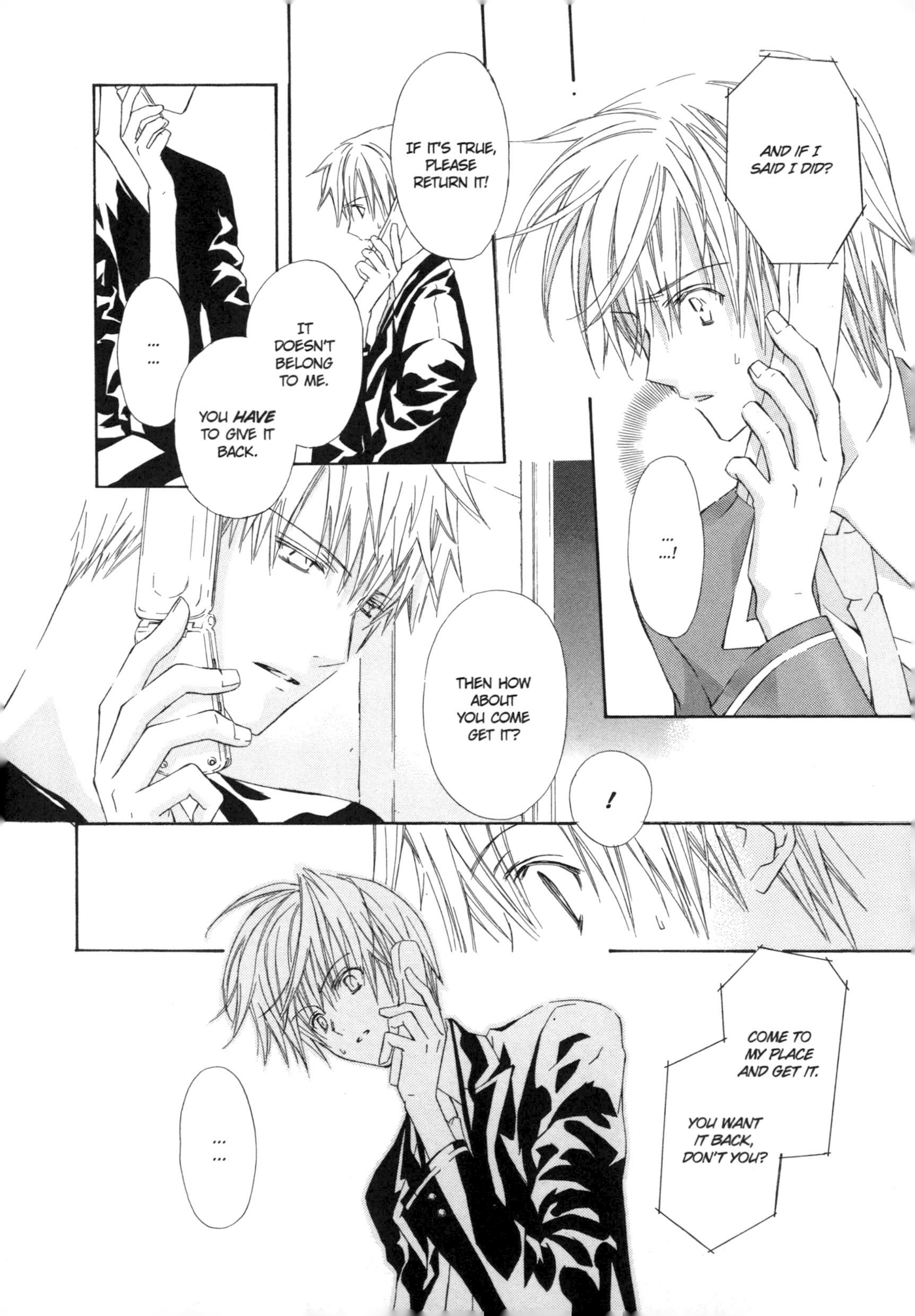
AND IF I SAID I DID?
IF IT'S TRUE, PLEASE RETURN IT!
... ...
IT DOESN'T BELONG TO ME.
YOU *HAVE* TO GIVE IT BACK.
... ...!
THEN HOW ABOUT YOU COME GET IT?
!
COME TO MY PLACE AND GET IT.
YOU WANT IT BACK, DON'T YOU?
... ...

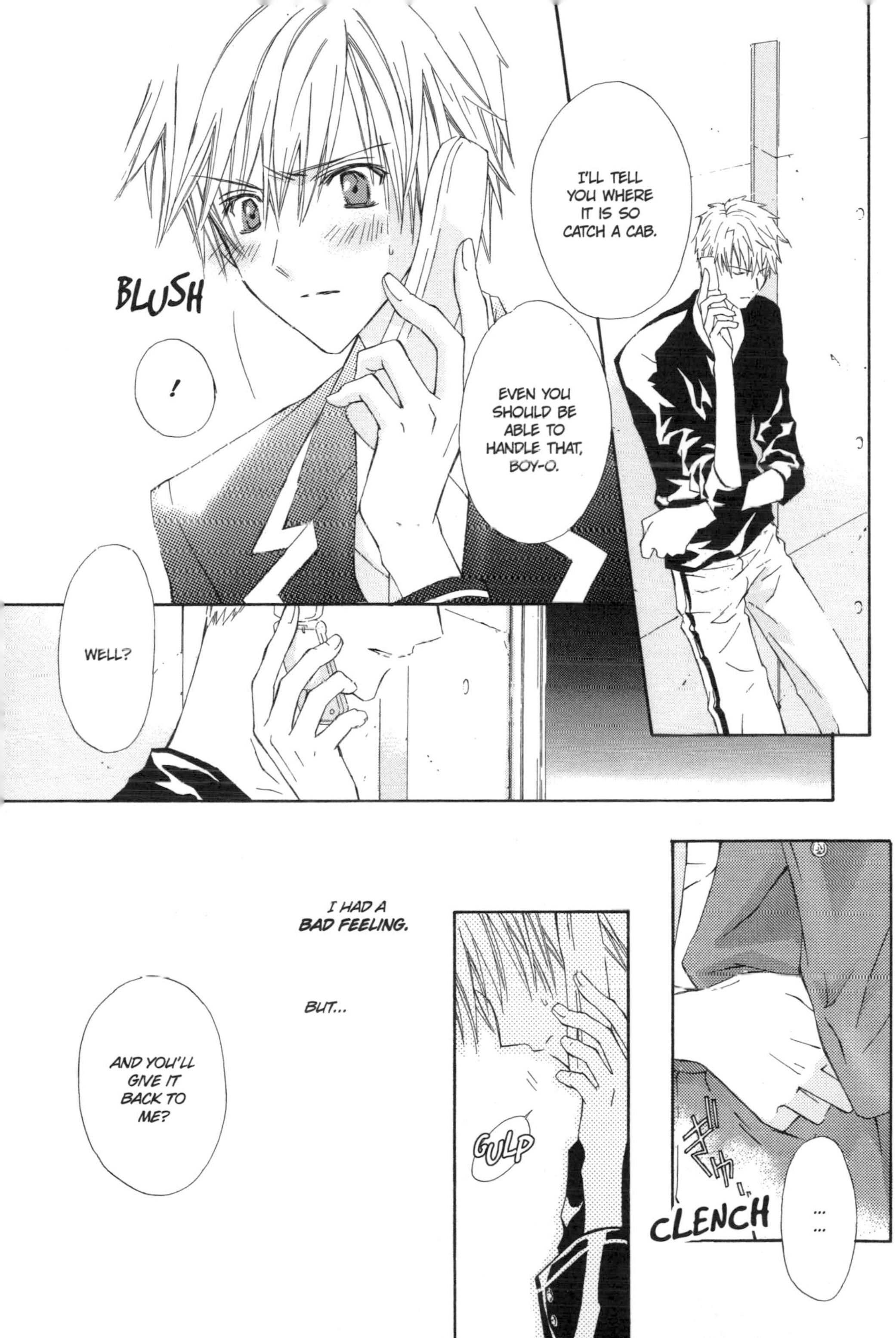
I'LL TELL YOU WHERE IT IS SO CATCH A CAB.
EVEN YOU SHOULD BE ABLE TO HANDLE THAT, BOY-O.
BLUSH
!
WELL?
CLENCH
... ...
GULP
I HAD A BAD FEELING.
BUT...
AND YOU'LL GIVE IT BACK TO ME?

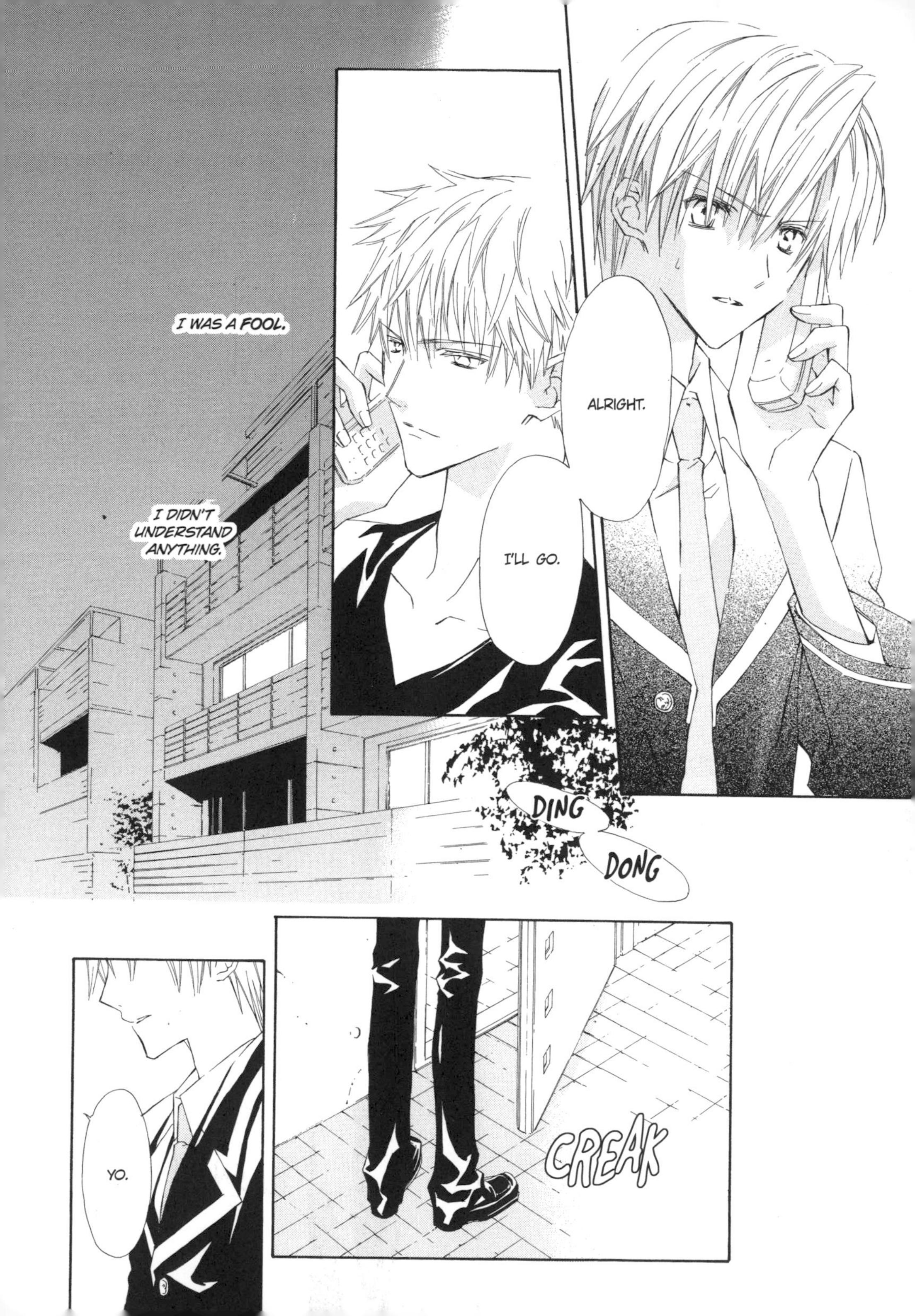
ALRIGHT.
I'LL GO.
I WAS A FOOL.
I DIDN'T UNDERSTAND ANYTHING.
DING
DONG
CREAK
YO.

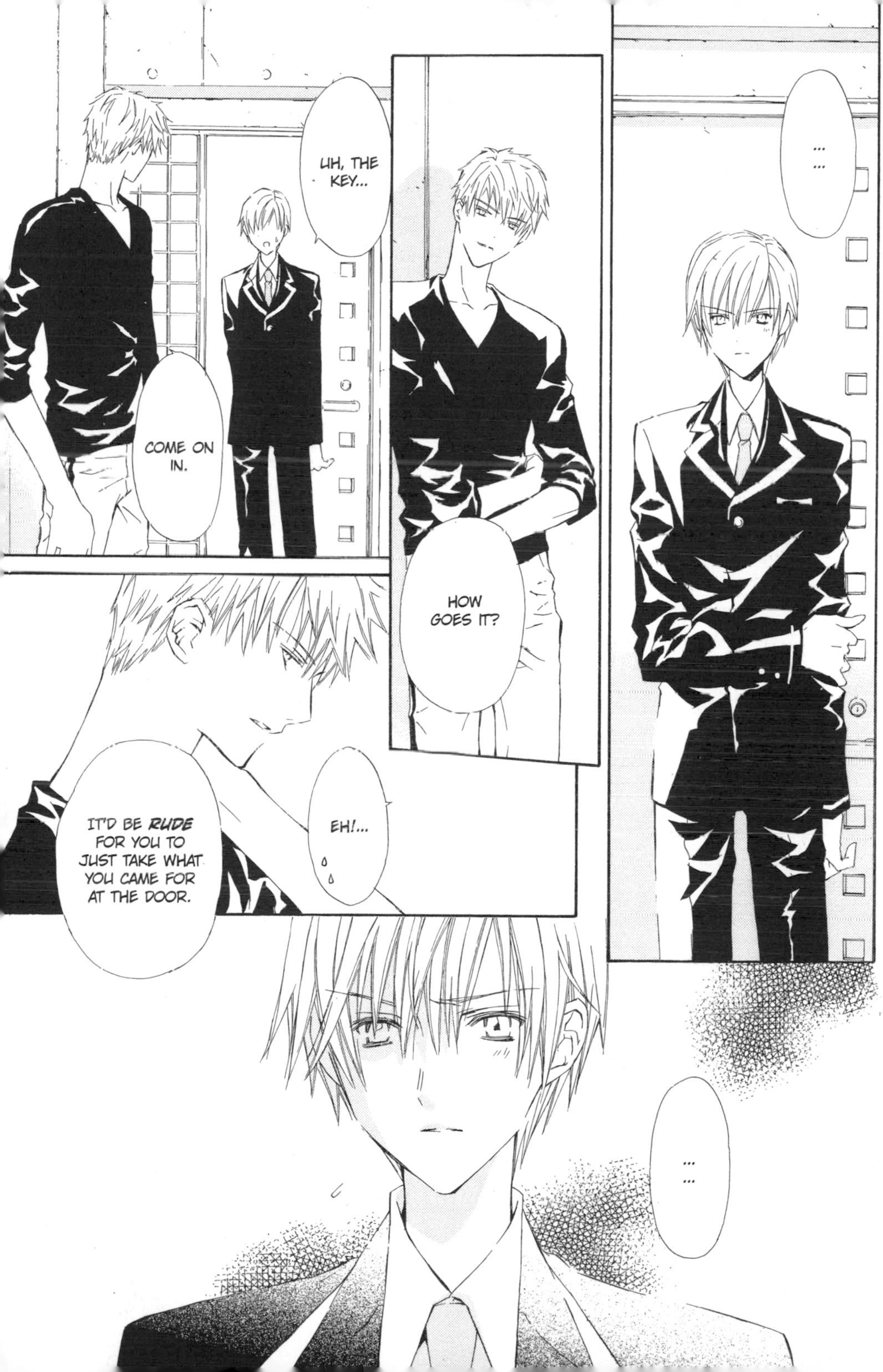
... ...
HOW GOES IT?
UH, THE KEY...
COME ON IN.
EH!...
IT'D BE **RUDE** FOR YOU TO JUST TAKE WHAT YOU CAME FOR AT THE DOOR.
... ...

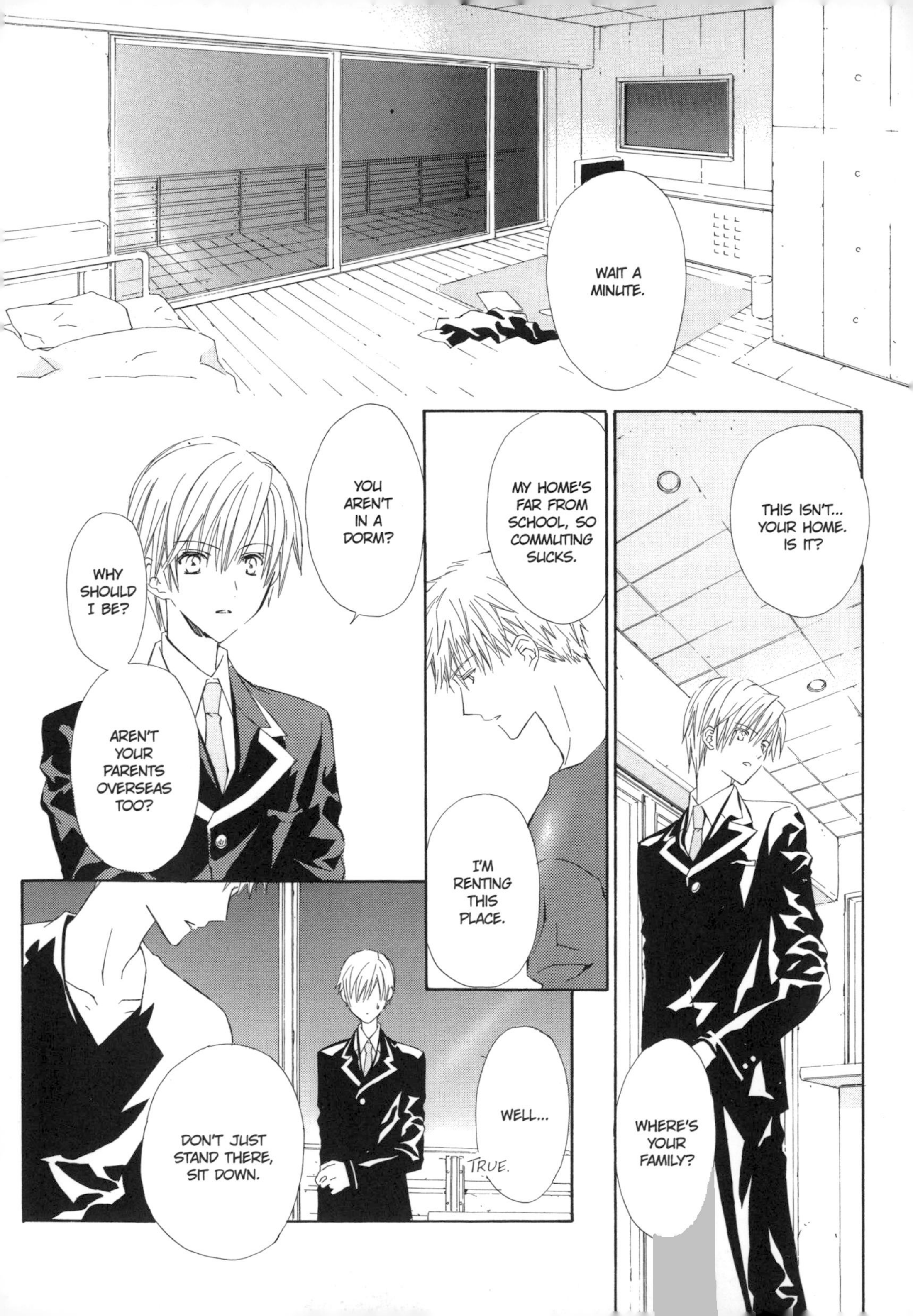
WAIT A MINUTE.
THIS ISN'T... YOUR HOME. IS IT?
WHERE'S YOUR FAMILY?
MY HOME'S FAR FROM SCHOOL, SO COMMUTING SUCKS.
I'M RENTING THIS PLACE.
YOU AREN'T IN A DORM?
WHY SHOULD I BE?
AREN'T YOUR PARENTS OVERSEAS TOO?
WELL...
TRUE.
DON'T JUST STAND THERE, SIT DOWN.

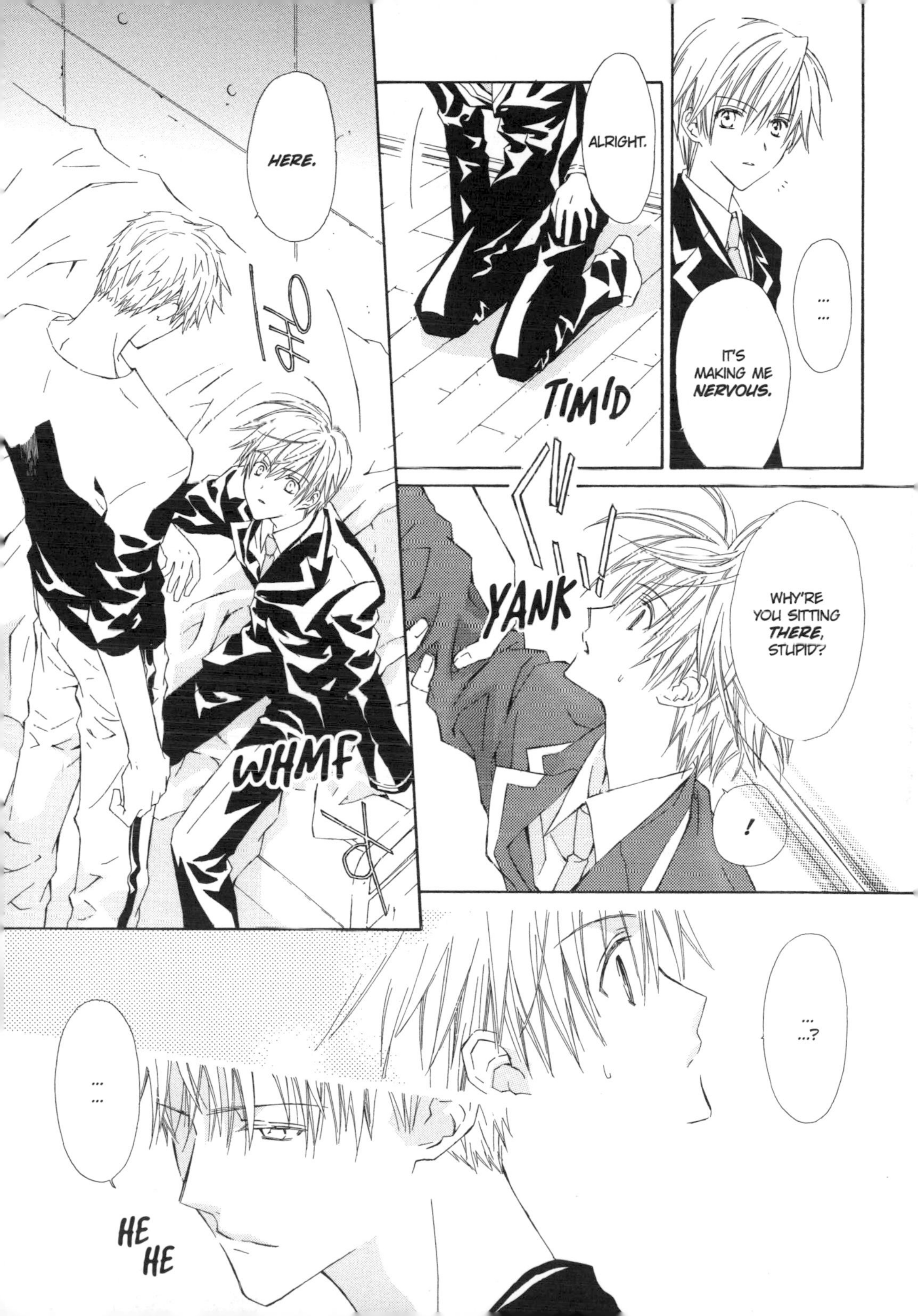

...
...
IT'S MAKING ME NERVOUS.
ALRIGHT.
TIMID
WHY'RE YOU SITTING THERE, STUPID?
YANK
!
HERE.
WHMF
...
...?
...
...
HE HE

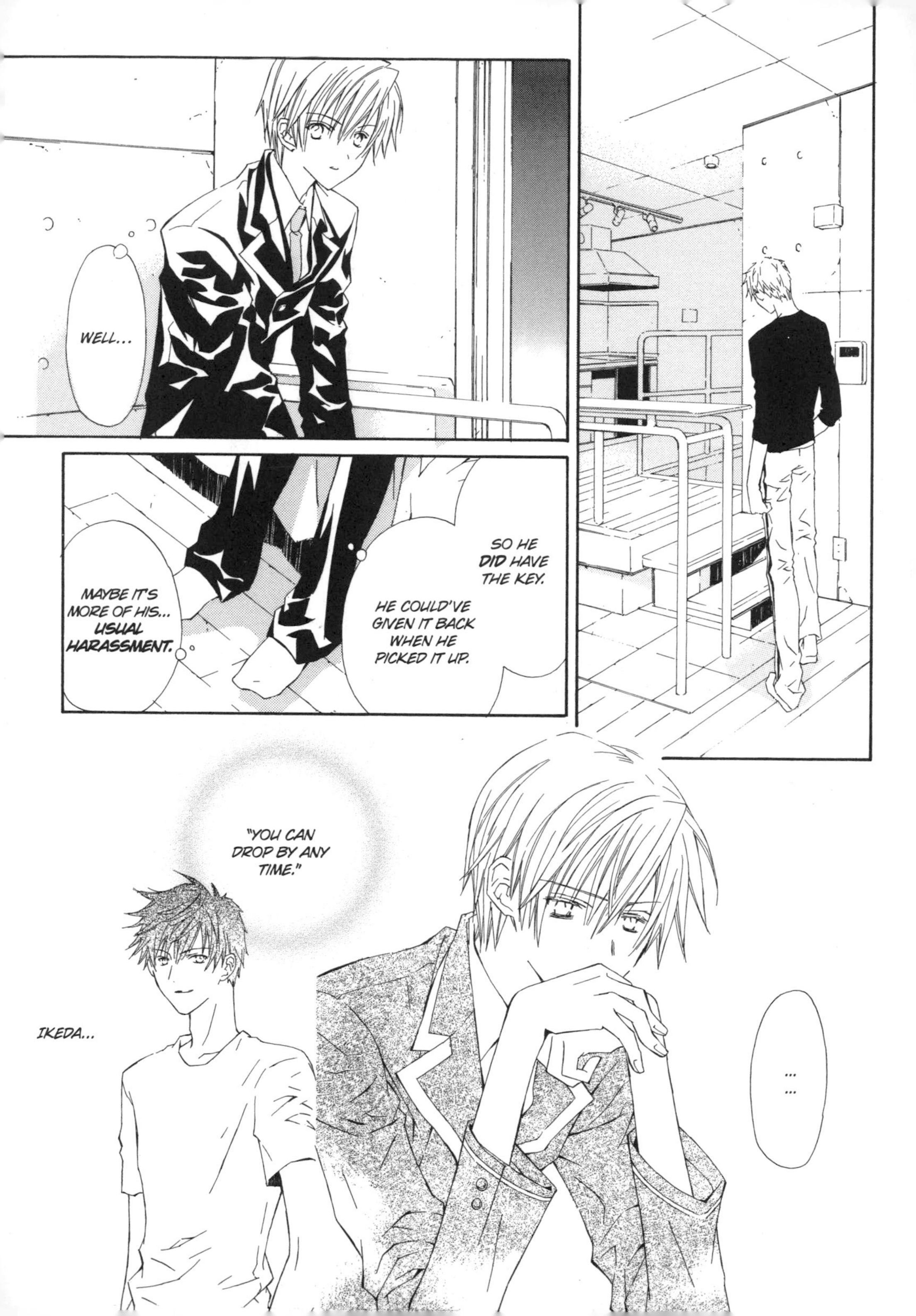
WELL...
SO HE DID HAVE THE KEY.
HE COULD'VE GIVEN IT BACK WHEN HE PICKED IT UP.
MAYBE IT'S MORE OF HIS... USUAL HARASSMENT.
"YOU CAN DROP BY ANY TIME."
IKEDA...
... ...

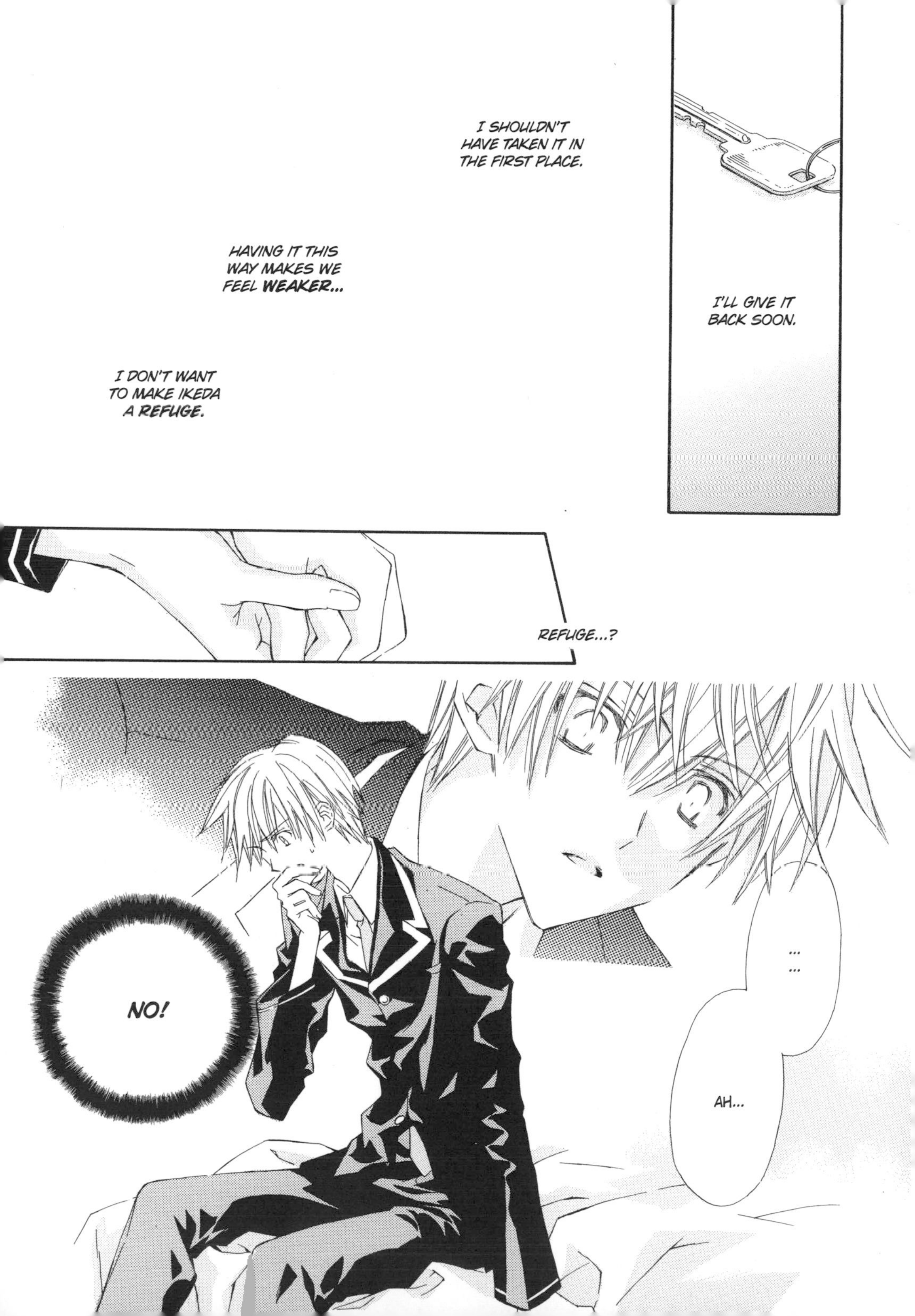
I'LL GIVE IT BACK SOON.
I SHOULDN'T HAVE TAKEN IT IN THE FIRST PLACE.
HAVING IT THIS WAY MAKES WE FEEL WEAKER...
I DON'T WANT TO MAKE IKEDA A REFUGE.
REFUGE...?
......
AH...
NO!

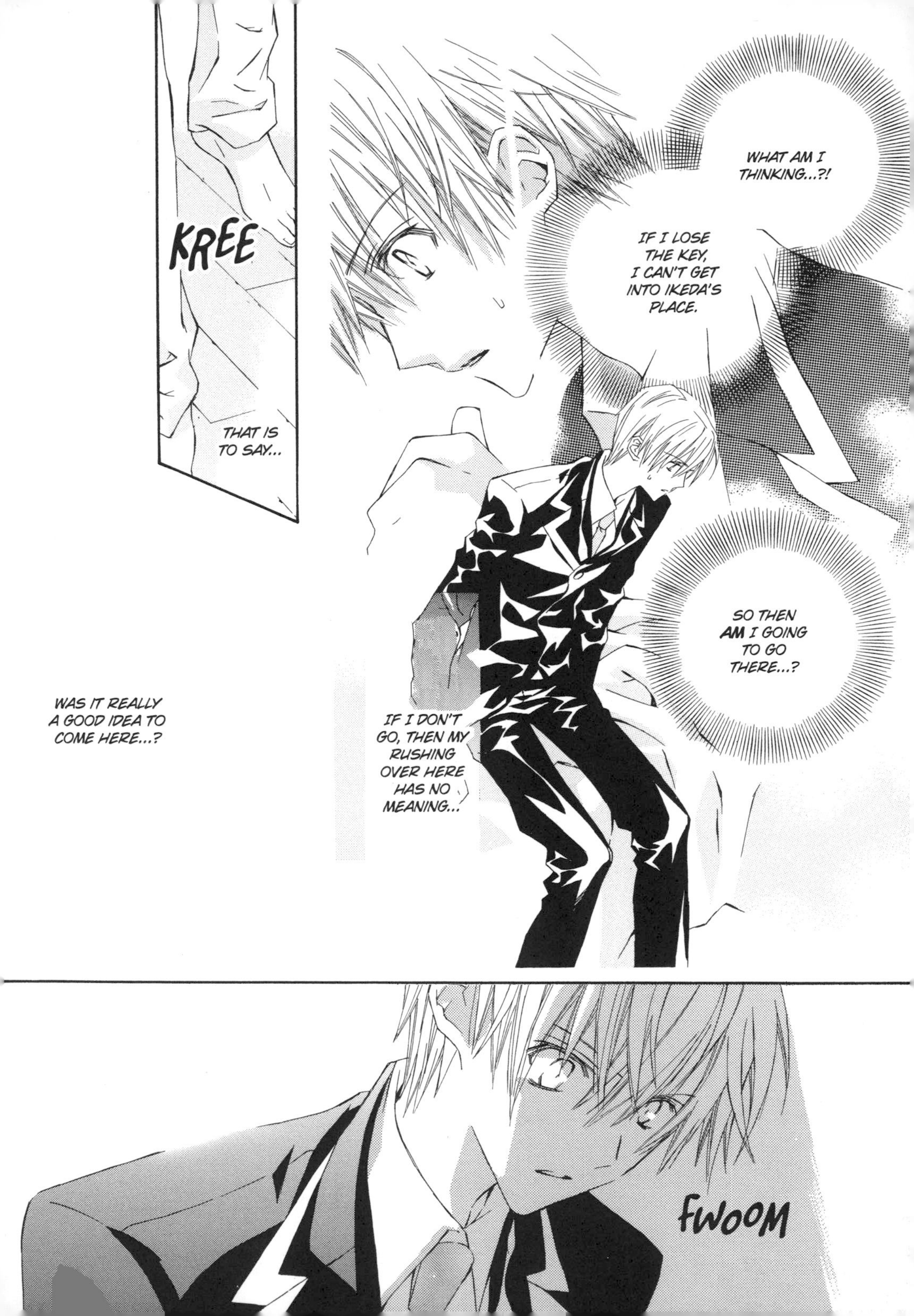
WHAT AM I THINKING...?!
IF I LOSE THE KEY, I CAN'T GET INTO IKEDA'S PLACE.
KREE
THAT IS TO SAY...
SO THEN AM I GOING TO GO THERE...?
IF I DON'T GO, THEN MY RUSHING OVER HERE HAS NO MEANING...
WAS IT REALLY A GOOD IDEA TO COME HERE...?
FWOOM

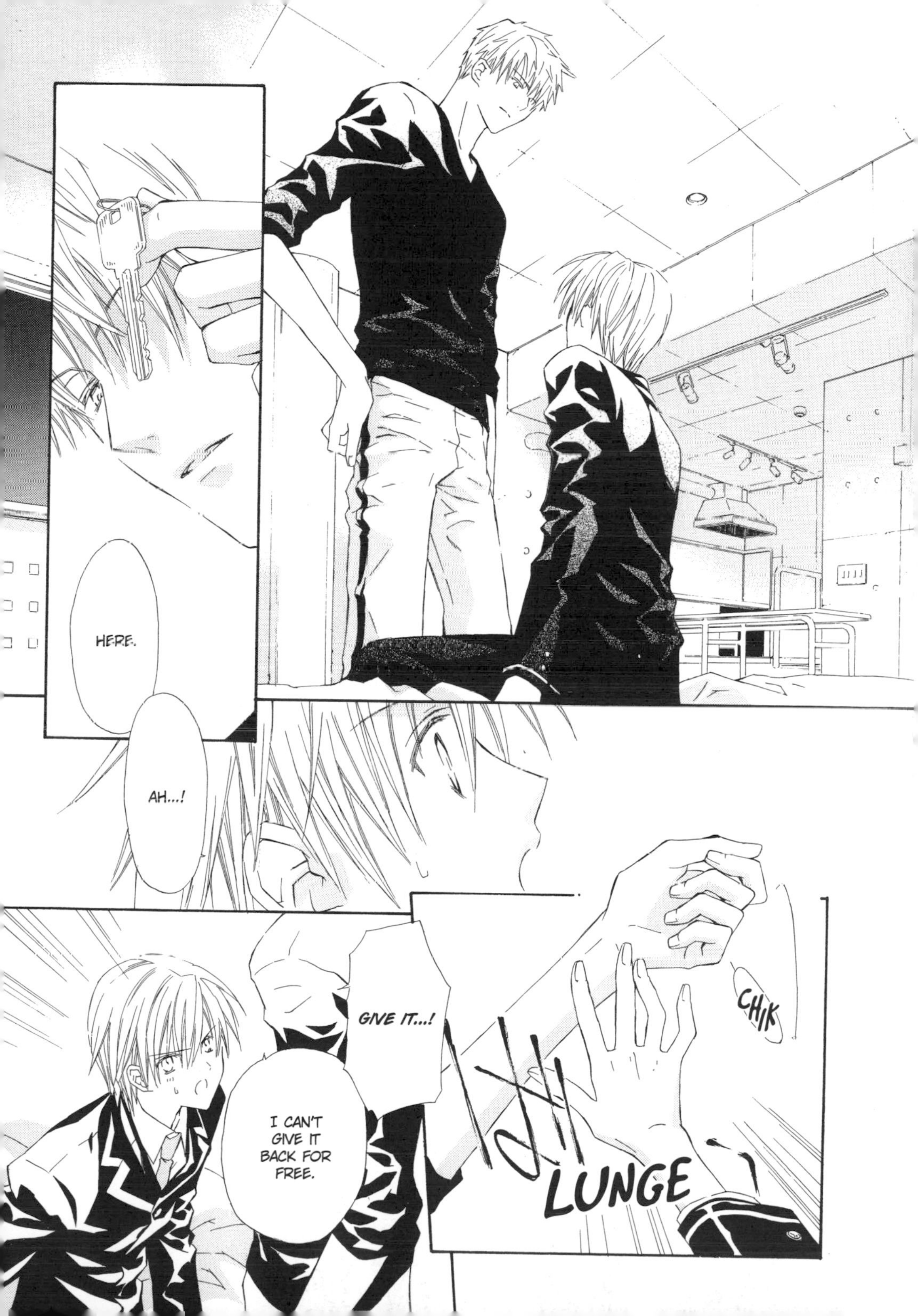
HERE.
AH...!
CHIK
LUNGE
GIVE IT...!
I CAN'T GIVE IT BACK FOR FREE.

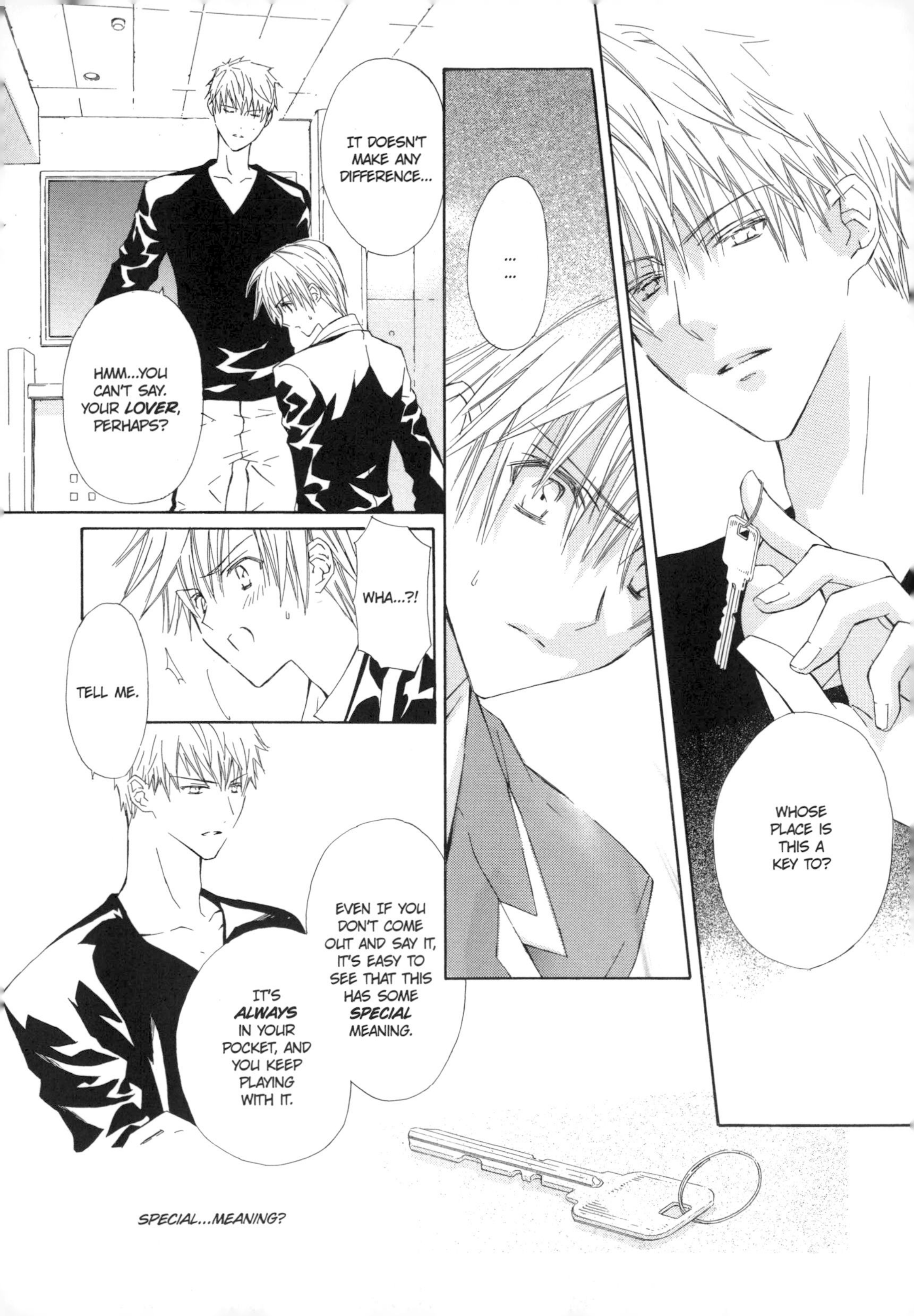
WHOSE PLACE IS THIS A KEY TO?
... ...
IT DOESN'T MAKE ANY DIFFERENCE...
HMM...YOU CAN'T SAY. YOUR **LOVER**, PERHAPS?
WHA...?!
TELL ME.
EVEN IF YOU DON'T COME OUT AND SAY IT, IT'S EASY TO SEE THAT THIS HAS SOME ***SPECIAL*** MEANING.
IT'S ***ALWAYS*** IN YOUR POCKET, AND YOU KEEP PLAYING WITH IT.
SPECIAL...MEANING?

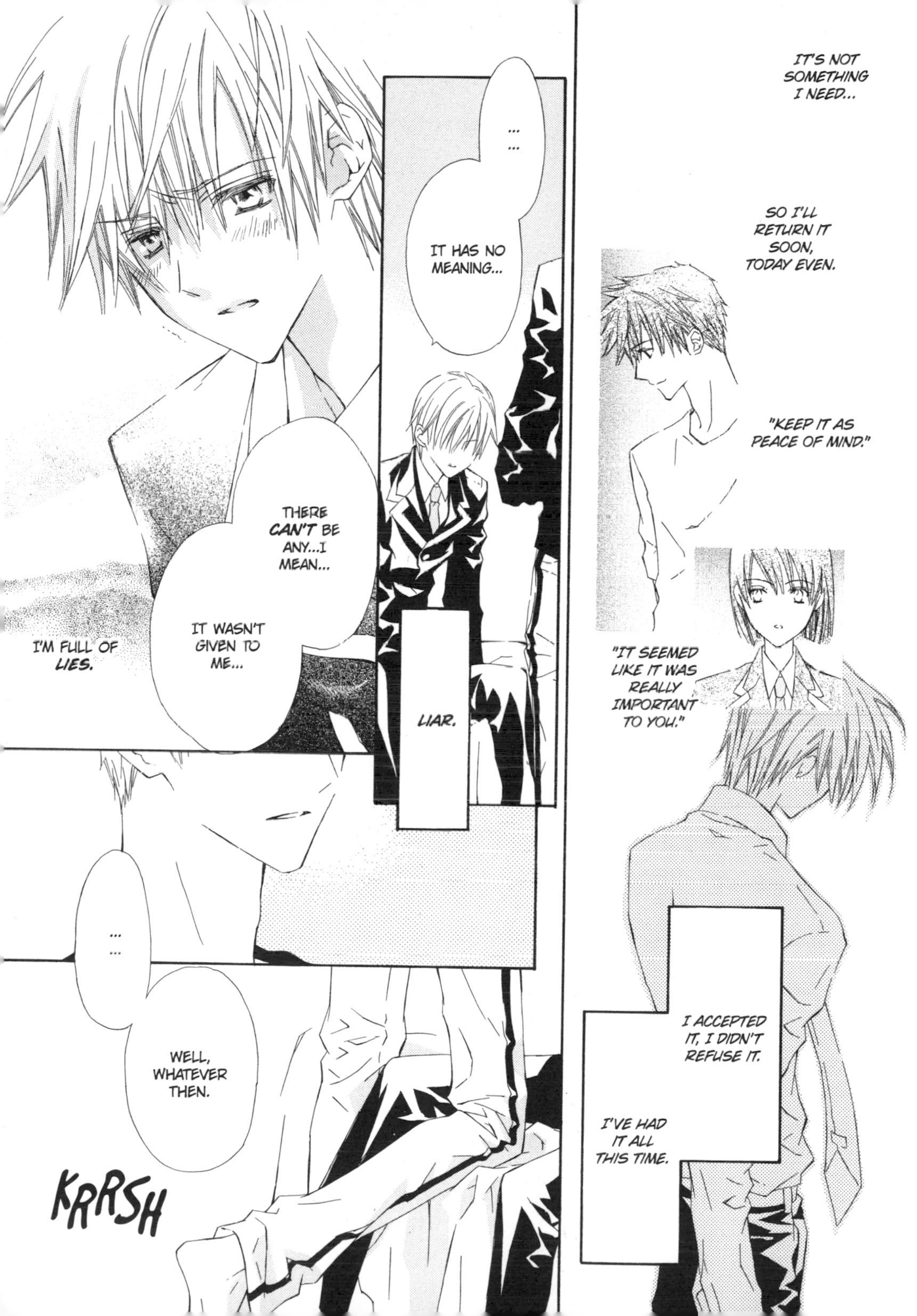
IT'S NOT SOMETHING I NEED...
SO I'LL RETURN IT SOON, TODAY EVEN.
"KEEP IT AS PEACE OF MIND."
"IT SEEMED LIKE IT WAS REALLY IMPORTANT TO YOU."
I ACCEPTED IT, I DIDN'T REFUSE IT.
I'VE HAD IT ALL THIS TIME.
... ...
IT HAS NO MEANING...
THERE CAN'T BE ANY...I MEAN...
IT WASN'T GIVEN TO ME...
I'M FULL OF LIES.
LIAR.
... ...
WELL, WHATEVER THEN.
KRRSH

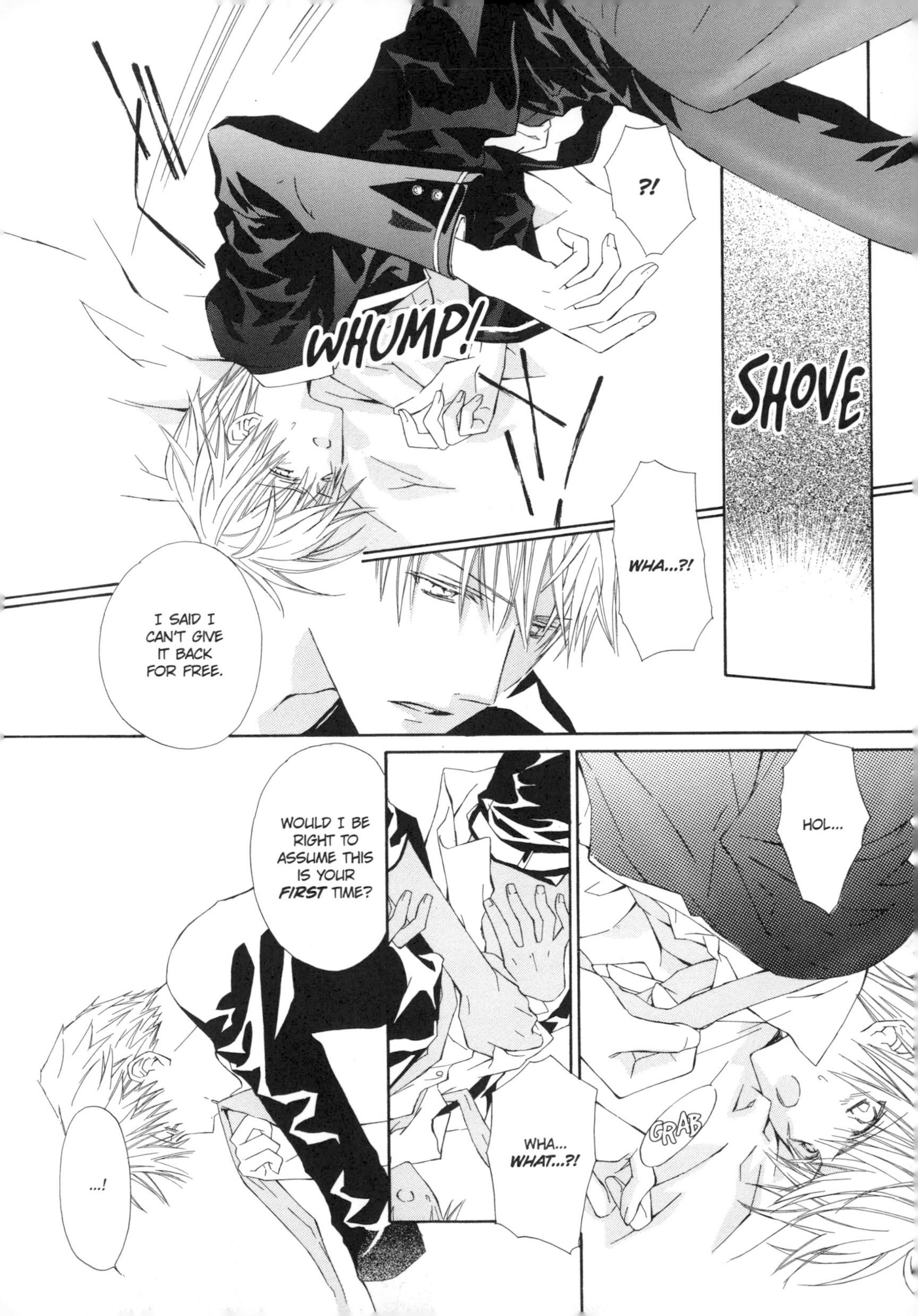
?!
WHUMP!
SHOVE
WHA...?!
I SAID I CAN'T GIVE IT BACK FOR FREE.
HOL...
GRAB
WHA... WHAT...?!
WOULD I BE RIGHT TO ASSUME THIS IS YOUR FIRST TIME?
...!

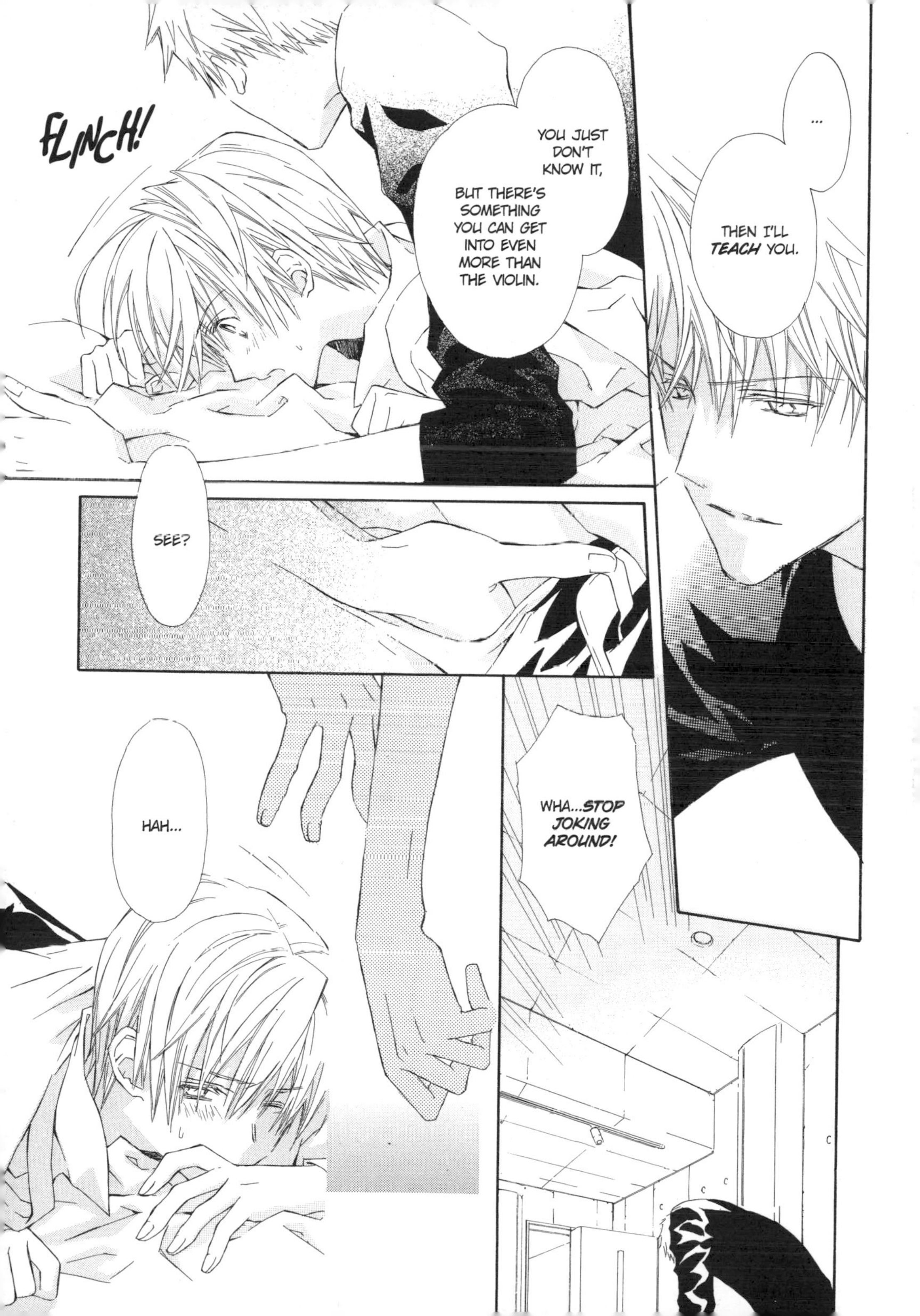
...
THEN I'LL TEACH YOU.
YOU JUST DON'T KNOW IT, BUT THERE'S SOMETHING YOU CAN GET INTO EVEN MORE THAN THE VIOLIN.
FLINCH!
SEE?
WHA...STOP JOKING AROUND!
HAH...

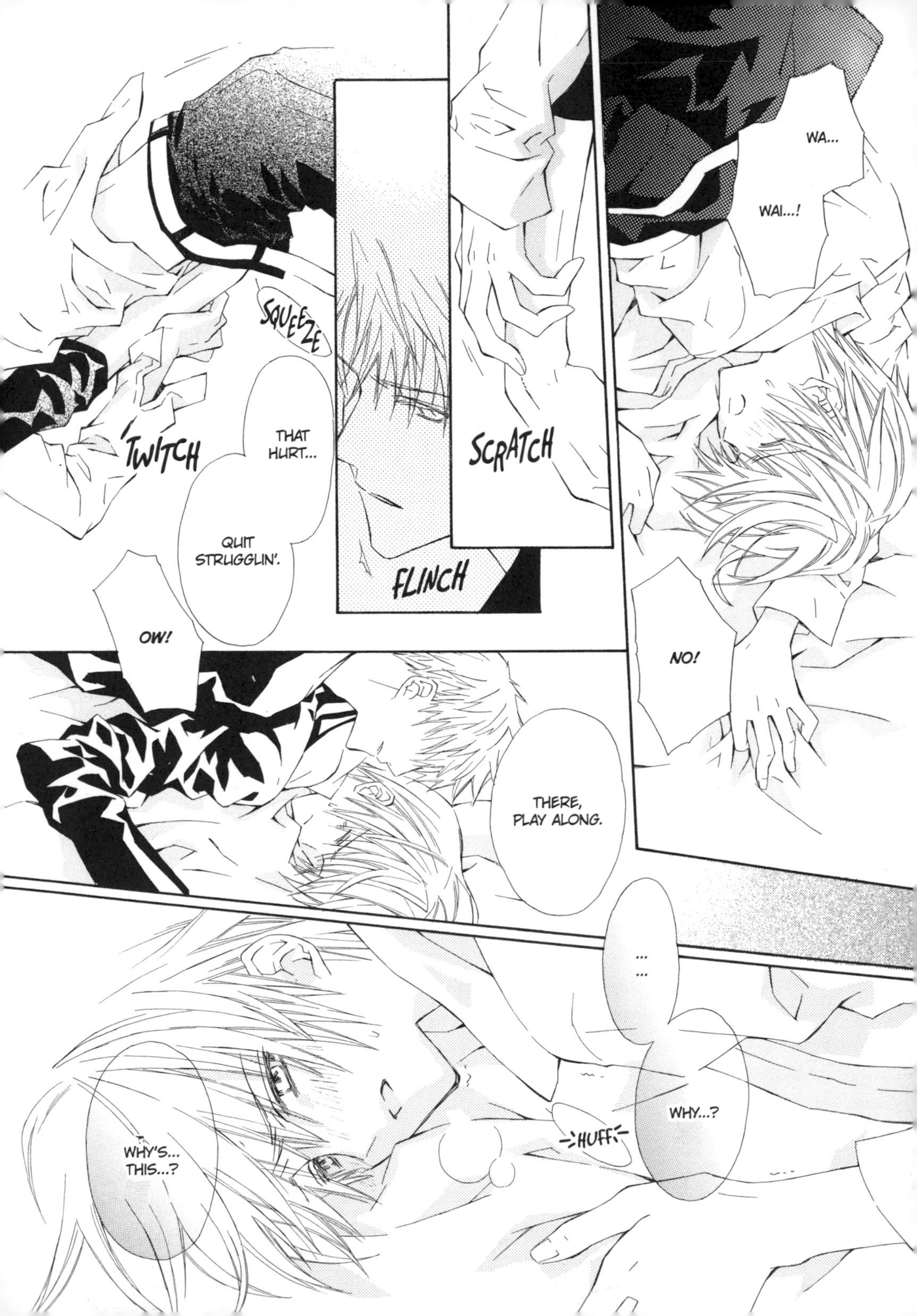
WA...
WAI...!
NO!
SCRATCH
FLINCH
SQUEEZE
THAT HURT...
TWITCH
QUIT STRUGGLIN'.
OW!
THERE, PLAY ALONG.
...
...
WHY...?
HUFF
WHY'S... THIS...?

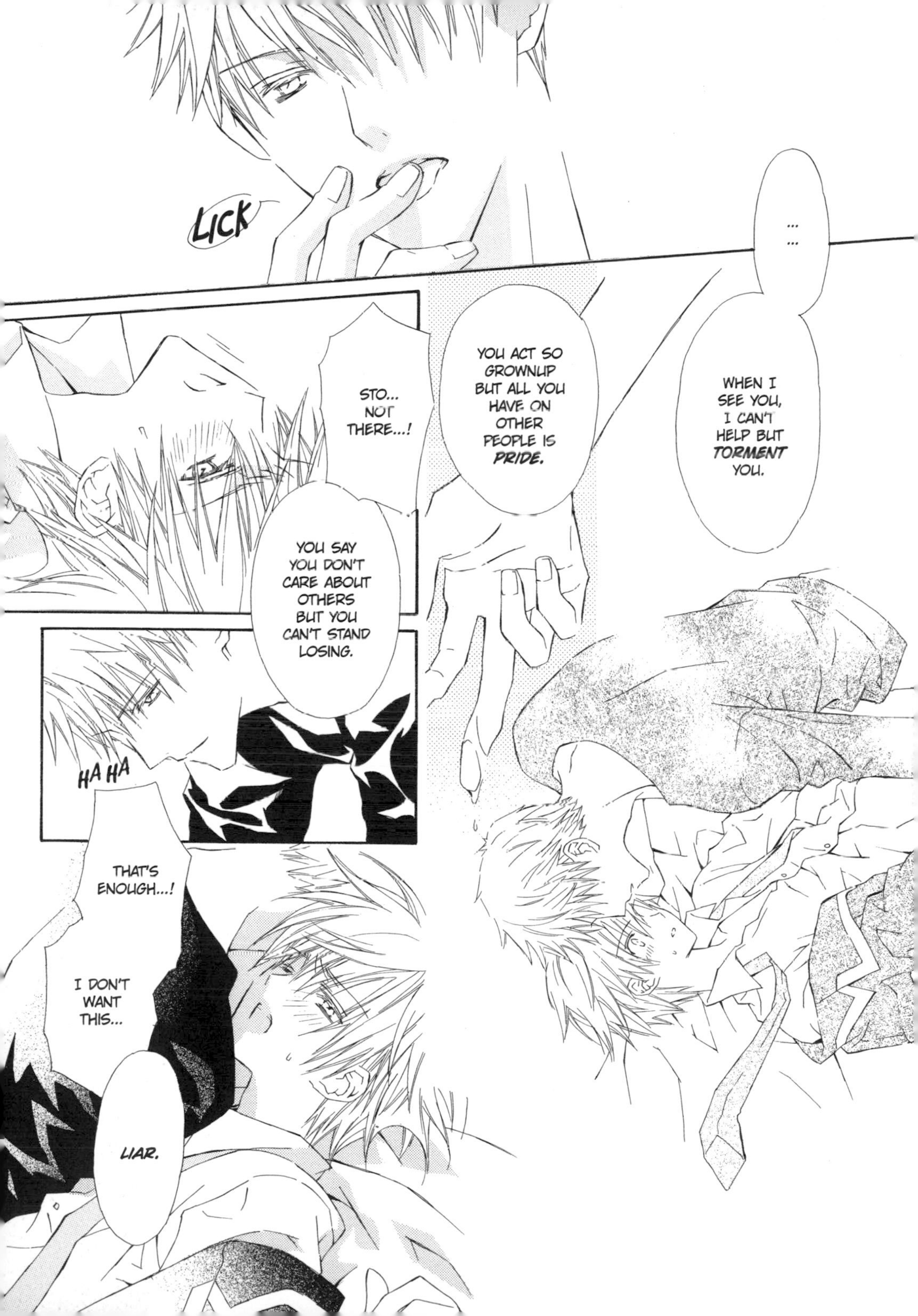
... ...
LICK
WHEN I SEE YOU, I CAN'T HELP BUT TORMENT YOU.
YOU ACT SO GROWNUP BUT ALL YOU HAVE ON OTHER PEOPLE IS PRIDE.
YOU SAY YOU DON'T CARE ABOUT OTHERS BUT YOU CAN'T STAND LOSING.
STO... NOT THERE...!
HA HA
THAT'S ENOUGH...!
I DON'T WANT THIS...
LIAR.

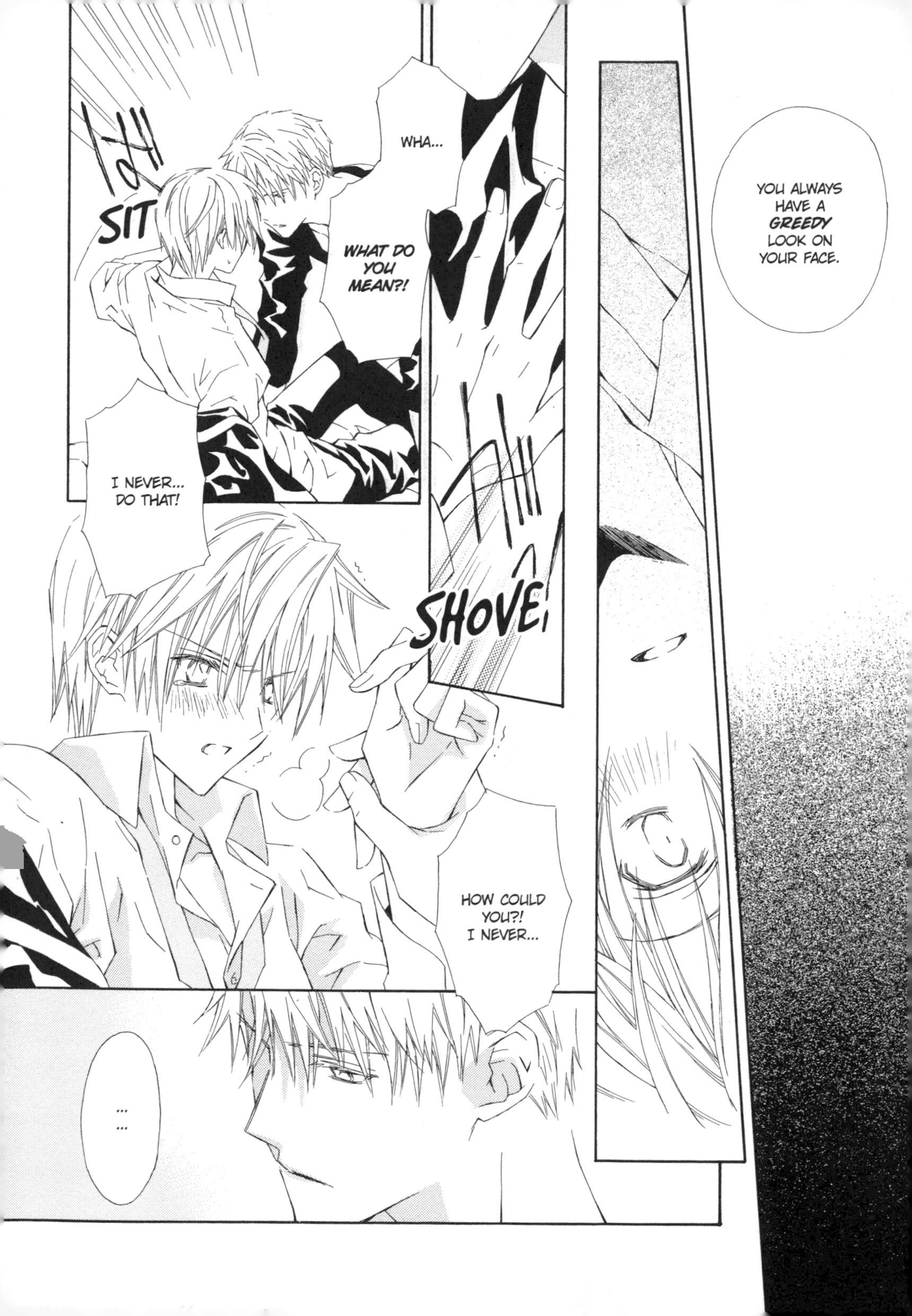
YOU ALWAYS HAVE A GREEDY LOOK ON YOUR FACE.
SHOVE
WHA...
WHAT DO YOU MEAN?!
SIT
I NEVER... DO THAT!
HOW COULD YOU?! I NEVER...
......

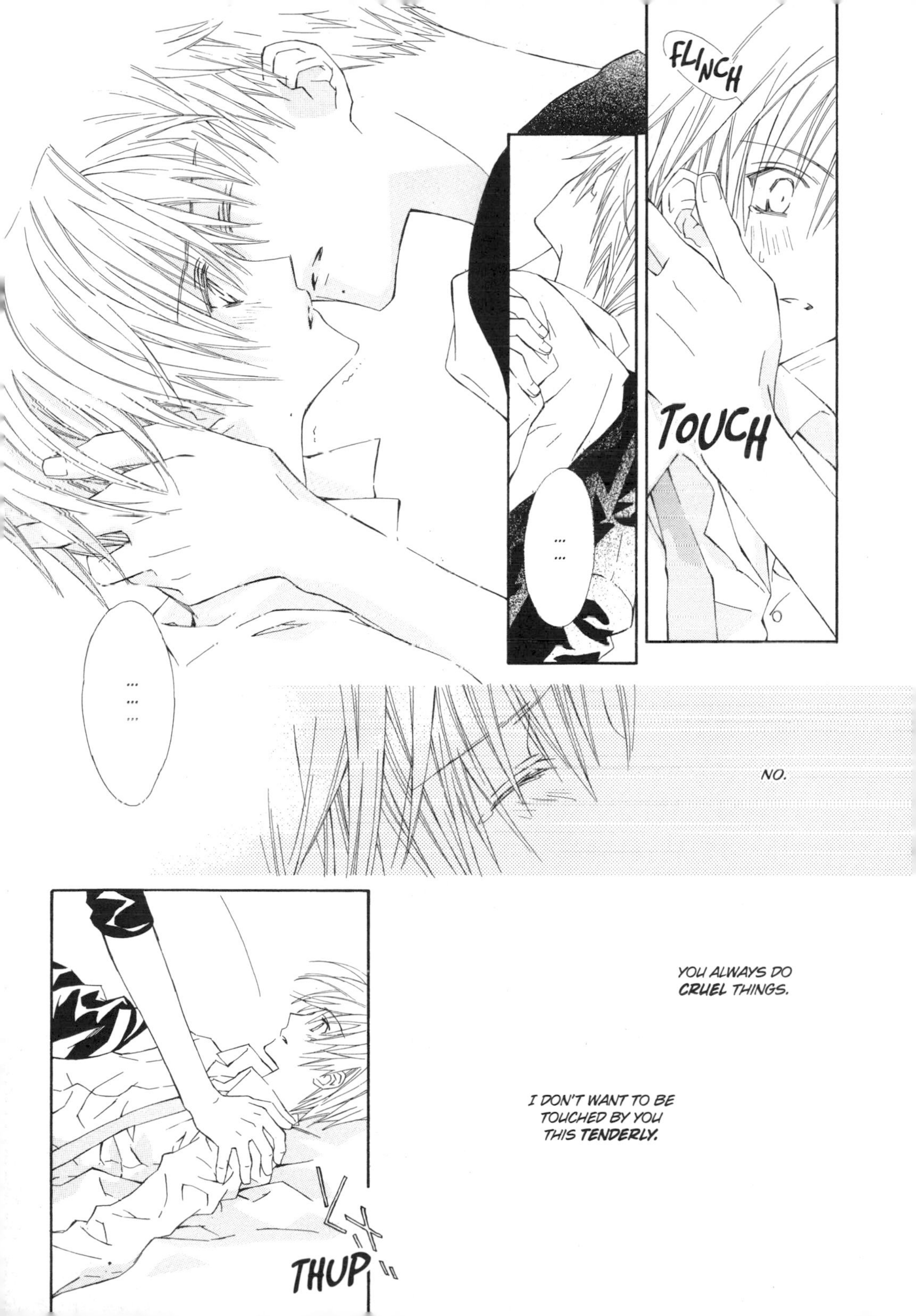
FLINCH
TOUCH
……
………
NO.
YOU ALWAYS DO CRUEL THINGS.
I DON'T WANT TO BE TOUCHED BY YOU THIS TENDERLY.
THUP

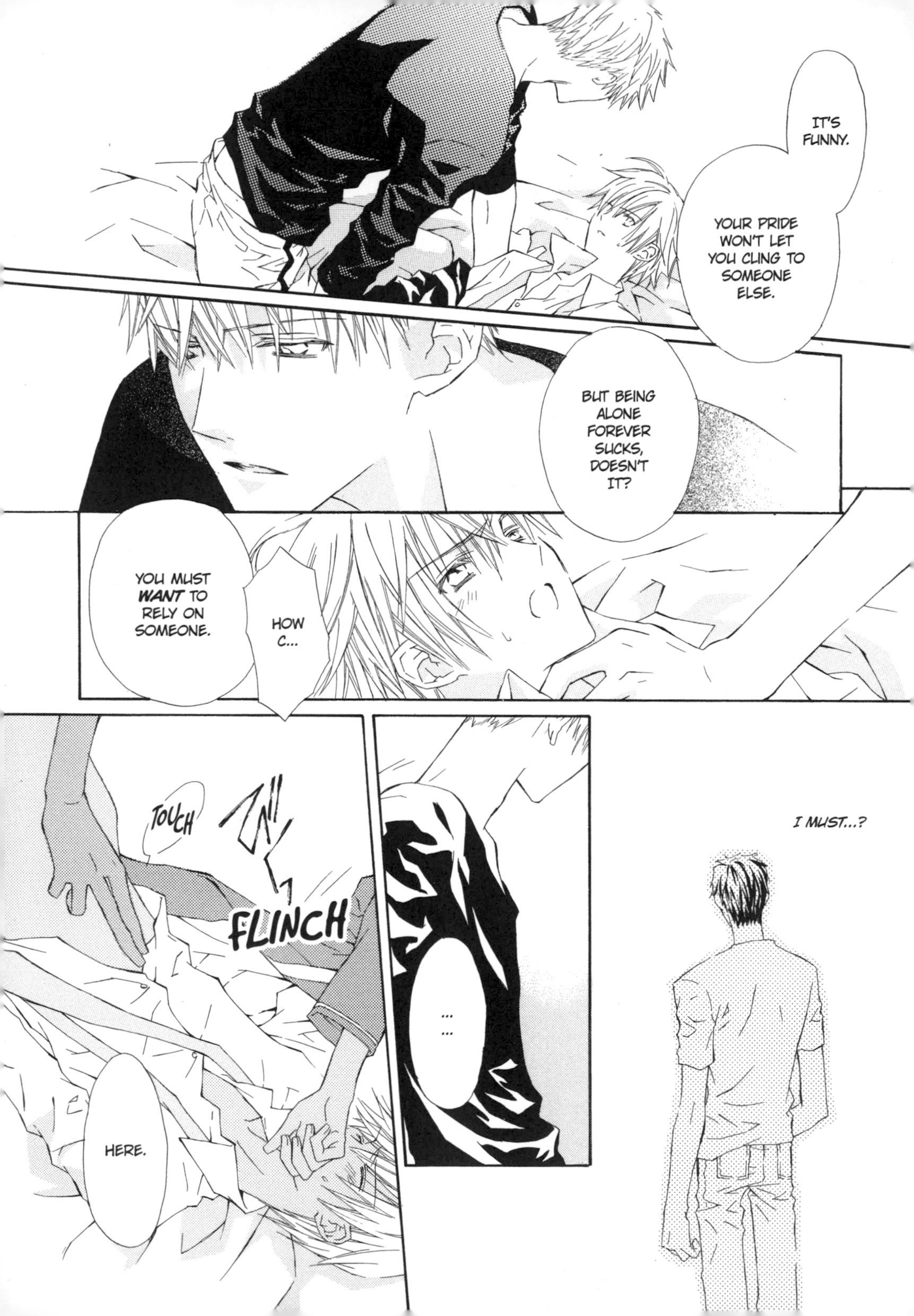
IT'S FUNNY.
YOUR PRIDE WON'T LET YOU CLING TO SOMEONE ELSE.
BUT BEING ALONE FOREVER SUCKS, DOESN'T IT?
YOU MUST *WANT* TO RELY ON SOMEONE.
HOW C...
I MUST...?
... ...
TOUCH
FLINCH
HERE.

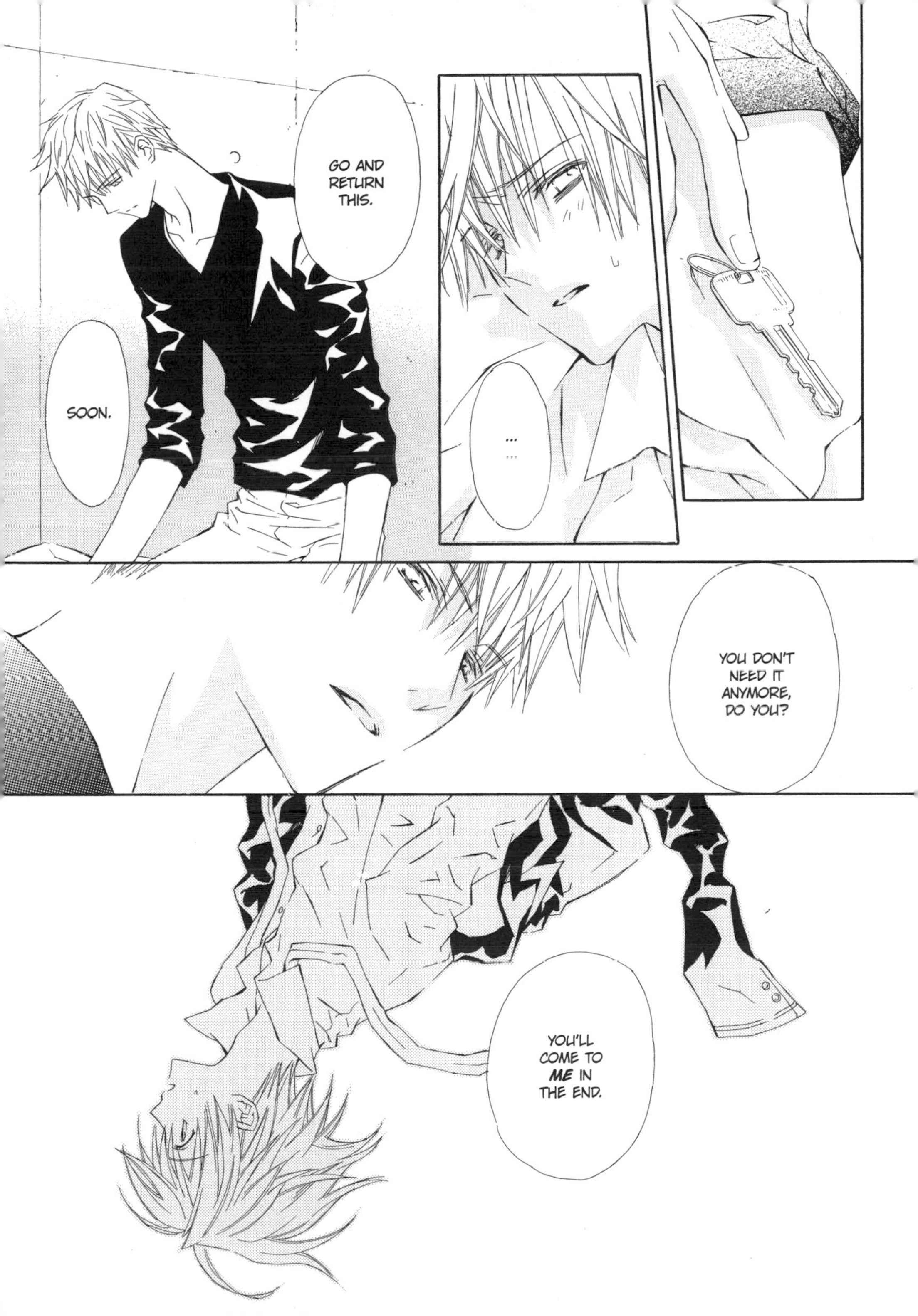
... ...
GO AND RETURN THIS.
SOON.
YOU DON'T NEED IT ANYMORE, DO YOU?
YOU'LL COME TO *ME* IN THE END.

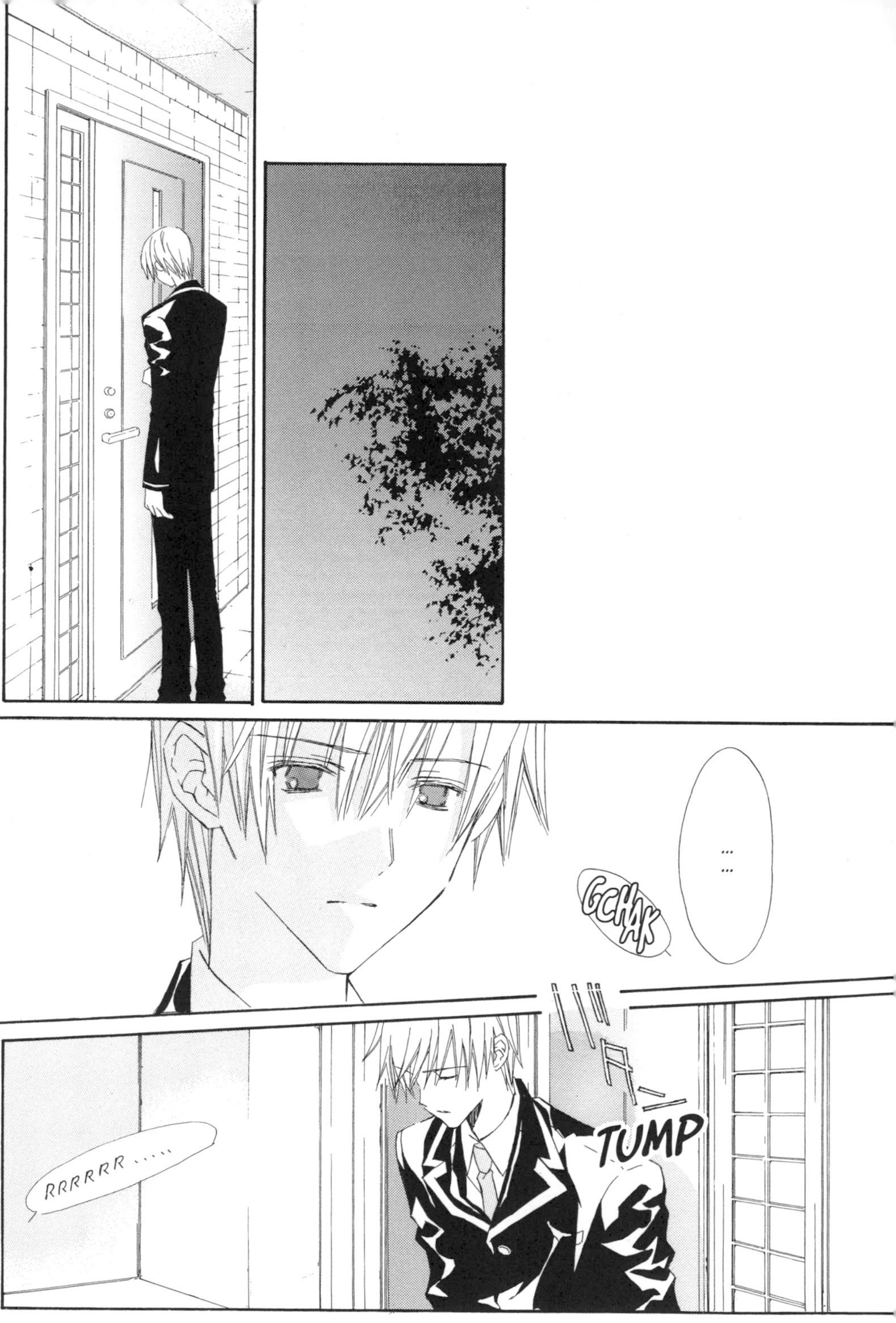
……
GCHAK
TUMP
RRRRRR……

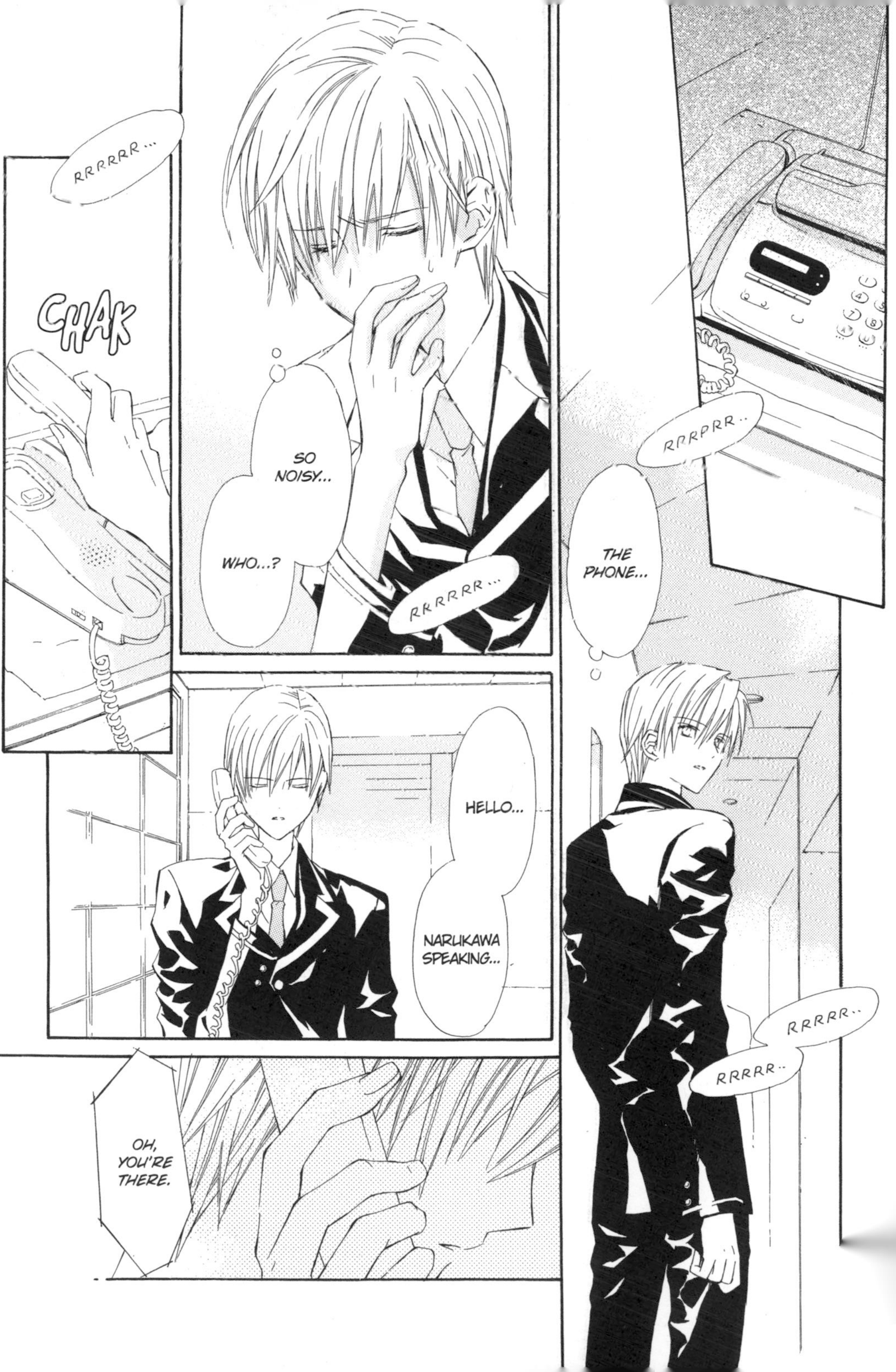

RRRPRR..
THE PHONE...
RRRRR..
RRRRR..
SO NOISY...
WHO...?
RRRRRR...
RRRRRR...
CHAK
HELLO...
NARUKAWA SPEAKING...
OH, YOU'RE THERE.

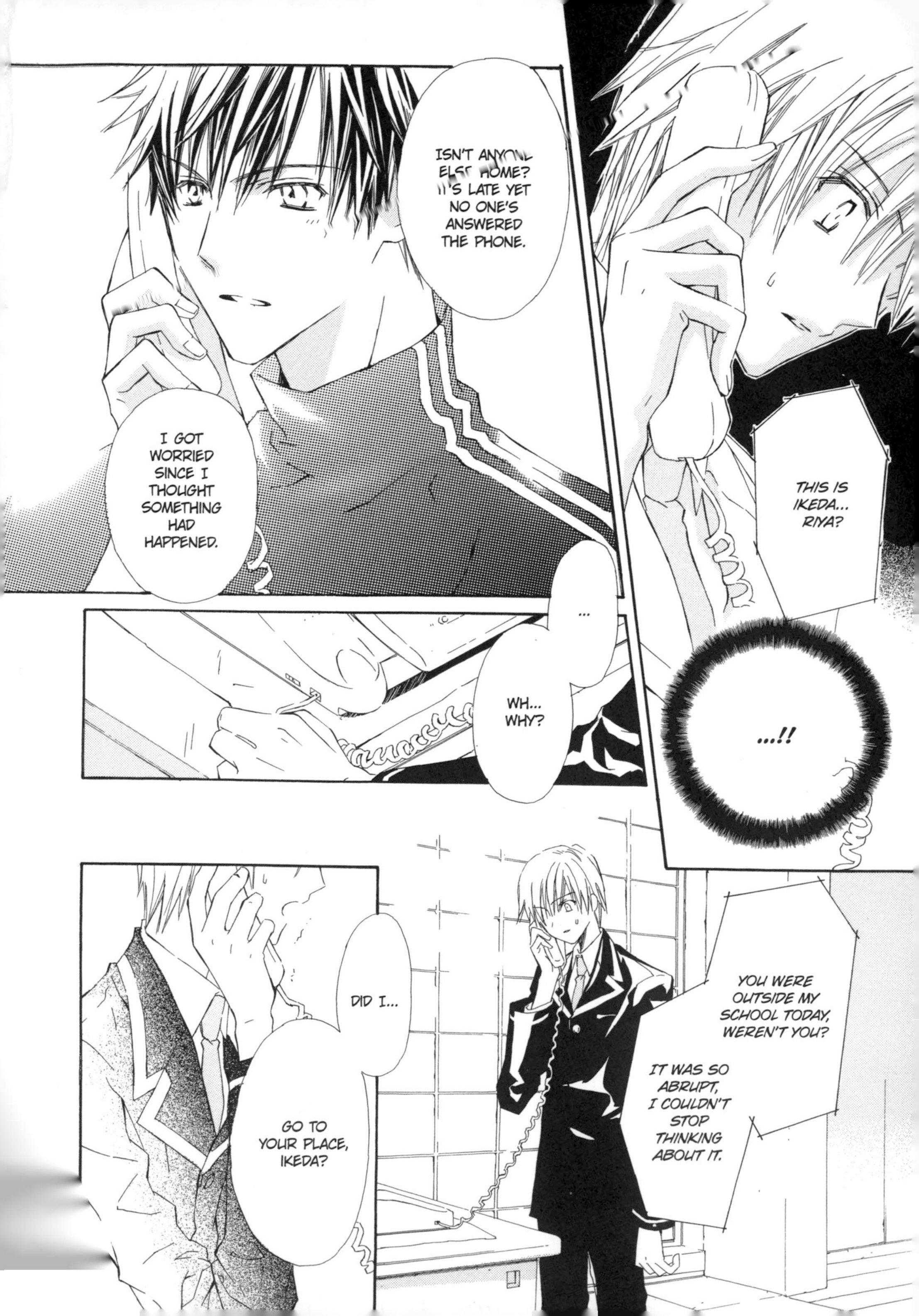
THIS IS IKEDA... RIYA?
...!!
ISN'T ANYONE ELSE HOME? IT'S LATE YET NO ONE'S ANSWERED THE PHONE.
I GOT WORRIED SINCE I THOUGHT SOMETHING HAD HAPPENED.
...
WH... WHY?
YOU WERE OUTSIDE MY SCHOOL TODAY, WEREN'T YOU?
IT WAS SO ABRUPT, I COULDN'T STOP THINKING ABOUT IT.
DID I...
GO TO YOUR PLACE, IKEDA?

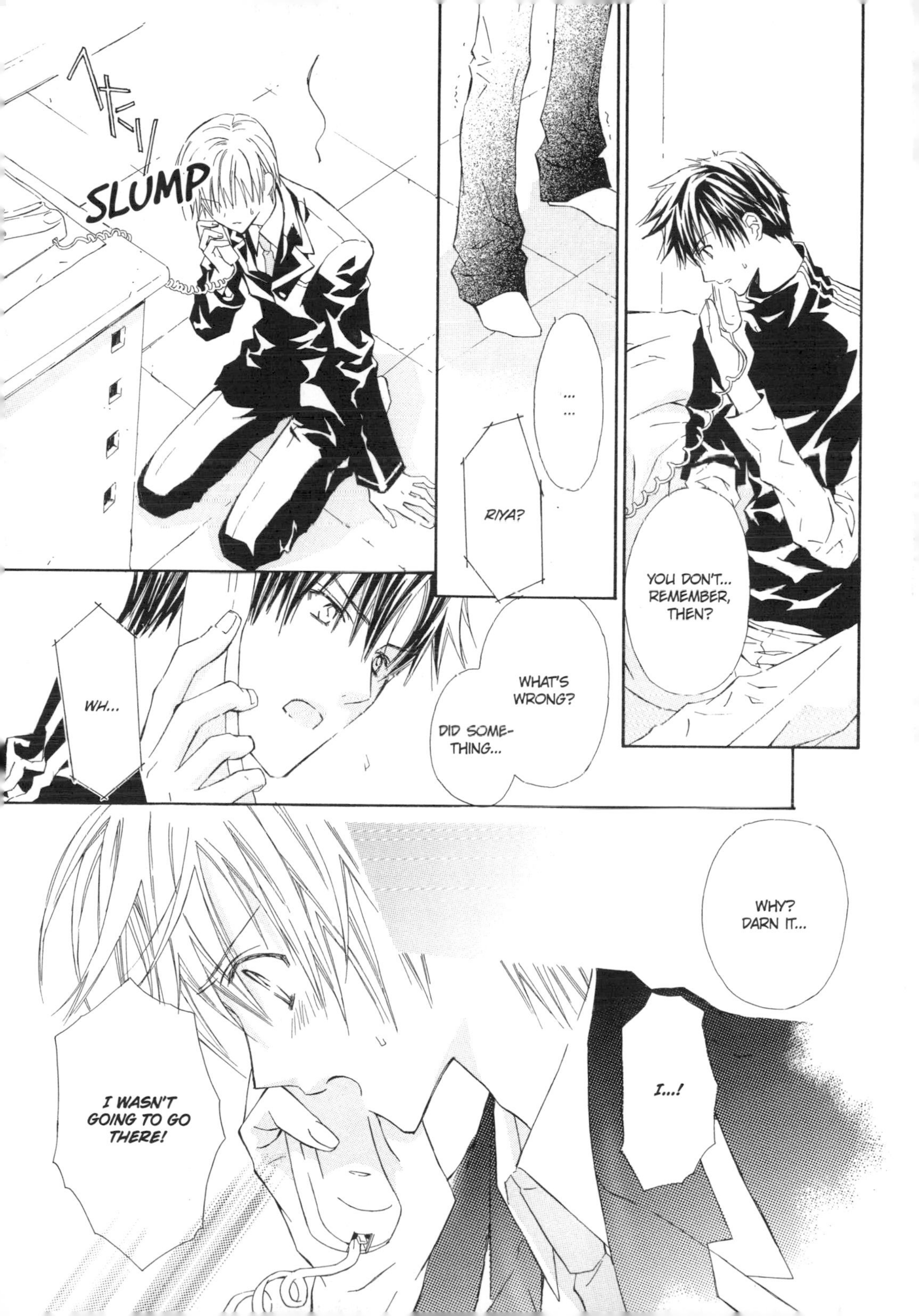

YOU DON'T... REMEMBER, THEN?
... ...
RIYA?
SLUMP
WHAT'S WRONG?
DID SOME-THING...
WH...
WHY? DARN IT...
I...!
I WASN'T GOING TO GO THERE!

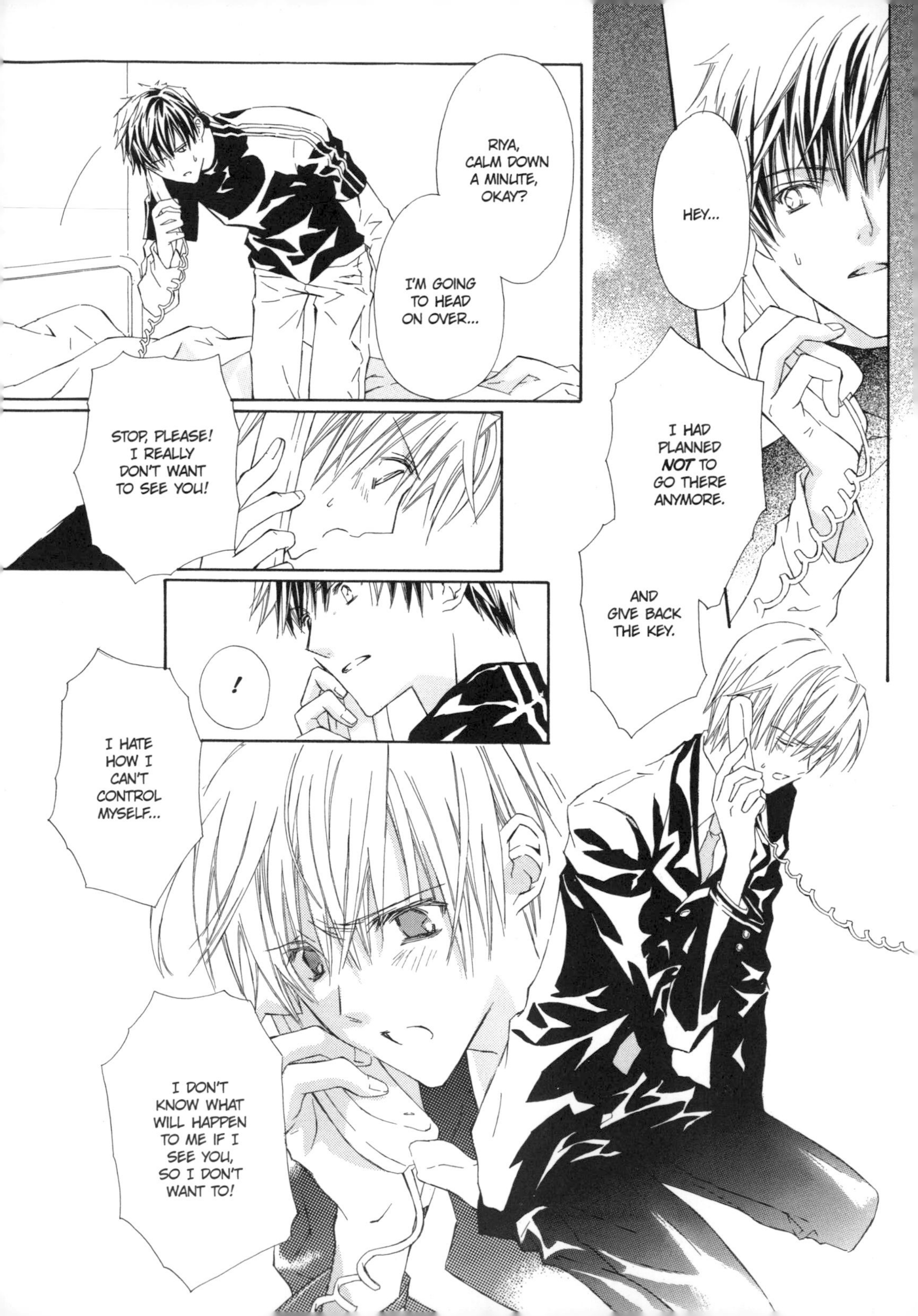
HEY...
I HAD PLANNED NOT TO GO THERE ANYMORE.
AND GIVE BACK THE KEY.
RIYA, CALM DOWN A MINUTE, OKAY?
I'M GOING TO HEAD ON OVER...
STOP, PLEASE! I REALLY DON'T WANT TO SEE YOU!
!
I HATE HOW I CAN'T CONTROL MYSELF...
I DON'T KNOW WHAT WILL HAPPEN TO ME IF I SEE YOU, SO I DON'T WANT TO!

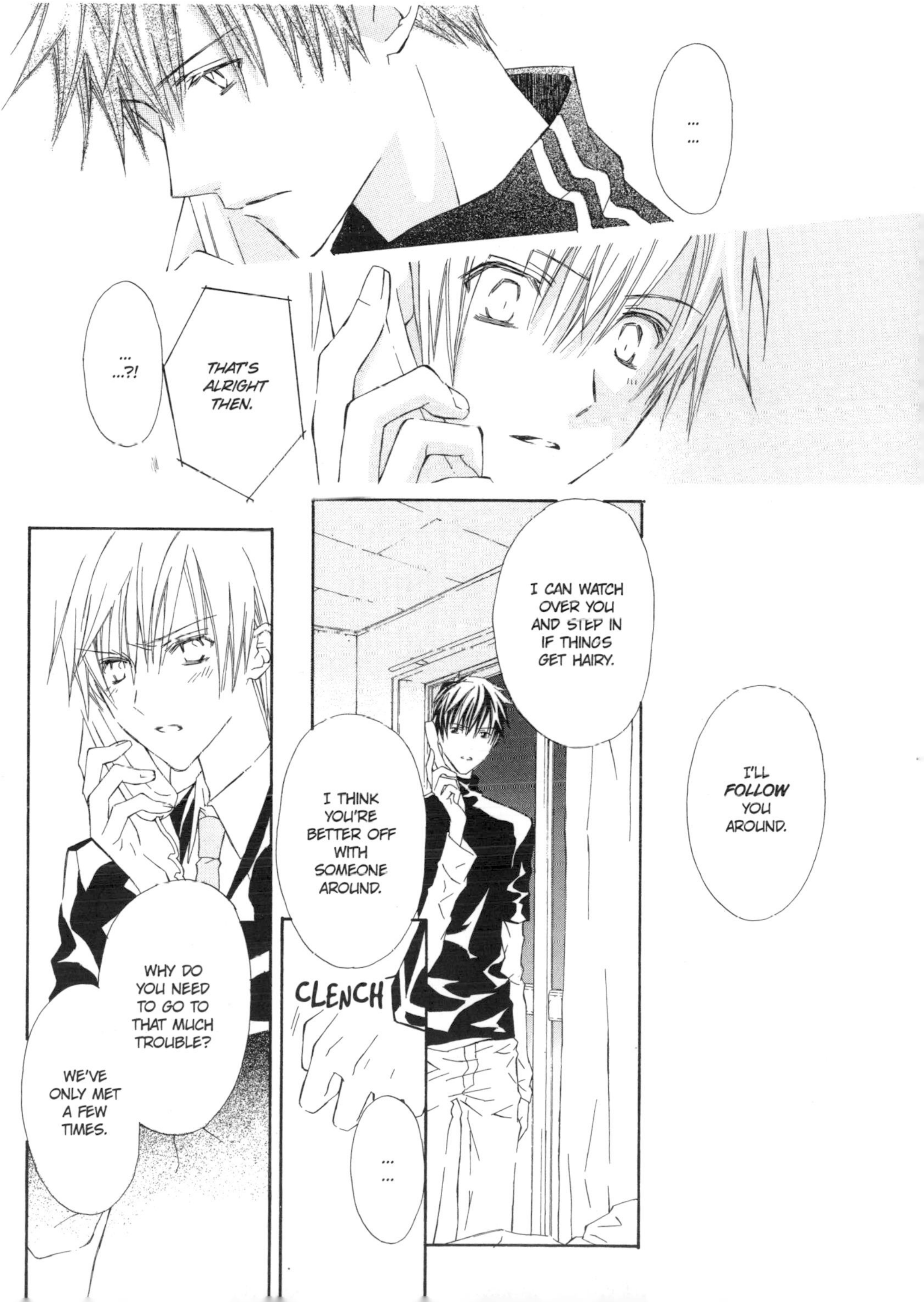
... ...
THAT'S ALRIGHT THEN.
... ...?!
I'LL *FOLLOW* YOU AROUND.
I CAN WATCH OVER YOU AND STEP IN IF THINGS GET HAIRY.
I THINK YOU'RE BETTER OFF WITH SOMEONE AROUND.
CLENCH
... ...
WHY DO YOU NEED TO GO TO THAT MUCH TROUBLE?
WE'VE ONLY MET A FEW TIMES.

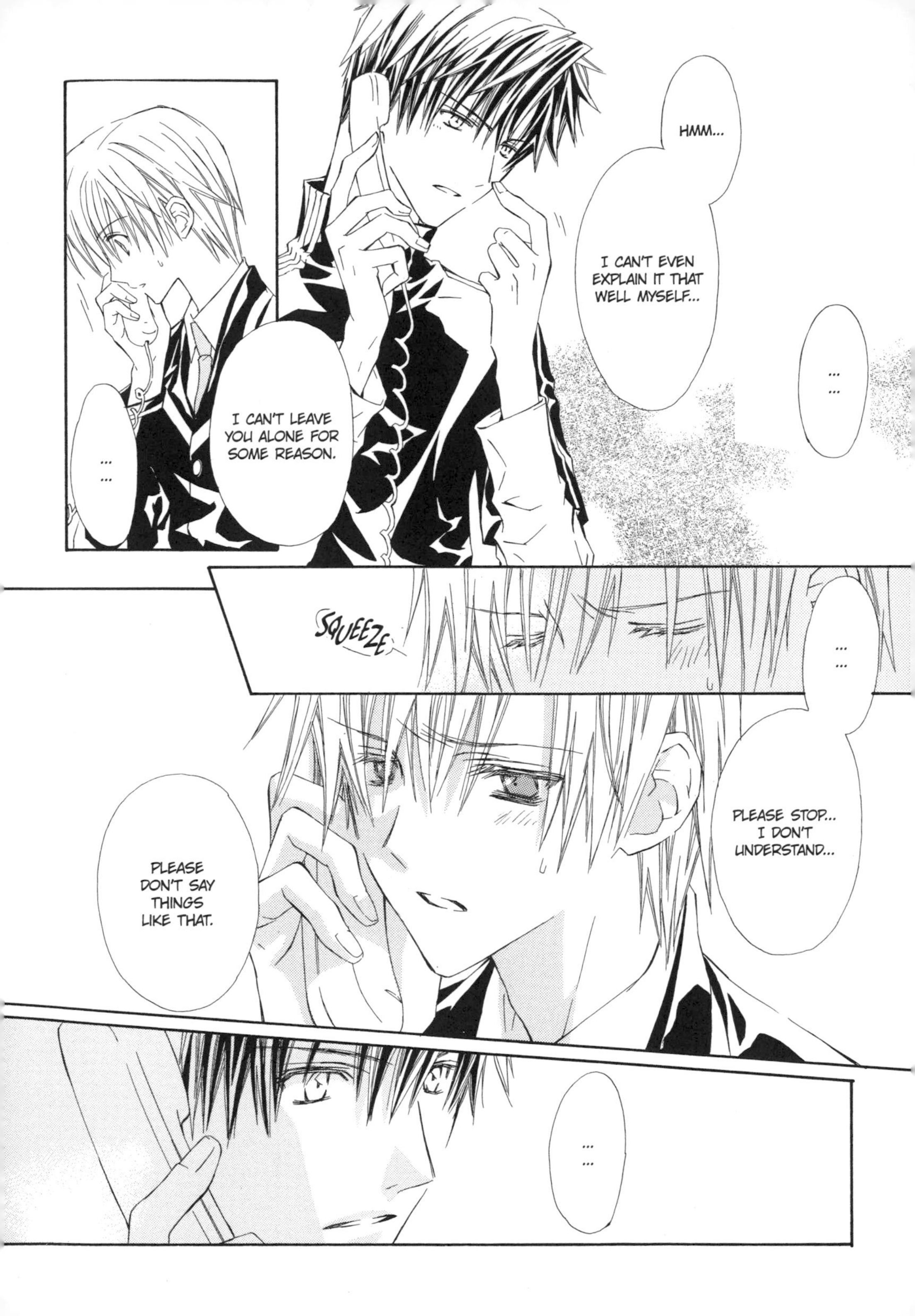

HMM...
I CAN'T EVEN EXPLAIN IT THAT WELL MYSELF...
... ...
I CAN'T LEAVE YOU ALONE FOR SOME REASON.
... ...
... ...
SQUEEZE
PLEASE STOP... I DON'T UNDERSTAND...
PLEASE DON'T SAY THINGS LIKE THAT.
... ...

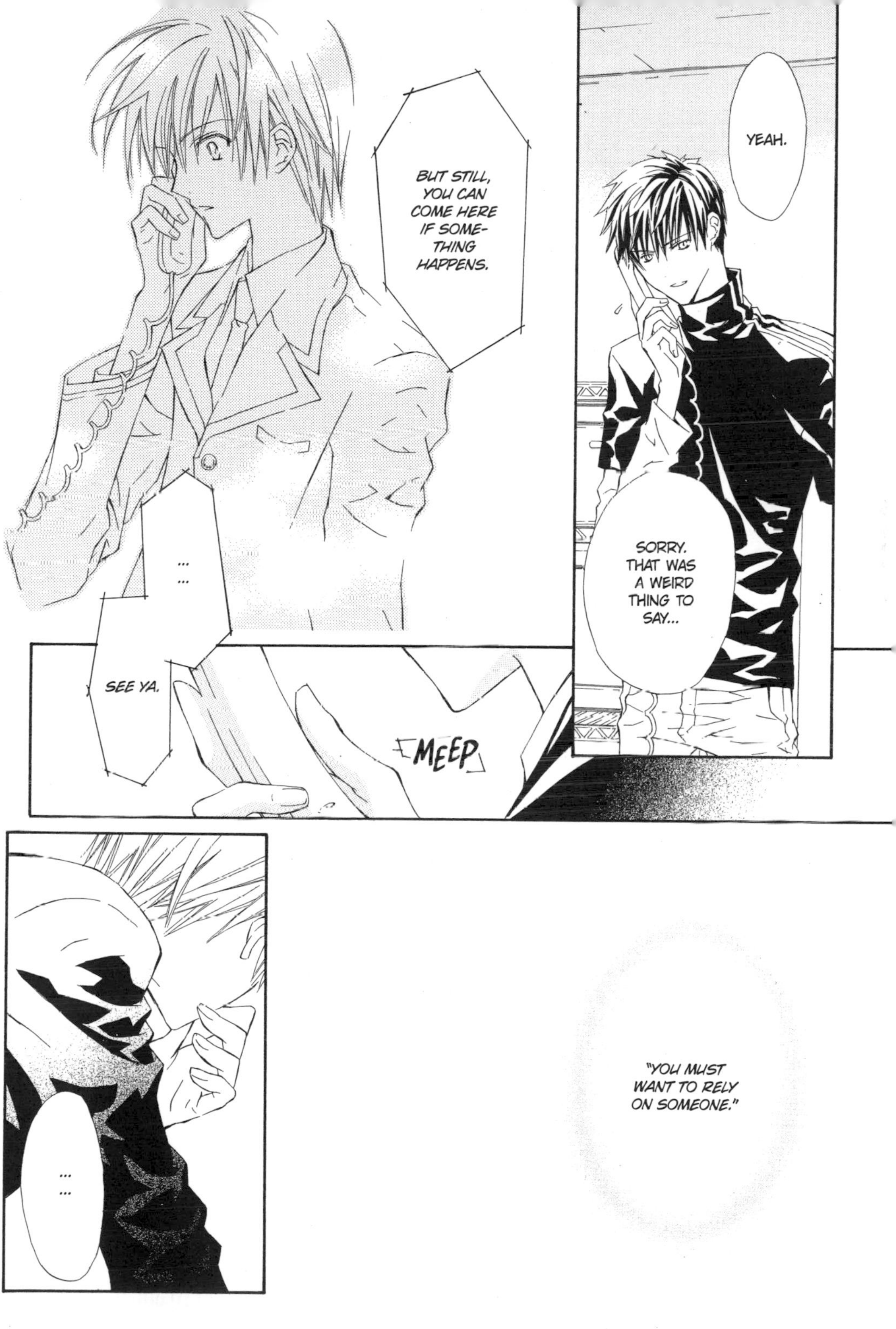
YEAH.
SORRY. THAT WAS A WEIRD THING TO SAY...
BUT STILL, YOU CAN COME HERE IF SOME-THING HAPPENS.
... ...
SEE YA.
MEEP
"YOU MUST WANT TO RELY ON SOMEONE."
... ...

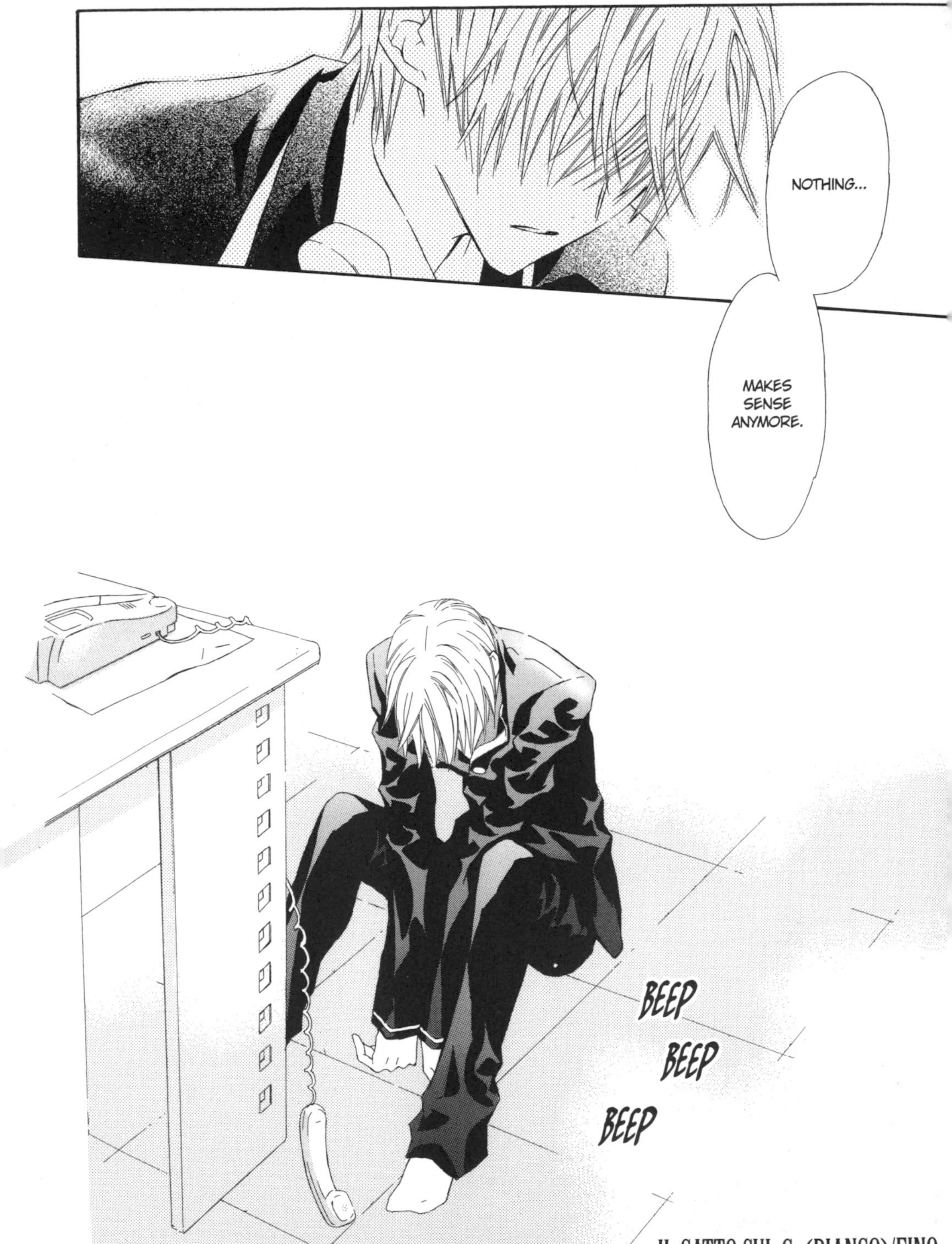
NOTHING...
MAKES SENSE ANYMORE.
BEEP
BEEP
BEEP

IL GATTO SUL G. (BIANCO)/FINO

G線上の猫

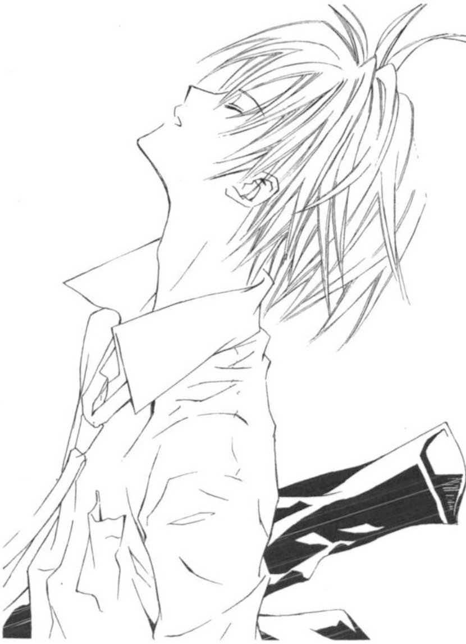

THE ATTRACTED PAIR.

"YOU CAN COME BY WHEN YOU WANT TO."

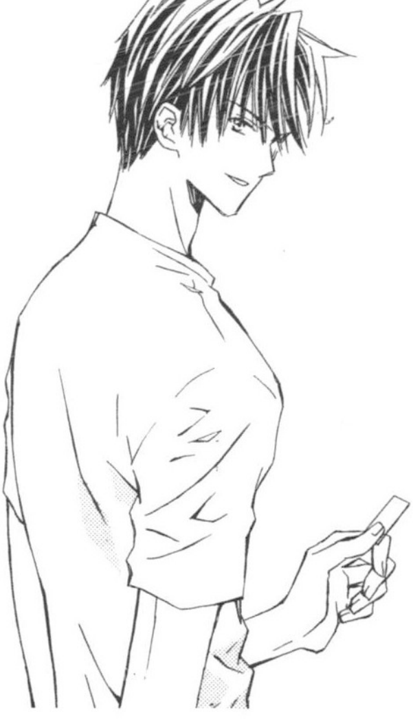

AND THE COLLIDING PAIR.

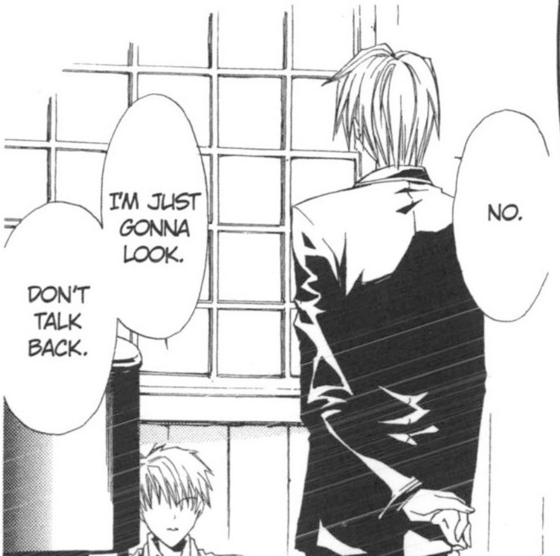
NO.
I'M JUST GONNA LOOK.
DON'T TALK BACK.

TO BE CONTINUED IN VOLUME 2

IL GATTO SUL G.

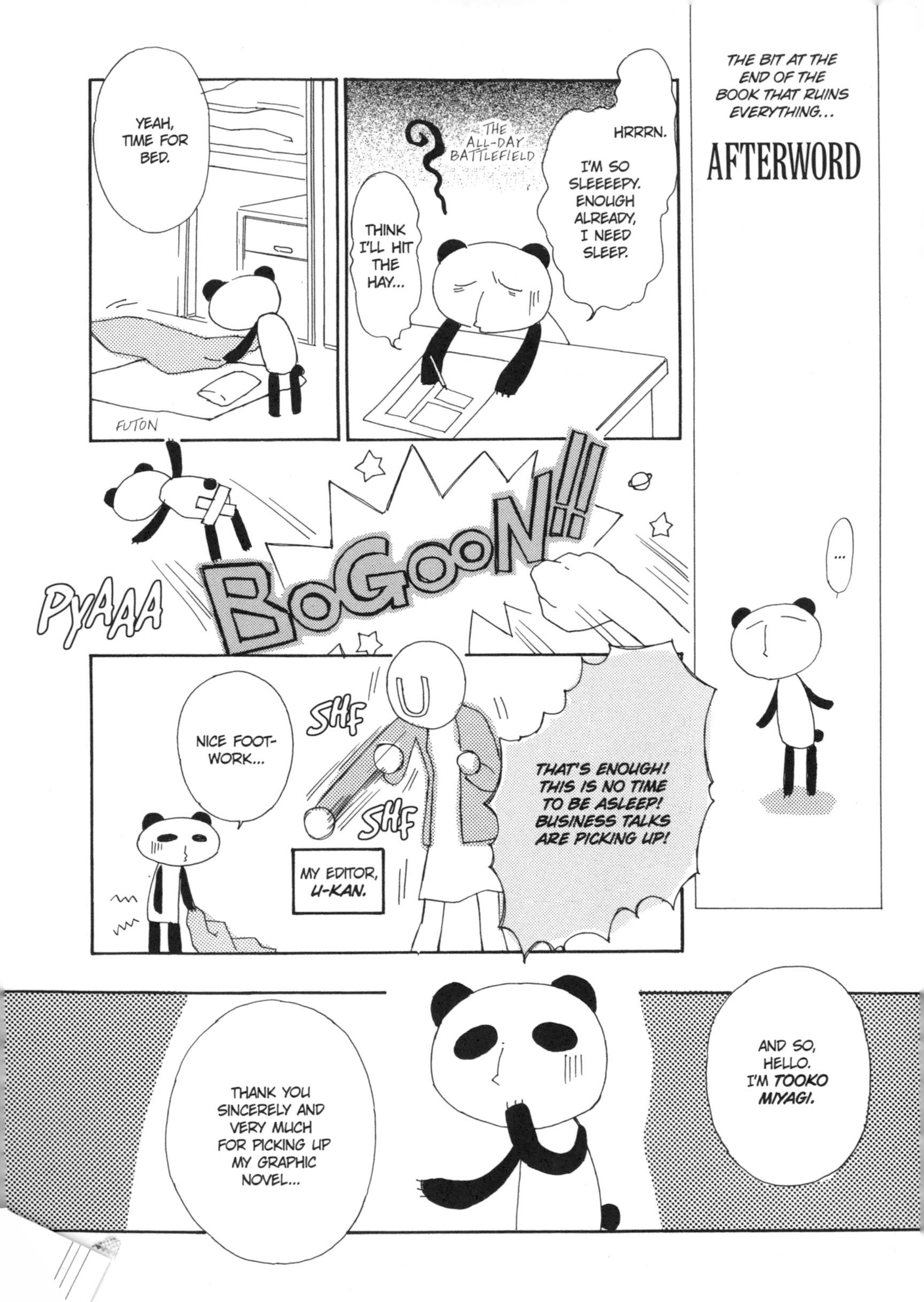
THE BIT AT THE END OF THE BOOK THAT RUINS EVERYTHING...
AFTERWORD
...
HRRRN.
I'M SO SLEEEEPY. ENOUGH ALREADY, I NEED SLEEP.
THE ALL-DAY BATTLEFIELD
THINK I'LL HIT THE HAY...
YEAH, TIME FOR BED.
FUTON
BOGOON!!!
PYAAA
THAT'S ENOUGH! THIS IS NO TIME TO BE ASLEEP! BUSINESS TALKS ARE PICKING UP!
SHF
SHF
MY EDITOR, U-KAN.
NICE FOOT-WORK...
AND SO, HELLO. I'M TOOKO MIYAGI.
THANK YOU SINCERELY AND VERY MUCH FOR PICKING UP MY GRAPHIC NOVEL...

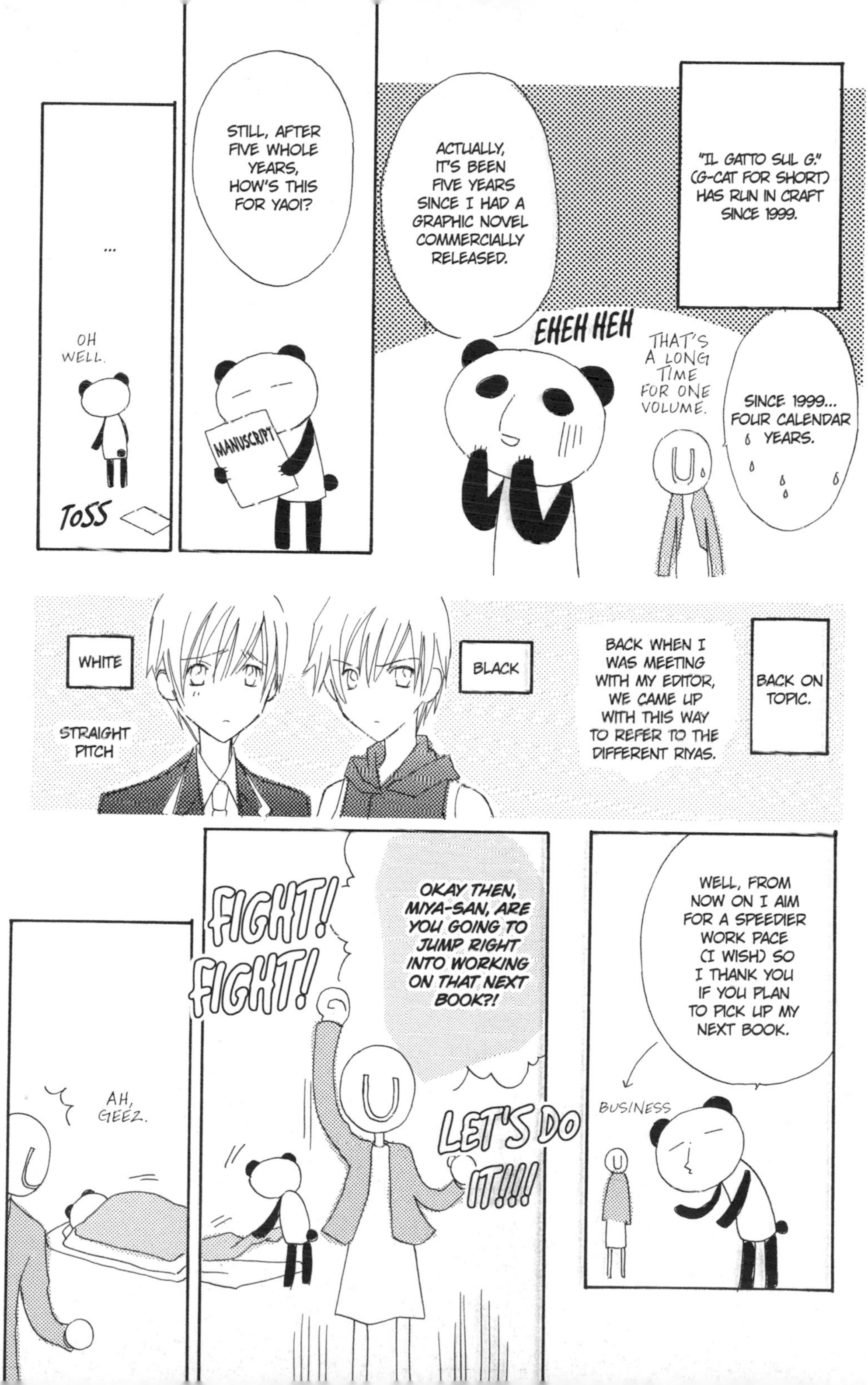
"IL GATTO SUL G." (G-CAT FOR SHORT) HAS RUN IN CRAFT SINCE 1999.
ACTUALLY, IT'S BEEN FIVE YEARS SINCE I HAD A GRAPHIC NOVEL COMMERCIALLY RELEASED.
EHEH HEH
SINCE 1999... FOUR CALENDAR YEARS.
THAT'S A LONG TIME FOR ONE VOLUME.
STILL, AFTER FIVE WHOLE YEARS, HOW'S THIS FOR YAOI?
MANUSCRIPT
...
OH WELL.
TOSS
BACK ON TOPIC.
BACK WHEN I WAS MEETING WITH MY EDITOR, WE CAME UP WITH THIS WAY TO REFER TO THE DIFFERENT RIYAS.
BLACK
WHITE
STRAIGHT PITCH
WELL, FROM NOW ON I AIM FOR A SPEEDIER WORK PACE (I WISH) SO I THANK YOU IF YOU PLAN TO PICK UP MY NEXT BOOK.
BUSINESS
OKAY THEN, MIYA-SAN, ARE YOU GOING TO JUMP RIGHT INTO WORKING ON THAT NEXT BOOK?!
FIGHT! FIGHT!
LET'S DO IT!!!
AH, GEEZ.

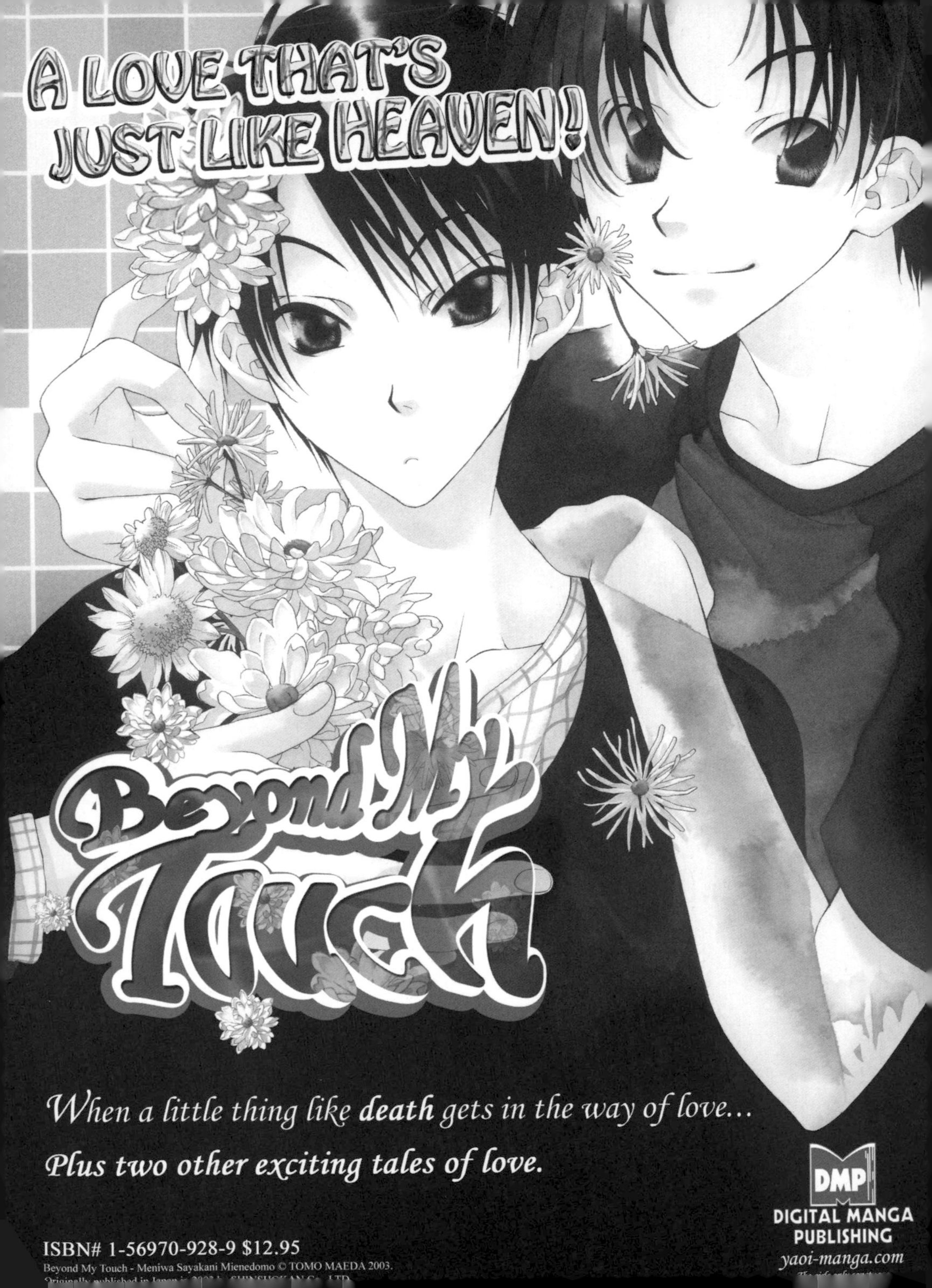
A LOVE THAT'S JUST LIKE HEAVEN!
Beyond My Touch
When a little thing like death gets in the way of love...
Plus two other exciting tales of love.
DMP
DIGITAL MANGA PUBLISHING
yaoi-manga.com
ISBN# 1-56970-928-9 $12.95
Beyond My Touch - Meniwa Sayakani Mienedomo © TOMO MAEDA 2003.

ALMOST CRYING

by Mako Takahashi

Please adopt me...

**Abandoned in a park as a child, Aoi finds a new home with Gaku.
Growing up brings new emotions, new love, and new jealousies.**

DMP

DIGITAL MANGA
PUBLISHING

yaoi-manga.com
The girls only sanctuary

ISBN# 1-56970-909-2 $12.95

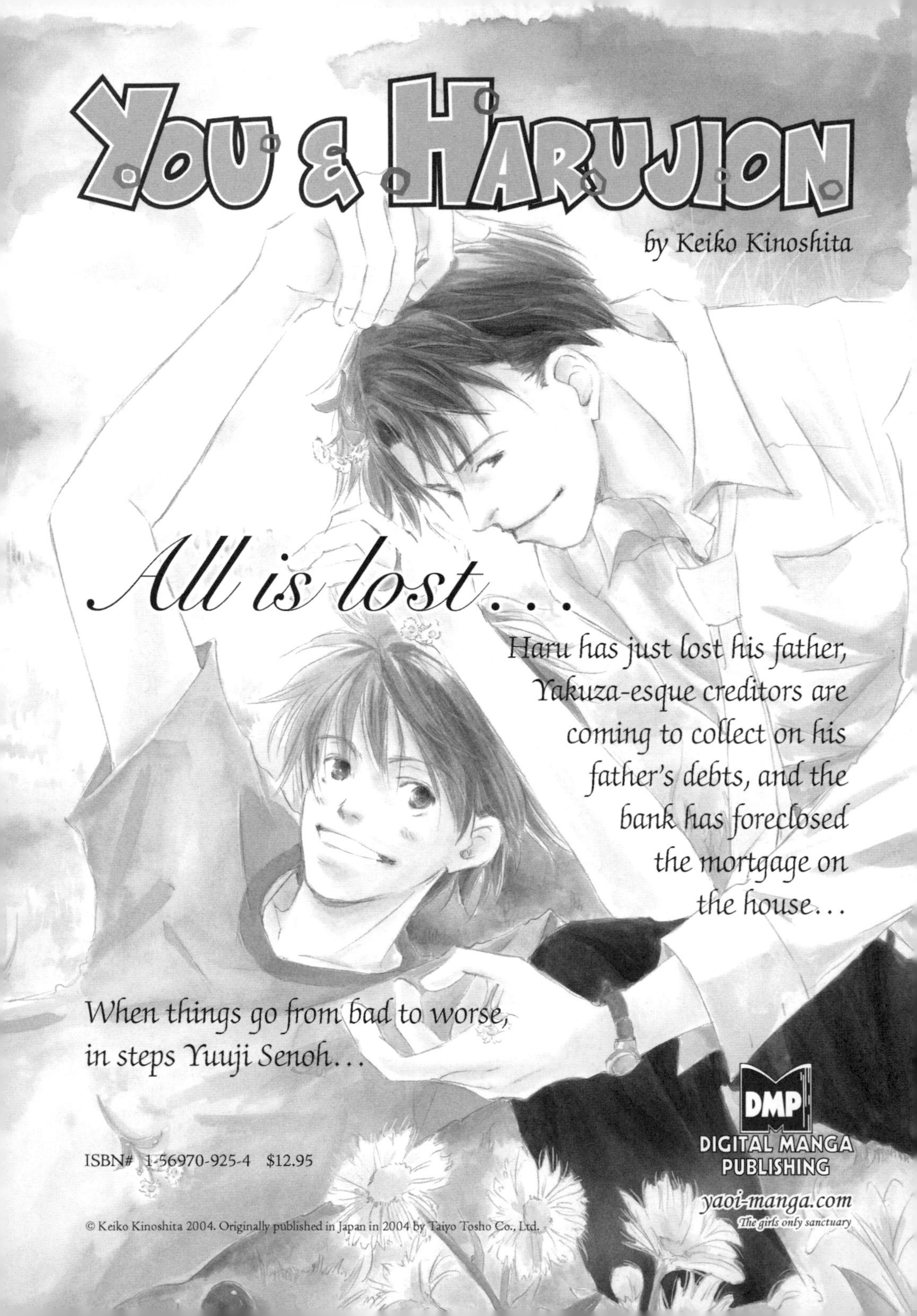
YOU & HARUJION
by Keiko Kinoshita
All is lost . . .
Haru has just lost his father, Yakuza-esque creditors are coming to collect on his father's debts, and the bank has foreclosed the mortgage on the house…
When things go from bad to worse, in steps Yuuji Senoh…
DMP
DIGITAL MANGA PUBLISHING
ISBN# 1-56970-925-4 $12.95
yaoi-manga.com
The girls only sanctuary
© Keiko Kinoshita 2004. Originally published in Japan in 2004 by Taiyo Tosho Co., Ltd.

LOST BOYS

*"Will you be
our father?"*

by Kaname Itsuki

A boy named "Air" appears at Mizuki's window
one night and transports him to Neverland.

ISBN# 1-56970-924-6 $12.95

© Kaname Itsuki 2004. Originally published in Japan in 2004 by Taiyo Tosho Co., Ltd.

DMP
DIGITAL MANGA
PUBLISHING

yaoi-manga.com
The girls only sanctuary

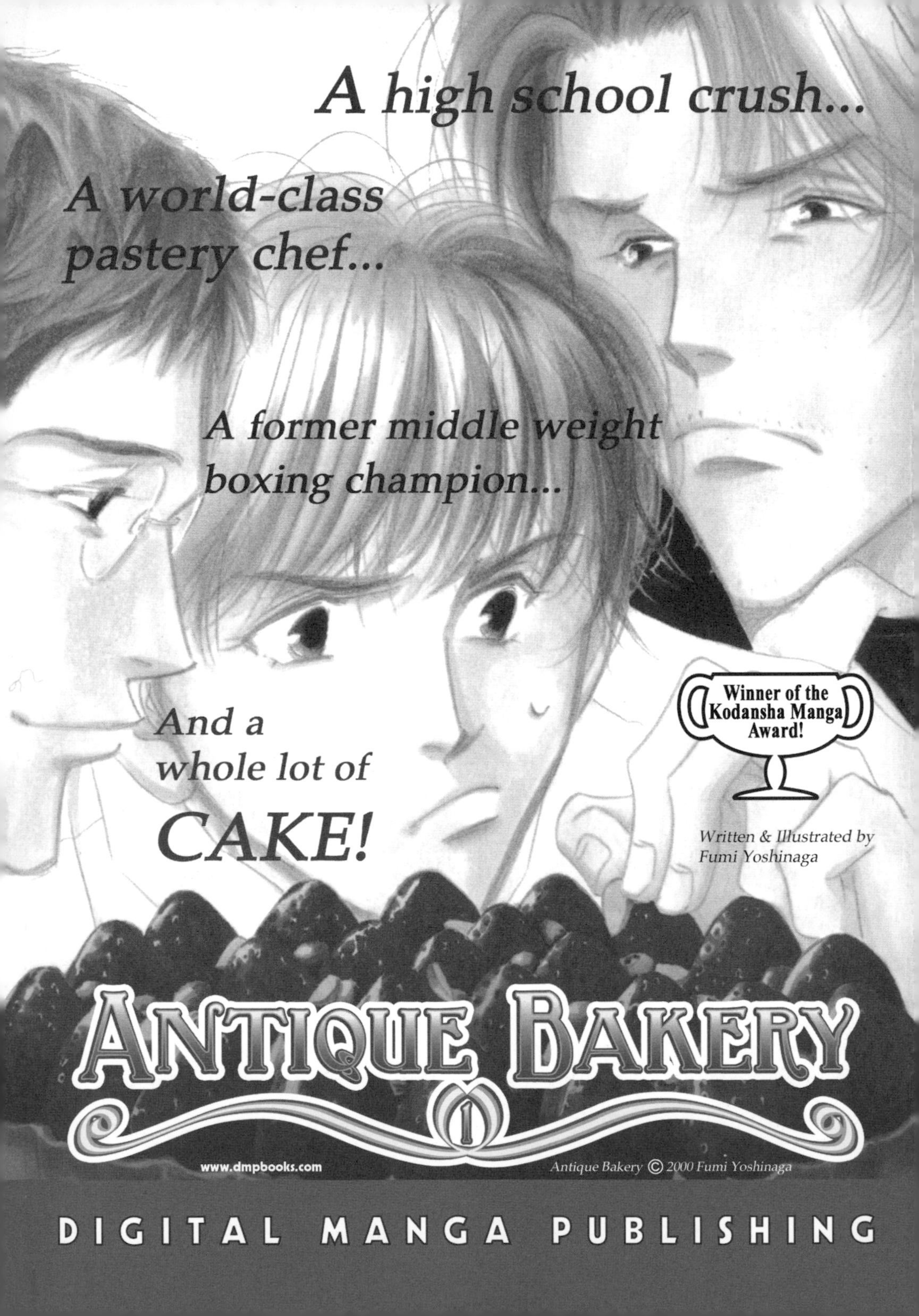

A high school crush...

A world-class
pastery chef...

A former middle weight
boxing champion...

Winner of the
Kodansha Manga
Award!

And a
whole lot of
CAKE!

Written & Illustrated by
Fumi Yoshinaga

ANTIQUE BAKERY

www.dmpbooks.com

DIGITAL MANGA PUBLISHING

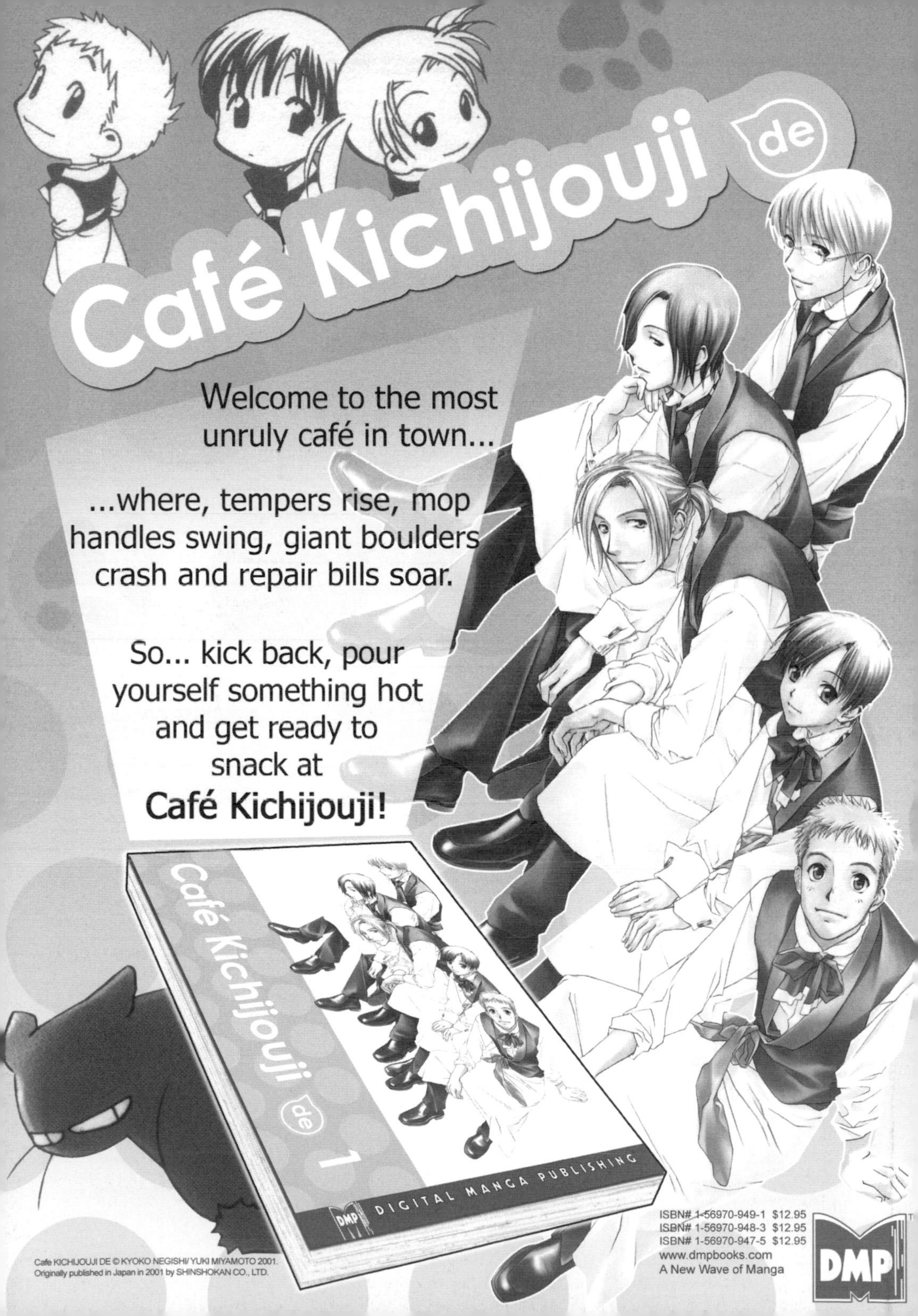
Café Kichijouji de
Welcome to the most unruly café in town...
...where, tempers rise, mop handles swing, giant boulders crash and repair bills soar.
So... kick back, pour yourself something hot and get ready to snack at
Café Kichijouji!
Café Kichijouji de 1
DIGITAL MANGA PUBLISHING
DMP
ISBN# 1-56970-949-1 $12.95
ISBN# 1-56970-948-3 $12.95
ISBN# 1-56970-947-5 $12.95
www.dmpbooks.com
A New Wave of Manga
DMP
Cafe KICHIJOUJI DE © KYOKO NEGISHI/ YUKI MIYAMOTO 2001.
Originally published in Japan in 2001 by SHINSHOKAN CO., LTD.

STOP

This is the back of the book!
Start from the other side.

***NATIVE MANGA* readers read manga from *right to left*.**

1
2
1
3
2
3
5
4
4
6
5
8
7
6

*If you run into our **Native Manga** logo on any of our books... you'll know that this manga is published in it's true original native Japanese right to left reading format, as it was intended. Turn to the other side of the book and start reading from right to left, top to bottom.*

Follow the diagram to see how its done.
Surf's Up!

NATIVE MANGA
READ RIGHT TO LEFT